To My Dear Friend
John Ehrenberg

*For reason is the light of the mind and without her
all things are dreams and phantoms.*
—BARUCH SPINOZA

*The motto of enlightenment is therefore: Sapere aude!
Have the courage to use your own understanding!*
—IMMANUEL KANT

I have always preferred freedom to everything else.
—VOLTAIRE

*The genuine synthesis will probably remain an
undiscovered country.*
—GOETHE

CONTENTS

RECLAIMING THE ENLIGHTENMENT

RECLAIMING THE ENLIGHTENMENT

Toward a Politics of Radical Engagement

STEPHEN ERIC BRONNER

COLUMBIA UNIVERSITY PRESS

NEW YORK

Columbia University Press
Publishers Since 1893
New York, Chichester, West Sussex
Copyright © 2004 Columbia University Press

Library of Congress Cataloging-in-Publication Data
Bronner, Stephen Eric
    Reclaiming the enlightenment / Stephen Eric Bronner.
        p.   cm.
    Includes bibliographical references and index.
    ISBN 0-231-12608-5 (cloth : alk. paper)
    ISBN 0-231-12609-3 (pbk. : alk. paper)
        1. Liberalism.   2. Enlightenment.   3. Political science—
    Philosophy.   I. Title.

JC574.B76 2004
320.51—dc22
                                    2004041312

Columbia University Press books are printed on
permanent and durable acid-free paper
Printed in the United States of America
c 10 9 8 7 6 5 4 3 2 1
p 10 9 8 7 6 5 4 3 2 1

PREFACE

WHAT FOLLOWS IS AN ATTEMPT TO RECLAIM THE ENLIGHTENMENT, with its peculiar tradition of theory and practice. Of course, the twenty-first century is not the eighteenth: there is clearly no exact symmetry between past and present. The analog it might provide for engaged intellectuals, no less than its ethical model for resisting oppressive structures of power, needs reinterpretation to meet new conditions. Rigid notions of progress have fallen by the wayside; no group or party can any longer claim to incarnate the ideals of humanity, and the intellectual too often identifies the university with the world. Images from television and film rather than words on the page now shape the public sphere. Liberal regimes have often been corrupted by imperialist ambitions and parasitical elites. Both the left and the right have championed totalitarianism. The new global expansion of capitalism, the rise of the bureaucratic state, media consolidation, thoughtless consumerism, disregard for the environment, and cultural relativism have all undermined the ideals of cosmopolitan tolerance, economic justice, democratic accountability, and the idea of the "good society" generally associated with the Enlightenment.

But, if the progressive intellectual can no longer guarantee the realization of reason's promise, it is still the liberal rule of law with its explicit privileging of civil liberty, the interventionist state as an agent of social justice, and cosmopolitan movements intent on demanding recognition of the "other," that serve as the precondition—the condition sine qua non—for bettering the lives of individuals, enabling them to expand the range of their experiences, which is the most basic meaning of progress. Current forms of engagement probably seem more pedestrian: perhaps that is the case. But political engagement is no less important than in earlier times. Universal interests remain real. It is only that the engaged intellectual can no longer indulge in the old romantic expectations of "changing the world" in one fell swoop.

Enlightenment intellectuals may have laced their political engagement with drama, but they never fell into the trap of demanding all or nothing. To view them as either utopians or totalitarians is philosophically untenable and historically absurd. They took the world as it was, and sought to deal with the problems that it presented in a pragmatic and principled way. But the world has changed. There is no longer an "agent" capable of realizing the emancipatory values of the Enlightenment. Neither "humanity" nor the proletariat nor the once colonized peoples can any longer be identified with what Hegel termed "the world spirit." There is also no longer a "republic of letters." But these changes are, too often, employed as an excuse for passivity. There is an even more diverse cosmopolitan community of critical intellectuals and there exists an even greater variety than heretofore of progressive organizations that deal—and often deal positively—with crucial issues ranging from world hunger to the protection of individual liberties to animal rights. Specifying an 'agent" of change or creating a hierarchy of causes is neither possible nor necessary. Teleology has fallen by the wayside and realizing freedom lacks any historical guarantee. The issue is no longer what party or social movement or interest group is joined; rather the issue concerns the initial decision to engage political reality and the choice of an ethical stance capable of fostering solidarity between organizations. That, indeed, is where the Enlightenment legacy still has a role to play.

Solidarity should not simply be assumed: the landscape of the left is still littered by ideological turf-wars inherited from the 1960s. Enlightenment political values are important not only because they contest narrow organizational ambitions that interfere with cooperative action, but also because they provide a historical and speculative orientation for progressive activists and intellectuals. That orientation virtually vanished following the fragmentation of the civil rights and poor peoples movements and the new popularity accorded the variants of postmodernism and—what perhaps lies at the root of them all—the "late" brand of critical theory associated with *Dialectic of Enlightenment* by Max Horkheimer and Theodor Adorno. In keeping with the decline of radical political parties, and the identification of resistance with the expression of subjectivity, the Enlightenment has been subjected to a new metaphysical form of "immanent" critique. Its *political legacy* has thus become a secondary concern.

The preoccupations of the philosophes with social and institutional reform , and what Max Weber termed the "elective affinity" between their values and progressive agents for change, now seem to receive scant attention.

This is all the more unfortunate since new transnational movements have come into existence, often confused in terms of how they should respond to "globalization," along with functioning transnational political institutions that still suffer from a deficit of loyalty. New communications technologies are providing new organizational possibilities for political resistance, expanding the range of available experiences, and opening the way for new understandings of the most diverse cultures. New forms of solidarity, reflected in the popular concern with "human rights," have challenged imperialist wars, outdated cultural norms, and authoritarian politics. The objective conditions for realizing the unrealized hopes associated with internationalism, liberal democracy, and social justice are already there; only the ideological willingness to embrace the assumptions underpinning these values is lacking. That is what provides the Enlightenment with a new salience for our time.

Humanity is not in the past, but rather in the making. Conservatism may have set the agenda since the last quarter of the twentieth century. But that does not justify the resignation and increasingly debilitating pessimism associated with so many current forms of "radical" thought. Genuinely progressive changes have occurred: dictators have fallen and more citizens of the world have been enfranchised; battles for economic justice have been won; racism and sexism are on the defensive; and there has been poetry—good poetry—after Auschwitz. Easy to downplay the gains, suggest that they have now been "absorbed"; and embrace a new version of the old and tired attitude known as "cultural pessimism." Cynicism always comes cheap. The real challenge lies in recognizing how the "system," which was never as "totally administered" as many would like to think has been changed for the better through social action inspired by Enlightenment ideals.

The closed society has become more open and—against the provincial, religious, exploitative, and authoritarian sources of opposition—it has the potential of becoming more open still. Deciding to enter the fray, however, becomes more difficult when relying on philosophical perspectives that leave their supporters wandering about lost in Hegel's night in which all cows are black. It is necessary to distinguish between traditions not by making reference to metaphysics, but rather by looking at the political and ideological conflicts between actual movements. Again, the radical democratic and egalitarian aspects of the Enlightenment have been betrayed often enough. But this recognition presupposes that there was indeed something to betray. Which promises made by the Enlightenment have been broken becomes apparent not from the standpoint of "negative dialectics," communitarian convictions, "pragmatism," or ethical relativism, but rather by taking seriously its universal understanding of liberty and progress.

To be sure: universalism can be found in western imperialist propaganda and notions like "the sun never sets on the British Empire." In reality, however, such universalism is not universal at all: it lacks reciprocity, an open discourse, and a concern with protecting the individual from the arbitrary exercise of power: That is what differentiates Enlightenment universalism from its imitators, provides it with a self-critical quality, and enables it to contest Euro-centrism and the prevalent belief in a "clash of civilizations." Let there be no mistake: it has no use for misguided tolerance. Refusals to entertain "western" criticisms can easily be used to insulate repressive non-western traditions from criticism if only because non-western elites can also be authoritarian. Enlightenment political theory was never willing to justify tradition simply because it exists. Its best representatives argued for tolerance over prejudice, innovation over stasis, the rights of the minority over the enthusiasms of the majority, and the moral autonomy of the individual over the revealed claims of religious authority. The radical moment of the Enlightenment lies in its universal assault on privilege and prejudice. Its reflexive and critical character enables its most distinctive political theory to call for constraining the arbitrary exercise of institutional power and expand the possibilities of individual experience in *both* western and nonwestern societies.

Enlightenment intellectuals provide an analogy for what contemporary intellectuals should strive to accomplish and a model of how to combat oppressive institutions, unjustifiable privileges, and anachronistic cultural practices. Viewing their political theory as the source of bureaucratic conformism or totalitarianism is a profound mistake. Their insistence upon demonstrating a plausible—not a perfect, but a plausible—connection between means and ends with respect to political action and social change was not merely to be directed against the ruling elites but against those who would resist them. They anticipated how the collapse of this connection would historically work against the interests of the lowly and the insulted. They sensed that it would turn individuals into a means for political ends and let them be seen as nothing more than economic "costs of production."

Resisting this state of affairs is the most radical purpose of the two most important political products of the Enlightenment: liberalism and socialism. Both inspired progressive mass movements and, for good reasons, inspire them still. The point of their intersection has become the intellectual point of departure for any genuinely progressive politics. Identification with the disenfranchised and the exploited from a cosmopolitan standpoint is the

necessary implication of this position. Such is the legacy of the Enlightenment. Making good on it, however, calls for privileging the satisfactions and
benefits of political interpretation over the esoteric and metaphysical va-
garies of fashionable pseudo-political philosophical currents. If philosophy
really has been an expression of what Novalis termed "transcendental home-
lessness," which I doubt, then perhaps it is time to confront the philosophical with the political and, finally, for the prodigal to return home.

ACKNOWLEDGMENTS

VARIOUS INDIVIDUALS READ ONE OR ANOTHER CHAPTER OF THIS manuscript, but I would particularly like to thank those of my students who participated in a seminar over the content of this book at Rutgers University and from whose comments and insights I benefited greatly: Eric Boehme, Sabrina Cywinski, Brian Graff, Aaron Keck, Geoff Kurtz, Marilyn LaFay, Margot Morgan, and Brian Stipelman. I am also grateful to Leslie Bialler for his help with copyediting the manuscript and Peter Dimock, my editor at Columbia University Press, for his support with the project.

RECLAIMING THE ENLIGHTENMENT

1

INTERPRETING THE ENLIGHTENMENT:
METAPHYSICS, CRITIQUE, AND POLITICS

IN THE AFTERMATH OF THE TERRORIST ATTACKS OF SEPTEMBER 11, 2001, amid the intellectual retrenchment consonant with the unending "war against terror," the Enlightenment legacy has become—more than ever before—a contested terrain. Human rights is often used as an ideological excuse for the exercise of arbitrary power; the security of western states has served as a justification for the constriction of personal freedom; and, with flags flying, Christian fundamentalists have called for the defense of western "values." The best of them—political liberty, social justice, and cosmopolitanism—are rooted in the Enlightenment, and they retain their radical character. But not only the right is distorting them. These values have also come under assault from important intellectual representatives of the left: anarchists, communitarians, postmodernists, half-hearted liberals, and authoritarian socialists. Intellectual and political disorientation has been the result. Ideas long associated with reactionary movements—the privileging of experience over reason, national or ethnic identity over internationalism and cosmopolitanism, the community over the individual, custom over innovation, myth over science—have entered the thinking of the American left. Its partisans have thus become increasingly unclear about the tradition into which they fit and the purposes their politics should serve. The collapse of intellectual coherence on the left reflects the collapse of a purposeful politics from the left. Reconstructing such a politics depends upon appropriating the Enlightenment to meet new conditions.

Conservatives have, ironically, been more clear-sighted. In the past, they deplored the "nihilism" of the Enlightenment[1]: its devastating assault on communal life, religious faith, social privilege, and traditional authority.

---

1. John Ralston, *Voltaire's Bastards: The Dictatorship of Reason in the West* (New York: Free Press, 1992); Alisdair MacIntyre, *After Virtue: A Study in Moral Theory* (Notre Dame: University of Notre Dame Press, 1984).

Conservatives, and those even farther to the right, consistently rejected Enlightenment concerns with individualism, dissent, secularism, reform, and the primacy of critical reflection. This differentiated them from the left. If many leading conservatives now insist upon the importance of "reason" in chastising radical reformers in the West and the advocates of Islam in the Orient, indeed, their "cultural" appropriation truncates the radical spirit of the Enlightenment and its critical ethos.[2] The defense of western civilization by conservative intellectuals is, unsurprisingly, mixed with anti-Enlightenment and anti-modern prejudices. They obsess about sexual license and the decline of family values, cultural "nihilism" and the loss of tradition, tolerance for divergent life-styles and the erosion of national identity. Their "west" is not the "west" of the Enlightenment. Those conservatives most concerned about the coming "death of the west," in fact, sound like their forefathers who feared "the age of reason" and later the destruction of privileges associated with an obviously white and Christian world.[3] Discussion of the Enlightenment has nonetheless become skewed to the right; the radical moment has dropped out. It is no longer treated as the razor that divides "left" and right." If there is any legitimacy to claims concerning the increasing irrelevance of fundamental political distinctions, indeed, here lies the historical source.

With its emphasis upon autonomy, tolerance, and reason—no less than its attack upon received traditions, popular prejudices, and religious superstitions—the Enlightenment was generally recognized as the foundation for any kind of progressive politics. *Dialectic of Enlightenment* by Max Horkheimer and Theodor Adorno, however, dramatically undermined that perception. Published in 1947, written in a period marked by the previously unimaginable slaughter of two world wars, the emergence of mass culture, bureaucratic states, and what Daniel Rousset called "the concentration camp universe," this book was an interdisciplinary experiment. Neither a work of history, anthropology, sociology, nor politics, it instead combined these disciplines to remarkable effect and turned the accepted notion of progress upside down. The scientific method of the Enlightenment, according to the authors, may have

2. Note the huge anthology in which essays deal with everything from "civil science" to "philosophical sex" without any concern for the political legacy of the Enlightenment. Cf. *Enlightenment, Passion, Modernity: Historical Essays in European Thought and Culture* edited by Mark S. Micale and Robert Dietle (Stanford: Stanford University Press, 2000).

3. Patrick J. Buchanan, *The Death of the West: How Dying Populations and Immigrant Invasions Imperil Our Country and Civilization* (New York: Thomas Dunne Books, 2002).

originally intended to serve the ideals of human liberation in an assault upon religious dogma. Yet the power of scientific reason ultimately wound up being directed not merely against the gods, but all metaphysical ideas—including conscience and freedom—as well. "Knowledge" became divorced from "information," norms from facts, and the scientific method, increasingly freed from any commitment to liberation, transformed nature into an object of domination, and itself into a whore employed by the highest bidder.

"Instrumental reason" was seen as merging with what Marx termed the "commodity form" underpinning capitalist social relations. Everything thereby became subject to the calculation of costs and benefits. Even art and aesthetic tastes would become defined by a "culture industry"—intent only upon maximizing profits by seeking the lowest common denominator for its products. Instrumental rationality was thus seen as stripping the supposedly "autonomous" individual, envisioned by the philosophes, of both the means and the will to resist manipulation by totalitarian movements. Enlightenment now received two connotations: its historical epoch was grounded in an anthropological understanding of civilization that, from the first, projected the opposite of progress. This gave the book its power: Horkheimer and Adorno offered not simply the critique of some prior historical moment in time, but of all human development. This made it possible to identify enlightenment not with progress, as the philistine bourgeois might like to believe, but rather—unwittingly—with barbarism, Auschwitz, and what is still often called "the totally administered society."

Such is the picture painted by *Dialectic of Enlightenment*. But it should not be forgotten that its authors were concerned with criticizing enlightenment generally, and the historical epoch known as the Enlightenment in particular, *yes* from the standpoint of enlightenment itself: thus the title of the work. Their masterpiece was actually "intended to prepare the way for a positive notion of enlightenment, which will release it from entanglement in blind domination."[4] Horkheimer and Adorno even talked about writing a sequel that would have carried a title something like "Rescuing the Enlightenment" (*Rettung der Aufklärung*).[5] This reclamation project was never completed, and much time has been spent speculating about why it wasn't. The reason, I believe, is that the logic of their argument ultimately left them with little positive

4. Max Horkheimer and Theodor W. Adorno, *Dialectic of Enlightenment* trans. John Cumming (New York: Herder & Herder, 1972), xvi.
5. Note the discussion in "Unserthema: die Rettung der Aufklaerung" on 3 October 1946 shortly before the book appeared in its 1947 edition. See Max Horkheimer, *Gesammelte Schriften* 20 Bde. hrsg. Alfred Schmidt und Gunzelin Schmid Norr (Frankfurt am Main: S. Fischer, 1989) 12: 594.

to say. Viewing instrumental rationality as equivalent with the rationality of domination, and this rationality with an increasingly seamless bureaucratic order, no room existed any longer for a concrete or effective political form of opposition: Horkheimer would thus ultimately embrace a quasi-religious "yearning for the totally other" while Adorno became interested in a form of aesthetic resistance grounded in "negative dialectics." Their great work initiated a radical change in critical theory, but its metaphysical subjectivism surrendered any systematic concern with social movements and political institutions. Neither of them ever genuinely appreciated the democratic inheritance of the Enlightenment and thus, not only did they render critique independent of its philosophical foundations,[6] but also of any practical interest it might serve.

Horkheimer and Adorno never really grasped that, in contrast to the system builder, the blinkered empiricist, or the fanatic, the philosophe always evidenced a "greater interest in the things of this world, a greater confidence in man and his works and his reason, the growing appetite of curiosity and the growing restlessness of the unsatisfied mind—all these things form less a doctrine than a spirit."[7] Just as Montesquieu believed it was the spirit of the laws, rather than any system of laws, that manifested the commitment to justice, the spirit of Enlightenment projected the radical quality of that commitment and a critique of the historical limitations with which even its best thinkers are always tainted. Empiricists may deny the existence of a "spirit of the times." Nevertheless, historical epochs can generate an ethos, an existential stance toward reality, or what might even be termed a "project" uniting the diverse participants in a broader intellectual trend or movement.[8]

The Enlightenment evidenced such an ethos and a peculiar stance toward reality with respect toward its transformation. Making sense of this, however, is impossible without recognizing what became a general stylistic commitment to clarity, communicability, and what rhetoricians term "plain speech." For their parts, however, Horkheimer and Adorno believed that resistance against the incursions of the culture industry justified the extremely difficult, if not often opaque, writing style for which they would become famous—or, better, infamous. Their esoteric and academic style is a far cry

---

6. Jürgen Habermas, *The Philosophical Discourse of Modernity: Twleve Lectures* trans. Frederic Lawrence (Cambridge: MIT Press, 1987), 116.

7. John C. Gagliardo, *Enlightened Despotism* (Wheeling, Illinois: Harlan Davidson, 1967), 20.

8. Peter Gay, *The Party of Humanity: Essays in the French Enlightenment* (New York: Norton, 1954), 112.

from that of Enlightenment intellectuals who debated first principles in public, who introduced freelance writing, who employed satire and wit to demolish puffery and dogma, and who were preoccupied with reaching a general audience of educated readers: Lessing put the matter in the most radical form in what became a popular saying—"Write just as you speak and it will be beautiful"—while, in a letter written to D'Alembert in April of 1766, Voltaire noted that "Twenty folio volumes will never make a revolution: it's the small, portable books at thirty sous that are dangerous. If the Gospel had cost 1,200 sesterces, the Christian religion would never have been established."[9]

Appropriating the Enlightenment for modernity calls for reconnecting with the vernacular. This does not imply some endorsement of anti-intellectualism. Debates in highly specialized fields, especially those of the natural sciences, obviously demand expertise and insisting that intellectuals must "reach the masses" has always been a questionable strategy.[10] The subject under discussion should define the language in which it is discussed and the terms employed are valid insofar as they illuminate what cannot be said in a simpler way. Horkheimer and Adorno, however, saw the matter differently. They feared being integrated by the culture industry, avoided political engagement, and turned freedom into the metaphysical-aesthetic preserve of the connoisseur. They became increasingly incapable of appreciating the egalitarian impulses generated by the Enlightenment and the ability of its advocates—Ben Franklin, Thomas Jefferson, James Madison, Thomas Paine, and Rousseau—to argue clearly and with a political purpose.[11] Thus, whether or not their "critical" enterprise was "dialectically" in keeping with the impulses of the past, its assumptions prevented them from articulating anything positive for the present or the future.

Reclaiming the Enlightenment is an attempt to provide the sequel that Horkheimer and Adorno never wrote in a style they refused to employ. Its chapters proceed in a roughly parallel manner and, given its interdisciplinary character, this book also has no intention of pleasing the narrow specialist in

---

9. Cited in ibid., 36.

10. Stephen Eric Bronner, "Critical Intellectuals, Politics, and Society" in *Imagining the Possible: Radical Politics for Conservative Times* (New York: Routledge, 2002), 73ff.

11. For the *philosophe*, "it was part of his new self-image as representative of society at large and of his pragmatic approach to affairs of the mind that he adhered to no academic protocol but wrote in whatever form would attract the widest interest, be most appropriate to the subject of the moment, and act with best narcotic effect on the official censors of church and state." Leonard Krieger, *Kings and Philosophers, 1689–1789* (New York: Norton, 1970), 155–56.

any particular field. In contrast to *Dialectic of Enlightenment*, however, what follows is not a collection of "fragments"—the subtitle that was dropped from the first English translation—and its "positive" appropriation rests upon a view of tradition that links theory and practice.[12] Little sympathy is wasted on meta-theory for its inability to deal with historical conflicts or even that the classic work by Horkheimer and Adorno is different from the postmodern works it inspired[13]: its intention, which was to criticize the Enlightenment from the standpoint of enlightenment itself, is not congruent with the result. The present volume considers the actual movements with which enlightenment ideals, as against competing ideals, were connected. It thus highlights the assault undertaken by the philosophes against the old feudal order and the international battle that was fought—from 1789 until 1939 and into the present—[14] between liberal and socialist forces imbued with the Enlightenment heritage and those forces of religious reaction, conservative prejudice, and fascist irrationalism whose inspiration derived from what Isaiah Berlin initially termed the "Counter-Enlightenment."[15] Without a sense of this battle, or what I elsewhere termed the "great divide" of modern political life, any discussion of the Enlightenment will necessarily take a purely academic form.

Dialectic of Enlightenment never grasped what was at stake in the conflict or interrogated its political history. Its authors never acknowledged that different practices and ideals are appropriate to different spheres of activity or that only confusion would result from substituting the affirmation of subjectivity, through aesthetic-philosophic criticism, for political resistance. Horkheimer and Adorno were no less remiss than their postmodern followers in ignoring the institutional preconditions for the free exercise of individual capacities. Striking indeed is how those most concerned about the "loss of subjectivity" have shown the least awareness about the practical role of genuinely democratic as against reactionary pseudo-universalism and the institutional lessons of totalitarianism.

---

12. Note the more extensive discussion in Stephen Eric Bronner, *Ideas in Action: Political Tradition in the Twentieth Century* (Lanham, MD: Rowman & Littlefield, 1999), 1ff.
13. Daniel Gordon, "On the Supposed Obsolescence of the French Enlightenment" in *Postmodernism and the Enlightenment: New Perspectives in Eighteenth-Century French Intellectual History* ed. Daniel Gordon (New York: Routledge, 2001), 206
14. Arthur Rosenberg, *Democracy and Socialism: A Contribution to the Political History of the Past 150 Years* (New York: Knopf, 1939).
15. Isaiah Berlin, "The Counter-Enlightenment" in *Against the Current: Essays in the History of Ideas* ed. Henry Hardy (New York: Viking, 1980), 1ff.

Enlightenment values are still not hegemonic or establishmentarian. \ Authoritarianism is still rampant, most inhabitants of the world still suffer under the strictures of traditionalism, and earn less than $2 per day. The Enlightenment was always a movement of protest against the exercise of arbitrary power, the force of custom and ingrained prejudices, and the justification of social misery. Its spirit was the expression of a bourgeois class on the rise against the hegemonic feudal values of the established society and its political ideals are still subordinate to those of traditionalism and authoritarianism in most of the world. There should be no mistake: though the philosophes were responding primarily to the world associated with "throne and altar," the ideals of these thinkers remain relevant for even for nations without a feudal past like the United States. Western nations still carry the scars of racism, sexism, homophobia, xenophobia, and class inequality.

Enlightenment thinkers evidenced anticipatory insights, speculations, and contradictory views on an extraordinary variety of issues. The less systematic the thinker, it is possible to assume, the more perverse the ways in which his or her ideas could be appropriated. Enlightenment thinkers, however, were rarely endorsed or embraced by conservative or fascist political movements: it is hard to imagine a bust of Locke or Voltaire sitting on the desk of Mussolini. The philosophes had their most profound impact on the Left: Locke and Kant influenced all manner of liberals, socialists, and anarchists. Beccaria, Holbach, and Adam Smith were deeply committed to moral development and social reform. Thomas Paine is among the founders of modern internationalism. There is hardly a genuinely democratic regime that is not indebted to Montesquieu. Enlightenment philosophers would inspire generations of those languishing under the weight of despotism and dogma. The extent to which their political contribution is forgotten is the extent to which the contemporary left will constantly find itself intellectually reinventing the wheel.

The Enlightenment privileged a critical reflection on society, its traditions, its ideologies, and its institutions. Its spirit was opposed from the beginning, both in terms of style and content, by the type of fanaticism evidenced yesterday by secular totalitarians and today by religious fundamentalists. Just as there is a spirit of the Enlightenment, there is a phenomenology of the anti-Enlightenment. The language of both has—often unwittingly—carried over into the modern age. A lack of awareness about the past, however, has undermined the ability to make sense of the present. Arguing that the Enlightenment with its emphasis upon civil liberties, tolerance, and humanism was—for example—somehow responsible for the "Terror" of the French Revolution or twentieth-century totalitarianism indulges the pseudo-dialectical sensibility without looking at political history, movements, or institutional practices. The entire political landscape is distorted by this view: its revision alone justifies the popular academic reinterpretation of the enlightenment legacy.

Understanding the current clash between secularism and religious fundamentalism in the present, no less than the most profound political conflicts of the past, calls for first recognizing that the "Counter-Enlightenment" was not some "dialectical" response to the success of the Enlightenment but an immediate response, born of fear and loathing, against everything associated with its spirit. Perversions of the original impulse still go unacknowledged. Enlightenment values run directly counter to the exercise of arbitrary power no less than the censorship, collectivism, and conformism of authoritarian or totalitarian regimes of both the left and the right. It was also not that the Enlightenment somehow blended with its opposite, the Counter-Enlightenment, but that—from the first—two traditions confronted one another. The hatred between them only intensified in the aftermath of the age of democratic revolution and the epic battle would culminate in Auschwitz.

This work does not treat the Enlightenment as a transhistorical anthropological dynamic, or a disembodied set of epistemological propositions, but rather as a composite of views unified by similar political ideals and social aims. As against contemporary critical theorists and postmodernists, the philosophes were clear about the basic values underlying their enterprise. They shared a fundamental concern with constricting the exercise of arbitrary institutional power and expanding the realm of individual autonomy. This connection between politics and ethics is growing weaker. Enough understand "experience" and intuition as enough in resisting power. But they are not enough. Indeed, since "Western civilization is essentially political, and politics has been its vital center throughout the modern period, . . . to restore ethical values means to revive political theory, and to achieve this what is needed is a return to the ideas of the eighteenth century, to pick up the threads where they were then dropped or broken off."[16]

That is the purpose behind this particular appropriation of the Enlightenment. Excellent research has been done on the tradition deriving from

16. Alfred Cobban, *In Search of Humanity: The Role of the Enlightenment in Modern History* (New York: George Braziller, 1960), 27.

Spinoza and lesser-known figures of the period concerned with fostering gender and racial equality as well as radical understandings of democracy and community: it is even legitimate to distinguish between the "radical" and the "conservative" or "moderate" Enlightenment.[17] But this is better done in hindsight. It was ultimately the "liberal" element that inspired progressive movements for suffrage, abolition of the slave trade, civil liberties, and progressive labor legislation during the nineteenth and twentieth centuries. The point was to highlight the rule of law and introduce constraints upon the arbitrary exercise of institutional power. These concerns made uncomfortable even "enlightened" monarchs like Frederick the Great who insisted that "the passions of rulers have no other curbs but the limits of their power." They also inspired virtually every major intellectual representative of the socialist labor movement from Eduard Bernstein to Rosa Luxemburg as surely as the best among the Bolsheviks, and libertarian anarchists like Gustav Landauer, Victor Serge, Augustin Souchy, and Murray Bookchin. The concerns of these radical heirs of the Enlightenment, if not always their solutions, retain their relevance.

Again: the political spirit of the Enlightenment crystallized around the principles connected with fostering the accountability of institutions, reciprocity under the law, and a commitment to experiment with social reform. Not in imperialism, or racism, or the manipulation of liberty, but in these ideals lies the basis of Enlightenment universalism. Democracy remains an empty word without it. Enlightenment universalism protects rather than threatens the exercise of subjectivity. It presumes to render institutions accountable, a fundamental principle of democracy, and thereby create the preconditions for expanding individual freedom. Such a view would inform liberal movements concerned with civil liberties as well as socialist movements seeking to constrain the power of capital. Reciprocity can be understood in the same way: it, too, underpins the liberal idea of the citizen with its inherently democratic imperative—against all prejudice—to include "the other" as well as the socialist refusal to identify the working person as a mere "cost of production." The Enlightenment notion of political engagement, indeed, alone keeps democracy fresh and alive.

Ideals such as these provide an enduring foundation for opposing contemporary infringements on individual rights and dignity by new global

---

17. Jonathan Israel, *Radical Enlightenment: Philosophy and the Making of Modernity 1650–1750* (Oxford: Oxford University Press, 2001); also, Margaret C. Jacob, *The Radical Enlightenment: Pantheists, Freemasons and Republicans* (London: Allen & Unwin, 1981).

forms of capitalism, the imperatives of the culture industry, and parochial biases of every sort. They constitute the radical quality of the Enlightenment, and its "positive" moment beyond the prejudices of its particular representatives. Too many on the fringes have been forgotten like the proto-socialist Mably or the proto-communist Morelly and, until the appearance of *Radical Enlightenment* (2001) by Jonathan Israel, even major intellectuals like Spinoza have not received the political recognition that they were due. But this volume is concerned with something other than uncovering the past. Its intent is instead to reinvigorate the present, salvage the enlightenment legacy, and contest those who would institutionally freeze its radicalism and strip away its protest character. Such an undertaking is important, moreover, since their efforts have been remarkably successful. Enlightenment thinking is seen by many as the inherently western ideology of the bourgeois gentleman, the *Vernunftrepublikaner* of the Weimar Republic, or characters like the "windbag" Settembrini who endured the sarcasm of totalitarians and the boredom of philistines in *The Magic Mountain* (1924) by Thomas Mann.

Reclaiming the Enlightenment views its subject less as a dead historical artifact than as the necessary precondition for developing any form of progressive politics in the present. Understanding the Enlightenment, in this way, calls for opposing current fashions and conceits. Despite the existence of superb classic studies on the Enlightenment,[18] the general trend of scholarship has tended to insist upon eliminating its unifying cosmopolitan spirit—its ethos—in favor of treating diverse national, religious, gender, generational, and regional "enlightenments." [19] There is indeed always a danger of reifying the "Enlightenment" and ignoring the unique and particular moments of its expression. Edward Gibbon was a very different historian than Hume; Goethe criticized the theory of color advanced by Newton; Hobbes understood the state differently than Montesquieu; Voltaire and Rousseau differed over the social role of the theatre; the atheistic materialism of the

---

18. Note in particular, Ernst Cassirer, *The Philosophy of the Enlightenment* trans. Fritz C. A. Koellen and James P. Pettegrove (Princeton: Princeton University Press, 1951).

19. "The Enlightenment has exploded. Coming under the immense weight of new scholarship, since the mid-Seventies, it has been fragmented into a plethora of Enlightenments. To the dismay of word processor spell-checkers, the plural form of the English term is currently used almost as often as the singular. In German, *Aufklärungen* is making a parallel entry. The French, whether by grammatical chance or by prophetic common wisdom, have always had *les lumières* in the plural mode." Fania Oz-Salzberger, "New Approaches towards a History of the Enlightenment: Can Disparate Perspectives Make a General Picture?" in *Tel Aviver Jahrbuch für deutsche Geschichte* Bd. XXIX (Gerlingen: Bleicher Verlag, 2000), 171.

Baron d'Holbach had little in common with the idealism of Kant. Different individuals in different circumstances produced different perspectives on reality. Nevertheless, what unified them made the cumulative impact of individual thinkers and national intellectual trends far greater than the sum of the parts.

Extraordinary was the way in which the philosophes evidenced a common resistance to parochial beliefs and the arrogance of power. By simply deconstructing the "Enlightenment", the forest gets lost for the trees. Radical tendencies within it like anti-imperialism thus often come to be seen either as historical anomalies or as simple interests of this or that thinker.[20] It also becomes easy to forget that even before 1789, the anti-philosophes of the Counter-Enlightenment were busy "reconciling and uniting their enemies well beyond their extreme differences, attributing to them common aims and common ends. Tautology aside, there is much truth to the claim that the Counter-Enlightenment invented the Enlightenment."[21]

If there was no "Enlightenment," but only discrete forms of intellectual activity falling loosely under its rubric, why should the political enemies of this international trend have been the same? These representatives of church and tradition—who so vigorously opposed democracy and equality, revolution and reform, cosmopolitanism and internationalism, skepticism and science—formed a "Counter-Enlightenment International" even before the French Revolution.[22] Academic historians have attempted to interpret the Enlightenment as a series of internal debates around important intellectual "flashpoints."[23] They have highlighted what the Enlightenment had in common with its enemies like the Church;[24] and the resentment of

---

20. Introducing the general category of "Enlightenment" is a practical necessity for understanding the plurality of particulars. Its existence is implicit in any study of the period or any other equally general concern like eighteenth-century thought. This often becomes evident, apparently against the intentions of the author, in an otherwise fine study where it is argued that: "A study of Enlightenment anti-imperialism offers a richer and more accurate portrait of eighteenth century political thought . . . and simultaneously . . . that 'the Enlightenment' *as such* and the notion of an overarching 'Enlightenment project' simply do not exist." Sankar Muthu, *Enlightenment Against Empire* (Princeton: Princeton University Press, 2003), 3, 264.

21. Darrin M. McMahaon, *Enemies of the Enlightenment: The French Counter Enlightenment and the Making of Modernity* (Oxford: Oxford University Press, 2001), 32.

22. Ibid., 106ff.

23. Dorinda Outram, *The Enlightenment* (Cambridge: Cambridge University Press, 1995), 3.

24. Carl Becker, *The Heavenly City of the Eighteenth Century Philosophers* (New Haven: Yale University Press, 1932).

its lesser known against its more famous representatives. [25] They have also emphasized the different connotations behind the terms Enlightenment, *Aufklärung, lumieres, Illuminismo.*

Nowhere is the political conflict between the Enlightenment and the Counter-Enlightenment, however, given center stage: it is as if the revolutionary quality of Cezanne were to be appreciated without referring to the most famous aesthetically conservative artists of his time. Perhaps in our apolitical age the primacy of such apolitical interpretations only makes sense. But the implications are clear: insofar as the savage political conflict between different ideologies is ignored, especially since it plays such an important role in understanding contemporary politics, the Enlightenment will be turned into a lifeless object of interest only to historical connoisseurs. The ability to evaluate its failings and those of its most important representatives is also, thereby severely compromised.

There weren't many saints among the philosophes. Even the most anticipatory form of philosophy retains residues, reactionary assumptions, and prejudices, from its historical context. Some figures of the Enlightenment look better than others with references to the stupidities of their time. But there is no comparing the views on women, religious minorities, and civil liberties of the philosophes with representatives of the Counter-Enlightenment who opposed every progressive measure to improve the condition of women, sought to keep Jews in the ghetto, and feared democracy and social reform like the plague. Usually ignored is the question concerning what it was reasonable to expect from these intellectuals in their own historical context. It is impossible to excuse Voltaire for his anti-Semitism, but that is because other of his contemporaries, like Lessing or Montesquieu, held more egalitarian and sophisticated views. Rousseau and Kant can be condemned for their support of the death penalty precisely because others like Beccaria and Voltaire understood its barbarity. But it is foolish simply to introduce an abstract standard of what is currently considered politically correct. Indeed, by reducing ideas to the prejudices of their usually white, male, and western authors, many supposedly progressive historical interrogations of the past actually wind up tossing the historical context by the wayside.

Confronting such biases in progressive terms is furthermore possible only from the standpoint of the Enlightenment with its liberal and socialist inheritance. There is little of organizational or ethical importance that the

25. Robert Darnton," The High Enlightenment and the Low-life of History in Pre-Revolutionary France" in *Past and Present*, 51 (1971), 81–115.

Counter-Enlightenment or the present assortment of "post-enlightenment" philosophies has to offer the struggle of the excluded and exploited. Viewing the Enlightenment as irremediably tainted by anachronistic prejudices only casts a plague on all houses. No need exists to compare the views of the philosophes and the fanatics: both are prejudiced with regard to race or sex or sexual practice and that is that. Forgotten is that the former can be held to their own ethical standards of progress while the latter cannot because they rejected those standards in the first place. This little volume seeks to illuminate not simply the "differences," but the *qualitative* differences between essentially progressive movements that embraced the political implications of the Enlightenment and essentially reactionary movements that resisted it.

Movements often show their weakness by the way in which they, whether consciously or unconsciously, appropriate the thinking of their adversaries. This is particularly true of the contemporary left. Enough "liberals" now suggest that liberal regimes must rest on a homogeneous national community with shared cultural values; others influenced by postmodern ideology view universal concepts as complicit with domination and as a threat to their particular identities; "western" ideas no less than the philosophies generating them are strenuously contested by self-styled radical anti-imperialists whose "nonwestern" beliefs are associated with indigenous religious traditions and romanticized visions of an organic society.[26] There are still those who laud the liberal heritage, often without admitting its complicity in the violence produced by capitalism, and others like Neil Postman who properly emphasized the importance of "building a bridge" to the eighteenth century in order to recapture its lost humanism.[27] But the more fashionable interpretations suggest that the Enlightenment has lost its relevance,[28] or that its importance was always overrated in comparison with the salacious and anti-authoritarian popular literature of the time.[29]

The Enlightenment may not have produced the best of all possible worlds and, admittedly, the importance of ideas and intellectuals is often

---

26. Rajani Kannepalli Kanth, *Breaking with the Enlightenment: The Twilight of History and the Rediscovery of Utopia* (Atlantic Highlands, NJ: Humanities Press, 1997), 94ff.

27. Neil Postman, *Building a Bridge to the 18th Century: How the Past Can Improve Our Future* (New York: Alfred A. Knopf, 1999).

28. John Gray, *Enlightenment's Wake: Politics and Culture at the End of the Modern Age* (London: Routledge, 1995).

29. Robert Darnton, *The Forbidden Bestsellers of Pre-Revolutionary France* (New York: Norton, 1995). For an excellent critique see Thomas Munck, *The Enlightenment: A Comparative Social History 1721–1794* (London: Arnold, 2000), pgs. 76ff and *passim*. Also, Reinhart Koselleck, *Kritik und Krise* (Frankfurt am Main: Sulu Kamp, 1973).

overestimated. But the philosophes surely shaped the progressive political discourse of modernity. Even their enemies have manipulated their line of argument. Too much time is now spent in abstract discussion of the tension between "liberty" and "equality" especially since, in general, right-wing movements—ranging from hard-line conservatives to old-fashioned totalitarians to the new supporters of fundamentalism—have had no trouble attacking both. It is true that establishmentarian elites employ the notion of rights to defend capitalist property relations and keep subaltern groups in their place. But it is also true that such an undertaking requires transforming what might be termed the protest character of the Enlightenment into a set of unassailable legal claims that benefit elites.

Democratic society was initially understood as an experiment that developed hand in hand with the liberation of the critical spirit. But the belief still persists that Enlightenment thinkers were preoccupied with finding a single absolute truth that explains all of reality, and the character of correct conduct in all circumstances.[30] Many radicals are also repulsed by the anti-populist sentiments and the toleration of religion exhibited by major representatives of the Enlightenment, their acceptance of the state, their sexist and racist prejudices, their elitism and their euro-centrism, their scientism and their eradication of subjectivity in the name of universal abstractions. That various philosophes harbored such beliefs is irrefutable; that the enlightenment ethos is reducible to them, however, is unsustainable.

What has been called the Enlightenment may no longer seem particularly radical: its most important values seem to have been realized.[31] Indulging in this belief, however, would be a mistake. The 11th of September only highlights what should already have been obvious: the need remains for an unrelenting assault on religious fanaticism not merely of the Islamic variety, but of the sort promulgated by "born again" Christians, biblical literalists, Protestant sects intent upon converting the Jewish infidels, and all those who would bring their revealed certainties—contested by others with other revealed certainties—into the mainstream of public life. The Enlightenment may have

---

30. Isaiah Berlin, "Giambattista Vico and Cultural History" in *The Crooked Timber of Humanity: Chapters in the History of Ideas* ed. Henry Hardy (New York: Vintage, 1992), 51; also, Alisdair MacIntyre, *Whose Justice, Which Rationality?* (Notre Dame, University of Notre Dame Press, 1988), 6.

31. Robert Anchor, *The Enlightenment Tradition* (Berkeley: University of California Press, 1967), 58.

32. David Sorkin, *Moses Mendelssohn and the Religious Enlightenment* (Berkeley: University of California Press, 1996).

had a transforming impact upon religion itself.[32] But its mainstream institutions fought against what Sir Karl Popper termed the "open society" virtually every step of the way. Every concession to the march of progress made by religion was the product of unremitting pressure by its opponents.

Reason is not the enemy of experience. Nothing is more foolish than to confuse a reactionary pseudo-universalism with the genuinely democratic universalism that underpins the liberal rule of law, the constraint of arbitrary power, and the free exercise of subjectivity. Probably no group of intellectuals, in fact, was more aware of the contributions offered by different cultures than the philosophes who prized the early agricultural societies that never encountered Christianity like the Amer-Indians and who looked with such respect at Tahiti, the Near East, and the Orient. Their information about these exotic regions was admittedly suspect, much of it was completely half-baked, and the philosophes often romanticized their subjects. But, still, they looked to these cultures as a source for new experiences and, generally speaking, the sympathy they extended to them was genuine. Skepticism concerning the inflexible claims of national and religious dogma links the Enlightenment with a political undertaking intent upon making society more democratic, more cosmopolitan, and more experimental.

Just as the philosophes saw science not merely as an ordering device but as a self-critical method that could be used in the fight for liberation from outdated prejudices and dogmas, their view of aesthetics called upon individuals to expand the realm of their experience. Rousseau was not alone in claiming that "the education of man begins at birth." Diderot called for the enjoyment of sexuality for its own sake and, though the Abbé Prévost may have warned against the dangers of unbridled passion and disrespect for superiors, his *Manon Lescaut* had the opposite effect: it also helped forge the image of America as a land without "the arbitrary laws of rank and convention."[33] Voltaire satirized the man who would understand the world through reason alone; and Kant understood aesthetic experience as a form of "purposeful purposelessness." The philosophes were not colorless academics or puritanical reformers, but individuals who gloried in their eccentricities and who sought not merely to educate their minds, but also to educate their sentiments and sensibilities.

Illuminating the spirit of the Enlightenment, the best that it had to offer, is the place to begin. But this involves envisioning a loose assemblage (

---

33. Anchor, *The Enlightenment Tradition*, 51.

of intellectuals as an international intellectual movement intent upon changing the world—ideologically, politically, socially, and economically. It means viewing the democratic revolutions in England, the United States, Europe, and beyond as part of a single undertaking. This requires a shift in interpretive perspective. Especially when the salience of the Enlightenment can no longer be taken for granted, when its values have come under attack from both the right and the left, more is necessary than analyzing a few thinkers or some abstract philosophical propositions about history, nature, and "man." It is a matter of presenting the Enlightenment as an overarching political enterprise and a living tradition—not merely in its ideas but in the actions it inspires.

2

IN PRAISE OF PROGRESS

MAX WEBER ALREADY ENVISIONED THE SPIRIT OF ENLIGHTENMENT "irretrievably fading" and a world comprised of "specialists without spirit, sensualists without heart."[1] But he was bitter about this development, which places him in marked contrast to much of contemporary opinion. The Enlightenment always had its critics. Beginning with the Restoration of 1815 and the new philosophical reaction to the French Revolution, however, they were almost exclusively political—if not necessarily cultural—adherents of the right: intelligent conservatives committed to organic notions of development like Edmund Burke, elitists seeking a return to the sword and the robe like Joseph de Maistre, racists intent on viewing world history as a battle between Aryans and Jews like Houston Stewart Chamberlain, and apocalyptics prophesying doom like Oswald Spengler. Today, however, many on the left forward a critique of the Enlightenment. The criticisms come in various guises: postmodernists consider the enlightenment as "essentialist," radical feminists view it as "male," and postcolonial thinkers disparage it as "Eurocentric." Communitarians condemn its individualism, religious radicals bemoan its skepticism, populists castigate its intellectualism, and the politicians of identity criticize its rejection of experience as the criterion of truth. Dogmatic Marxists dismiss the Enlightenment as "bourgeois," anarchists are repelled by its reliance on the state, and ecologists by its belief in science and technology. Followers of the Frankfurt School still view it as the unwitting source of modern totalitarianism. Left critics of the Enlightenment form a motley crew and, perhaps, this reflects the current disarray of progressive forces. Still there is something that, ultimately, binds all of them: a basic discomfort with the notion of progress.

1. Max Weber, *The Protestant Ethic and the Spirit of Capitalism* trans. Talcott Parsons (New York: Schocken, 1958), 182.

Forged amid the scientific revolution, the birth of modern idealism, and the struggle for political liberty, the term "progress" is usually seen as having been coined by Fontenelle. But it is unnecessary to employ the word to believe in its feasibility. Progress is the crucial category for talking about change, autonomy, and drawing qualitative distinctions. The current understanding of progress, however, has become impoverished. The category has been flattened out. It is a travesty to reduce "progress" to the disenchantment of the world, the dissolution of myths, and the substitution of "knowledge for fancy."[2] Progress is, above all, an attack on "the illusion of finality":[3] closure, certainty, and utopia.

Enlightenment thinkers believed that they were changing the world by formalizing empirical data under the abstract laws of nature that were open to testing and observation. But these thinkers also knew that normative concerns were intertwined with the quantitative extension of knowledge.[4] They recognized that religion rested on revealed claims and that the aristocracy justified its privileges by invoking a mythical past. Acceptance of such beliefs no less than social evils now became understood less as the result of original sin than ignorance and prejudice or those assumptions and opinions, customs and traditions, preserved from critical reflection.[5] With this change in the causation of misery and the new emphasis on reason came, quite logically, the desire to better the condition of humanity. In the first instance, this meant throwing off the veils of stupidity imposed by centuries of ideological oppression. *The Magic Flute* indeed expressed this fundamental assumption of the Enlightenment that no "dialectic" would ever fully ruin:

2. Max Horkheimer and Theodor W. Adorno, *Dialectic of Enlightenment* trans. John Cumming (New York: Herder & Herder, 1972), 3

3. J. B. Bury, *The Idea of Progress: An Inquiry into Its Origin and Growth* (New York: Dover, 1987), 351.

4. "Perhaps no other century is so completely permeated by the idea of intellectual progress as that of the Enlightenment. But we mistake the essence of this conception, if we understand it merely in a quantitative sense as an extension of knowledge indefinitely. A qualitative determination always accompanies quantitative expansion; and an increasingly pronounced return to the characteristic center of knowledge corresponds to the extension of inquiry beyond the periphery of knowledge. One seeks multiplicity in order to be sure of unity; one accepts the breadth of knowledge in the sure anticipation that this breadth does not impede the intellect, but that, on the contrary, it leads the intellect back to, and concentrates it in, itself." Ernst Cassirer, *The Philosophy of the Enlightenment* trans. Fritz C.A. Koelln and James P. Pettigrove (Boston: Beacon Press, 1951), 5.

5. Darrin M. McMahon, *Enemies of the Enlightenment The French Counter-Enlightenment and the Making of Modernity* (Oxford: Oxford University Press, 2001), 141.

The rays of the sun
Drive away the night;
Destroyed is the hypocrite's
Hidden might.

The Enlightenment idea of progress ultimately implied something very simple and very dramatic: transforming the invisible into the visible, the ineffable into the discursive, and the unknown into the known. Hobbes put the matter well when he noted in *De Cive* (1642) that "there is a certain clue of reason whose beginning is in the dark; but by the benefit of whose conduct, we are led, as it were, by the hand into the clearest light." It is secondary whether this meant clarifying the workings of electricity, translating ethical intuitions into discursive statements, the activities of the market into economic laws, or fears about human nature into institutions capable of constraining arbitrary power: Hegel only rendered absolute what had been the guiding impulse, the regulative principle, of the general trend toward "enlightenment" when he based his *Phenomenology of Mind* on the famous assumption that "there is nothing in the essence of object that does not become evident in the series of its appearances." Marx would echo this sentiment and provide it with an even more radical material formulation in the second of the "Eleven Theses on Feuerbach" where he writes:

The question whether objective (*gegenständliche*) truth can be attributed to human thinking is not a question of theory but is a *practical* question. In practice man must prove the truth, that is, the reality and power, the this-sidedness (*Diesseitigkeit*) of his thinking. The dispute over the reality or non-reality of thinking which is isolated from practice is a purely *scholastic* question.

The Enlightenment envisioned progress as the process of bringing what had once been shrouded in darkness into the light. This meant not simply recognizing existing differences among people of different cultures as morally legitimate,[6] but also what is institutionally required in order that people may safely exercise their differences. The crucial issue was, for this reason, never the "subjectivity of the subject." Advocates of the Enlightenment instead sought to foster the moral autonomy of the individual over established

6. Richard Rorty, *Truth and Moral Progress: Philosophical Papers* (Cambridge: Cambridge University Press, 1998), 11.

traditions and the critical use of rationality against what Ernst Cassirer termed "mytho-poetical thinking." This enabled them to link progress with the extension of freedom and the exercise of the intellect.

Some may have believed that morality would ultimately flourish in each and every individual. More important was the insistence that conditions should allow for debating the moral claims of traditional authorities and religious institutions.[7] The respect accorded "reason" by the Enlightenment was intertwined with a belief in the need to cultivate common decency and a sense of compassion,[8] what Voltaire termed a "softening" of the worst customs, prejudices, and instincts: there is indeed something legitimate about the claim that he and many of his friends were "more inspired by a hatred of cruelty than a love of truth."[9] The attempt to "soften" the vices of humanity, in any event, reaches back to the earliest cultures: Jewish law condemned the torture of animals; the Buddha spoke of "selflessness" and compassion for suffering; Confucius saw himself as part of the human race; Hinduism lauded the journey of life; and Jesus articulated the Golden Rule. Herein is the anthropological grounding for the historical experience of Enlightenment. Without even making specific reference to the West, it thus becomes possible to envision a certain development of "civility" and feeling for "civilization,"[10] which should be considered the substance of progress.

All of this requires respect for the ideals of fairness and reciprocity. These notions underpinning the liberal rule of law make it possible to contest the prejudices and arbitrary privileges incorporated in any number of positive laws. A notion of reason that prizes freedom is therefore implicitly informed by a certain sensibility. Only the more vulgar among the philosophes, in this vein, ignored the role sentiments and passions play in human affairs.

---

7. "If a serious debate over moral problems, as distinguished from an unquestioning acceptance of views established by tradition or authority, is any test of morality, then the age of the Enlightenment was the most moral of all ages." Alfred Cobban, *In Search of Humanity: The Role of the Enlightenment in Modern History* (New York: George Braziller, 1960), 89.

8. As a very young man, Horkheimer found this emphasis upon compassion philosophically formulated in Schopenhauer and—without considering it part of the anthropological trend of Enlightenment and a fundamental theme among all the great philosophes—his interest in this German pessimist remained with him the rest of his life. Note the discussion in Stephen Eric Bronner, *Of Critical Theory and Its Theorists* 2nd Edition (New York: Routledge, 2002), 76ff.

9. Cobban, *In Search of Humanity*, 66.

10. Norbert Elias, *Uber den Prozess der Zivilisation* 2 Bde. (Frankfurt am Main: Suhrkamp, 1997) 1:149–50.

Voltaire and most of his friends, for example, were sharply critical of the mechanical materialism of Holbach. Crucial for the Enlightenment was not whether sentiments and passions were important, obviously they were, but whether they could be influenced by reason. The philosophes were thus concerned with adapting state and society to the developing wants and faculties of citizens and the given social relations to the standards of freedom.[11] They employed "progress" to attack the institutions and ideas of a bygone age in the name of the reason, rights, and interests of the individual. It was precisely their contempt for dogma, prejudice, and privilege—their reliance on critique for political purposes—that provoked the most violent opposition. Confronting tradition and questioning authority, indeed, rendered the Enlightenment notion of progress unique and highlights its contemporary salience.

Enlightenment understandings of progress may not have been "dialectical," but they contested both the classical view of change as a circular "revolution"—with its inevitable transitions from monarchy to tyranny to democracy to mob rule to aristocracy to oligarchy and back to monarchy—as well as the religious belief in an increasingly imminent millennium whose realization would fulfill a predestined purpose and, apocalyptically, recreate paradise.[12] Condorcet, Helvetius, Priestly, and a few others may have waxed poetic about the future, but their relation to antiquity and even to the more recent past was not simply negative. Most Enlightenment thinkers, in keeping with the ancients, surrendered belief in the redemption of the past while, in keeping with the western religious tradition, retained some belief in an emancipated future. And so, situated in the world while retaining a certain longing for paradise, its most important representatives acknowledged that progress would never be complete. Leibniz put it well in his *On the Ultimate Origination of Things* when he wrote: "there always remain in the abyss of things slumbering parts which have yet to be awakened, to grow in size and worth, and in a word, to advance to a more perfect state. And hence no end of progress is ever reached."

Something will always be missing: freedom will never become fully manifest in reality. The relation between them is *asymptotic*. Therefore, most

11. Herbert Marcuse and Franz Neumann, "Theories of Social Change" in Herbert Marcuse, *Collected Papers: Technology, War and Fascism* ed. Douglas Kellner (New York: Routledge, 1998) 1:119.
12. Karl Löwith, *Meaning in History* (Chicago: University of Chicago Press, 1967); Ernest Lee Tuveson, *Millennium and Utopia: A Study in the Background of the Idea of Progress* (New York: Harper, 1964), 6.

philosophes understood progress as a regulative ideal, or as a postulate,[13] rather than as an absolute or the expression of some divine plane or the foundation for a system.[14] Even in scientific terms, progress retained a critical dimension insofar as it implied the need to question established certainties. In this vein, it is misleading simply to equate scientific reason with the domination of man and nature.[15] All the great figures of the scientific revolution —Bacon, Boyle, Newton—were concerned with liberating humanity from what seemed the power of seemingly intractable forces. Swamps were everywhere; roads were few; forests remained to be cleared; illness was rampant; food was scarce; most people would never leave their village. What it implied not to understand the existence of bacteria or the nature of electricity, just to use very simple examples, is today simply inconceivable. Enlightenment figures like Benjamin Franklin, "the complete *philosophe*,"[16] became famous for a reason: they not only freed people from some of their fears but through inventions like the stove and the lightning rod they also raised new possibilities for making people's lives more livable.

Critical theorists and postmodernists miss the point when they view Enlightenment intellectuals in general and scientists in particular as simple apostles of reification. They actually constituted its most consistent enemy. The philosophes may not have grasped the commodity form, but they empowered people by challenging superstitions and dogmas that left them mute and helpless against the whims of nature and the injunctions of tradition. Enlightenment thinkers were justified in understanding knowledge as inherently improving humanity. Infused with a sense of furthering the public good, liberating the individual from the clutches of the invisible and inexplicable, the Enlightenment idea of progress required what the young Marx later termed "the ruthless critique of everything existing."

13. "Believers in progress never thought empirical validation likely or even possible when the referent was as abstract and vast as humanity or civilization. The point is that for these believers there was no more necessity for empirical proof of universal progress than there was for a geometrical proposition—or, if one was religious, for a commandment or other injunction in the Bible." Robert Nisbet, *The History of Progress* (New York: Basic Books, 1980), 7.

14. Peter Gay, *The Enlightenment* 2 vols. (New York: Norton, 1995 edition) 1:132

15. Cf. Horkheimer and Adorno, *Dialectic of Enlightenment*, 4.

16. Note the wonderful sketch by Henry Steele Commager, *The Empire of Reason: How Europe Imagined and America Realized the Enlightenment* (London: Phoenix, 1978), 21; Richard Wolin, *The Terms of Cultural Criticism: The Frankfurt School, Existentialism, Poststructuralism* (New York: Columbia University Press, 1992), 3.

This regulative notion of progress was never inimical to subjectivity. Quite the contrary: progress became meaningful only with reference to real living individuals.

Enlightenment thinking did not mechanically identify progress with the chronological passing of time or, usually, mere technological development. It was instead always seen as entailing a moral commitment to expanding self-awareness and the possibilities for exercising judgment. This was as true for Immanuel Kant, who viewed progress from the standpoint of the species, as for Moses Mendelssohn, who identified it with the increasing capacities for self-reflection by the individual. Both saw the root of progress in the growing possibilities for criticism and the development of human capacities. Progress thus became the rallying cry for attacking the privileges and dogma associated with the status quo. It was undoubtedly what led Diderot to exclaim that freedom would only be realized when the last aristocrat had been strangled with the entrails of the last priest. The outburst was revealing but so were the words of Tom Paine who probably best expressed the general position of the philosophes when he noted in 1795 that "the vanity and presumption of governing beyond the grave is the most ridiculous and insolent of all tyrannies. Man has no property in man, neither has one generation a property in the generations that are to follow."

To be sure, from the beginning, "progress" was open to perversion. It was capable of being projected back into the past, thereby justifying the exploitation of those considered lower on the evolutionary scale, and it could be identified with an escalator that moves society ever upward. The idea was always in danger of becoming regimented and stripped of its critical character. But it is absurd to doubt the fundamentally liberating vision with which the notion of progress should remain associated. It always projected a world perhaps best described in *The Future of Progress* by Condorcet who so avidly hoped that one day:

> . . . the sun will shine only on free men who know no other master but their reason: when tyrants and slaves, priests and their stupid or hypocritical instruments, will exist only in works of history and on the stage; and when we shall think of them only to pity their victims and their dupes; to maintain ourselves in a state of vigilance by thinking on their excesses; and to learn how to recognize and so to destroy, by force of reason, the first seeds of tyranny and superstition, should they ever dare to reappear amongst us.

Like the notion of Enlightenment itself,[17] of course, progress can be interpreted in two ways. It can be seen as a modern historical phenomenon inspiring the Enlightenment of the seventeenth and eighteenth centuries. But progress can also be understood as an anthropological tendency demanding the sacrifice of subjectivity and desire, the domination of inner and outer nature, for the purpose of survival and conquest: Odysseus was its symbol in *Dialectic of Enlightenment*. He surrendered his name and identity in order to survive, he used logic in order to illuminate the unknowable, and his saga is marked by his ever increasing attempt to exert mastery over himself and nature:[18] his fate is thereby seen by Horkheimer and Adorno as emblematic of a process whose liquidation of subjectivity would culminate in the number tattooed on the arm of the concentration camp inmate.[19] The historical and the anthropological notions of progress thereby converged. Critique of the Enlightenment would now require a critique of civilization.

And this is legitimate when considering the way in which people of color, Native Americans, or inhabitants from other premodern cultures, were trotted around the European capitals for analytical inspection and treated like animals in the zoo. François Truffaut provided a moving and representative portrait of this in his movie *The Wild Child* where a waif born outside of "civilization," grown up among wolves and in virtual isolation, is captured and "educated" according to the scientific strictures and "civilized" ideals. The film identified progress with a moral escalator leading from the supposedly primitive, emotional, and childlike to the modern, rational, and adult. This view would indeed influence later forms of teleological thinking that paid little mind to those whom Engels derisively called "peoples without history" (*geschichtslosen Völker*),[20] and who understood progress as an abstract standard to be met and imposed from the outside—through imperialism—

17. Enlightenment comprises both a historically specific scientific "theory of knowledge," which was developed in Europe during the seventeenth and eighteenth centuries in contesting theological dogma, as well as an anthropological struggle with error and superstition. Max Horkheimer, "Die Aufklärung" in *Gesammelte Werke* (Frankfurt am Main: Fischer, 1989) 13:571.
18. Horkheimer and Adorno, *Dialectic of Enlightenment*, 46ff.
19. For an alternative view of the Odyssey, which highlights its critical reflexivity, humanism, and sense of nuance, see the famous opening chapter of Erich Auerbach, *Mimesis: The Representation of Reality in Western Literature* trans. Willard R. Trask (Princeton: Princeton University Press, 2003 ed.)
20. Note the illuminating study by Roman Rosdolsky, *Friedrich Engels und das Problem der 'Geschichtslosen Völker* from the Archiv für Sozialgeschichte Bd. 4 (Verlag für Literatur und Zeitgeschehen: Hannover, 1964).

rather than fostered and cultivated from within diverse cultures.[21] Even by resisting repressive customs in order to expand the range of individual experience and the existing wealth of knowledge, however, the pre-modern community will be undermined by becoming entangled in a "foreign" debate. To this extent, indeed, the critique of progress will always become intertwined with the critique of modernity.

Rousseau introduced this critique by claiming that "our minds have been corrupted in proportion as the arts and sciences have improved." His *Discourse on the Arts and Sciences* (1749), which won him a prize from the Academy of Dijon and made him famous, challenged the value of progress and reflection in the name of authentic intuition and an unadulterated view of nature. But his essay was not concerned with resurrecting the "noble savage"—a term Rousseau never employed—as his critics like Voltaire would later insist. It also was inspired less by provincial resentment than the hatred of opulence inherited from the Reformation, the critique of courtly manners, leveled by Moliere in *Les précieuses ridicules*, and the egalitarianism cherished by the self-styled "citizen of Geneva." Rousseau knew that there was no going back to some golden age, which was also the case for Horkheimer and Adorno, though—in contrast to them—his critique of "progress" evidenced a a political purpose. Rousseau had little sympathy for what would become the longings of nineteenth-century reactionaries for the heroic, the aristocratic, the hierarchical, or some mythic past with which to challenge the introduction of democracy and the "masses." He never showed any inclination to restore the medieval past or the privileges of a self-selected elite and, until he neared the end of his life, a church protected by dogma.

"Necessity raised thrones," Rousseau wrote, "and the arts and sciences support them." Nature alone, rational in its laws, might provide a standard for criticizing the corruption fostered by civilization. His vision was profoundly critical and populist. Rousseau identified with the "simple souls," the exploited and disenfranchised, and he sought to articulate the sentiments appropriate to a democratic community. His radicalism derived from a willingness to identify progress—or, better, the way it was understood by a foppish court and an increasingly materialist bourgeoisie—with inauthenticity and

21. A critique of those who would identify the Enlightenment with imperialist ideology, and a perspective linking progress with the expression of cultural difference, is provided by Sankar Muthu, *Enlightenment Against Empire* (Princeton: Princeton University Press, 2003), 4,7.

alienation.[22] These themes would become pillars of romanticism and, long before the young Marx, they appear in *The Sorrows of Young Werther* by Goethe and also in the beautiful lines from Hölderlin's *Hyperion*:

> Barbarians from times past grown still more barbaric through effort, and knowledge, and even religion. Profoundly incapable of any sublime feeling, depraved to the core. . . . Manual workers do you see but not human beings (*Menschen*), thinkers but not human beings, masters and servants, youths and propertied persons but no human beings—is this all not like a battlefield in which hands and arms and torn-off limbs lie strewn among one another, their spent life-blood running into the sands?[23]

Amid the disorientation and fragmentation, the products of a burgeoning capitalist division of labor, it became a question for "romantic anticapitalism" (Lukács) of restoring wholeness to the human being as well as a harmony between human beings and nature that had never existed. The romantic assault on progress was undertaken in terms of a utopian ideal that conservatives denied and genuine reactionaries sought to discover in the mists of the past. Critics from the left would, soon enough rely not merely on Rousseau but also on Hegel, whose work highlighted the "inverted world" of an alienated consciousness, and Marx, who borrowed the term in describing the "commodity form" and its aim of supplanting "use value" with "exchange value," issues of quality with matters of quantity, and the interests of working people with the requirements of capital accumulation. Instrumental reason and the commodity form could thus be seen fusing in a production process—predicated on "alienation" (*Entfremdung*) and "reification" (*Verdinglichung*)[24]—that turned the individual into a tool for the division of labor and the accumulation of capital.

Many on the radical left were thus led to conclude that the "revolution" should no longer be directed merely against capitalism or an authoritarian form of government but rather against an "alienated" totality and a "reified" set of social relations. It was no longer a question of instituting a more humane

22. Marshall Berman, *The Politics of Authenticity: Radical Individualism and the Emergence of Modern Society* (New York: Atheneum, 1970).

23. Friedrich Hölderlin, *Werke und Briefe* 3 Bde. Hrsg. Friedrich Beissner und Jochen Schmidt (Frankfurt am Main: Insel, 1969) 1:433.

24. Georg Lukács, *History and Class Consciousness: Studies in Marxist Dialectics* trans. Rodney Livingstone (Cambridge: MIT Press, 1971), 83ff.

economic system with a republican regime and new secular modes of thinking. It was instead a matter of turning the historical "revolution into an anthropological apocalypse. The transformative act thereby became burdened
with ever more utopian goals ranging from the abolition of money and the division of labor to the elimination of the family and the creation of democratic "soviets" or workers' councils. Such utopian hopes were raised during the
"heroic period" of the Russian Revolution from 1918–23. With its passing,
however, they were dashed. Exaggerated optimism made way for an equally
exaggerated pessimism. Progress seemed invalidated by Auschwitz and Hiroshima, the costs of two world wars, and a failed revolution. It made sense to
suggest that: "the curse of irresistible progress is irresistible regression."[25]

No longer would the idea of progress be understood from the material
standpoint of policies, movements, and institutions. It would instead speak
to securing the individuality threatened by mass society and a notion of freedom now seen only in the tension between subjectivity and the system intent upon eliminating it.[26] The point of progress for the new radicals was to
foster "resistance" with no purpose other than the existential affirmation of
subjectivity in terms of aesthetic experience, metaphysical speculation, or
the utopian "longing for the totally other."[27] Increasing the choices available
to individuals now meant nothing more than reinforcing a "totally administered society;"[28] insisting upon "tolerance" would produce only a false
sense of autonomy; mass education could, by definition, only prove "mass
deception;" while greater affluence merely strengthened the "happy consciousness." The positive manifestation of progress thereby became identified with furthering the extension of un-freedom, the practice of exploitation and imperialism, or—more dramatically—what might be understood
as the connection between "the sling-shot and the atom bomb."[29]

Critical theory identified genuine progress with resisting the worst evil: it
became a matter of plugging holes in a shoddy dike against an ever more violent flood. What should be preserved remained unclear, however, and what
should be supported even less so. But this was only logical. The interpretation had become completely contradictory: progress required resistance

---

25. Horkheimer and Adorno, *Dialectic of Enlightenment.*, 36.
26. Theodor W. Adorno, *Zur Lehre von der Geschichte und von der Freiheit* (Frankfurt am
    Main: Suhrkamp, 2001), 27
27. Max Horkheimer, *Die Sehnsucht nach dem ganz Anderen* (Hamburg: Fischer, 1970), 70.
28. Adorno, *Zur Lehre von der Geschichte und von der Freiheit*, 22
29. Ibid., 20.

against the existing society yet political action necessarily involved the use of instrumental reason. The only possible move was to turn resistance into a metaphysical or aesthetic stance. In turn, however, this stripped progress of its political rationale, its moral appeal, and its critical character. What remained was a hope more wistful than militant: "Too little of what is good has power in the world for progress to be expressed in a predicative judgment about the world, but there can be no good, not a trace of it, without progress."[30]

The next step was inevitable: the critics of meta-narrative, perhaps the best definition of postmodernism,[31] would create a meta-narrative of their own. Progress would no longer merely be "cursed" with regression but instead become identified with regression *tout court:* modernity with its reliance on scientific reason and "totalizing ideologies" would now be seen as the source of the holocaust.[32] The new subjectivists—fashionable purveyors of a metaphysical version of critical theory, "postcolonial" thinkers, poststructuralists, philosophers of identity—would thus find themselves increasingly incapable of recognizing that modernity "affects man in two ways simultaneously: he becomes more independent, self-reliant, and critical, and he becomes more isolated, alone, and afraid. The understanding of the whole problem of freedom depends upon the very ability to see both sides of the process and not to lose track of one side while following the other."[33]

Hegel and Marx had still viewed the march of alienation in concert with the possibility of its conquest. Their judgment of material development depended on the human resources it liberated. They understood "progress" as the establishment of conditions that would expand the possibilities for critical reflection, or foster the "self-determination" (*Selbsttaetigkeit*) of the proletariat, and they used it to confront the more degrading expressions of intellectual and material oppression. They privileged speculative intelligence and empirical knowledge—as against will and subjectivity—in order to enhance the ability of the individual to deal with nature and society. The communists would later subordinate this understanding of progress to a stultifying determinism and a form of technological ambition run amok. Any

---

30. Theodor W. Adorno, "Progress," in *Critical Models: Interventions and Catchwords* (New York: Columbia University Press, 1998),146.
31. Jean-François Lyotard, *The Postmodern Condition: A Report on Knowledge* trans. Geoff Bennington and Brian Massumi (Minneapolis: University of Minnesota Press, 1984), xxiv.
32. Zygmunt Bauman, *Modernity and the Holocaust* (Ithaca: Cornell University Press, 1991), 17 and *passim*.
33. Erich Fromm, *Escape from Freedom* (New York: Holt, 1965 ed.), 124.

historical or political point of reference was thereby lost. This indeed makes it incumbent upon new forms of critical theory to highlight the radical moment of "progress" that was expressed by the philosophes in theory and fought for by their followers in practice.

Again it is a matter of sense and sensibility: Odysseus is not the only, or even necessarily the best, symbol of Enlightenment. There is also Prometheus, who paid dearly for stealing fire from the gods, and Icarus who dared to fly, and crashed to his death when his wings of wax melted in the sun. The Enlightenment identified progress less with some abstract notion of freedom—expressed in the interplay between subjectivity and system—than with fostering the will to know and the fight against prejudice, the insistence upon tolerance and reciprocity, the demand for a democratic public sphere, and the accountability of institutions. Its representatives sought a flowering of freedoms that the individual might actually employ: intellectual freedom and the right to hold views counter to those already established; economic freedom to pursue personal economic advantage beyond the limitations then still determined by birth; and, finally, the political freedom secured in institutions based on the liberal rule of law and popular sovereignty.[34] Not to understand the Enlightenment idea of progress in terms of the struggle for these practical freedoms is not to understand it at all.

The idea of progress was always—anthropologically as well as historically—less about the eradication of subjectivity and the domination of nature than the possibility of personal liberation, popular empowerment, and overcoming the spell of myth and nature. Progress is an inherently rational idea. But it does not call for belief in the omnipotence of reason, the superfluous character of passion, or the existence of an objective solution to every problem.[35] Neither Condorcet nor Kant provided an ontological foundation for progress and even the most rabid believer in progress, an adamant atheist and technological enthusiast, like Holbach could write in his *System de la nature* that "it is not given man to know everything; it is not given him to know his origins; it is not given him to penetrate to the essence of things or to go back to first principles." The issue for the philosophes was not the discovery of absolute truth but the establishment of conditions in which truth might be pursued. Or, to frame the matter in terms of a new critical theory with

34. Leonard Krieger, *The German Idea of Freedom: History of a Political Tradition* (Chicago: The University of Chicago Press, 1957), 3
35. Gay, *The Enlightenment* 1:141–45.

some sense of the concrete, the extent to which progress manifested itself was the extent to which claims could be treated as provisional.

Reason and knowledge were never the enemies of progress. But their enemies were also the enemies of progress. David Hume, in this vein, liked to say that "ignorance is the mother of devotion." Unreflective passion offers far better support than scientific inquiry for the claims of religion or the injunctions of totalitarian regimes. The scientific method projects not merely the "open society," but also the need to question authority. This was already evidenced in the *Meno* when Socrates showed that he could teach mathematics to a slave and in *The Republic* when, exhibiting the frustration of the anti-intellectual, Thrasymachus insisted that justice is the right of the stronger. On one point, however, the most famous adversary of Socrates was right: his position suggested that whether the moral possibilities of progress are realized is not the province of philosophy but of politics. This would have radical implications. Upsetting the divine structure of things marked the Enlightenment notion of progress. Its advocates privileged liberty over order and the communicable power of discourse over the incommunicable experience of grace. These new values would serve as the points of reference for all other values: order would no longer be employed as an excuse to smother liberty, but rather be understood as the precondition for its pursuit.[36] Order always preceded liberty for the philosophes: it was seen as providing the rules and procedures for "constituting" the liberty enjoyed by citizens through the protection of the state.[37]

Enlightenment thinkers were aware that while nature obeys fixed laws, history is a varied spectacle. But this insight resulted in neither an unyielding commitment to forging a system resulting in what has once again become the fashionable belief that we are at "the end of history, or a some postmodern conviction that all is rupture:[38] In his *Philosophy of History* (1766), Voltaire introduced the term "philosophical history" to contest religious dogmas emphasizing predestination and the like as well as indicate that the struggle for rationality furnishes coherence for the manifold struggles undertaken in the name of freedom.[39] His *Essay on the Manners and*

36. Krieger, *Kings and Philosophers*, 182.
37. Eric R. Boehme, "The Power to Harm: Institutionalized Risk, Political Development, and Citizenship in the United States" (PhD Dissertation, Rutgers University, 2003), 12.
38. Stephen Eric Bronner, "The End of History Revisited," in *Imagining the Possible: Radical Politics for Conservative Times* (New York: Routledge, 2002), 195ff.
39. Voltaire, *The Philosophy of History* (New York: Citadel, 1965)

Spirit of Nations (1756), in the same vein, had already articulated a general vision of historical development. It lacked the usual unrelenting emphasis on western experience and "great" individuals because it identified progress with what might be termed a critical reflection on the pursuit of progress. Voltaire made clear that history combines human creation with the interpretation of what has been created and that the latter alone should be identified with progress. The importance of his historical work derives from its insight that the struggle for self-understanding is a human struggle. The communicable character of this understanding or "consciousness" of progress, indeed, turns history into a shared enterprise.

The belief that enlightenment values are somehow intrinsically "western" is surely parochial and most likely racist. Just as money, the division of labor, and class conflict can be found in precapitalist cultures like Egypt, Greece, and Rome, so is it the case that liberal and cosmopolitan values usually identified with western thinking in general and the Enlightenment in particular were expressed in any number of nonwestern societies—including the three great civilizations of India, China, and Islam[40]—by religious figures like Mohammed and the Buddha; political leaders from Cyrus the Great, who allowed each nation to choose its religion and keep its customs, to the sixteenth-century leader Akbar who condemned slavery and the immolation of widows; and philosophers like Plotinus, Avicenna, Averroes, who highlighted the cosmological elements of the classical heritage and generated a tradition that extended from Giordano Bruno over Spinoza and Leibniz to Ernst Bloch. Amid the civil wars and religious conflicts of the premodern world, enough reflective people of compassion, appalled by religious fanaticism and the devastation of war insisted upon fairness and the rule of law, and highlighted the sanctity of the individual conscience and the plight of the lowly and the insulted. In a fine essay,[41] Amartya Sen has made western intellectuals aware of what we should have been more aware of from the beginning: nonwestern and premodern thinkers had also emphasized the "pursuit of reason" rather than "the reliance on tradition." The idea of progress, of making the solutions to conflict more civilized, is not simply a western idea.

This does not mean that all regions and nations embraced the idea of progress—along with its liberal, egalitarian, and cosmopolitan implications—

---

40. J. M. Roberts, *The History of the World* (Middlesex: Penguin Press, 1976).
41. Amartya Sen, "East and West: The Reach of Reason," in *New York Review of Books* (July 20, 2000), 33–38.

or that all will ever do so to the same degree. This is not the venue in which to examine the complex reasons why capitalism and the modern notion of progress were generated in the West. But it is necessary to emphasize that progress and enlightenment values are not the preserve of a geographic entity.[42] Intellectual tendencies that seek to promote such an understanding of progress have existed within diverse cultures and manifold traditions, and these have something to offer for the vision of a liberated society. It would be the height of arrogance, for example, to suggest that a Chinese tradition harking back three thousand years is somehow invalidated by the philosophical efforts of a small minority of European intellectuals writing between 1650 and 1800 or to deny that Gandhi could justify his vision of a multi-ethnic, democratic order from within his own religious understanding. The belief that achieving a genuine consensus on moral issues calls upon all participants in the discourse to think through arguments in the same way is absurd. The quest for humanitarian values has taken many paths in the past and it will do so, again, in the future.

"Progress" is rooted in the Socratic dictum "know thyself" with its insistence upon critical reflection and the concern of those like St. Augustine and Angelus Silesius, seeking to understand what constitutes a genuine revelation, who employed the term "authenticity." Kant or Locke or Rousseau did not conjure such ideas and categories out of thin air. But there is a danger in underestimating their contributions and viewing these thinkers as simply refashioners of classical preoccupations or religious concerns with immortality and grace.[43] Indeed, if absolute rupture is the only criterion for determining what is new, then nothing will ever be new under the sun: it can always be shown that somebody else got there first.

42. "Of course, it is not being claimed here that all the different ideas relevant to the use of reasoning for social harmony and humanity have flourished equally in all civilizations of the world. That would not only be untrue; it would also be a stupid claim of mechanical uniformity. But once we recognize that many ideas that are taken to be quintessentially Western have also flourished in other civilizations, we also see that these ideas are not as culture-specific as is sometimes claimed. We need not begin with pessimism, at least on this ground, about the prospects of reasoned humanism in the world." Ibid., pg. 36

43. Thus, Carl Becker could suggest in his *The Heavenly City of the Eighteenth-Century Philosophers* (1932) that the philosophes were really engaged in little more replacing the longing for paradise with a longing for recognition by posterity and reconstructing the "heavenly city" of St. Augustine along secular lines." For a withering critique, see by Peter Gay, "Carl Becker's Heavenly City," in *The Party of Humanity: Essays in the French Enlightenment* (New York: Norton, 1971), 188ff.

The Enlightenment of the seventeenth and eighteenth centuries may have relied more on the past than is usually assumed; its advocates may ultimately have rendered self-conscious prior aspirations involving the role of the intellect and the possibilities for its exercise. But the Enlightenment also reflected the radical vision of a rising bourgeoisie that grew out of the feudal system with its capitalist mode of production, its republican goals, and its new secular culture. Even the majority in Europe did not initially embrace its worldview. The "western" ideals of the Enlightenment were opposed by all established feudal institutions like the church and premodern classes like the aristocracy and the peasantry, and—following the failure of the Revolutions of 1848—even by the majority of the bourgeoisie. Its representatives soon surrendered the original political radicalism of their class for new commitments to the authoritarian state and imperialism. Thus, while the Enlightenment may have arisen in the West, its initial challenge was to conquer the prejudices of the West.

Various developments facilitated the attack on the past. Too often forgotten is the influence of the geographical findings made by great explorers like Captain Cook—the opening of the African interior as well as the encounter with Australia and Siam—no less than the daring anthropological investigations of thinkers like Buffon who extended the age of the earth millions of years into the past.[44] There is indeed a sense in which the Enlightenment reflected what was becoming a far deeper paradigmatic shift in the experience of space and time. A new planetary perspective served as the precondition for the new ideas of "humanity" and universal "rights." It enabled the philosophes to articulate in secular form those universal ideals of freedom for which dissidents, usually inspired by religion, had struggled from time immemorial in different ways and in different cultures.

Enlightenment thinkers could not jump out of their historical skin. Many of them exhibited elitist and racist traits: Africa was given little respect and anti-Semitism was common. But such prejudices were contradicted by the universal principles predicated on reciprocity—and the view of nature—in which the philosophes believed. Eurocentrism did not define

---

44. "While others enlarged the world of space, Buffon expanded the world of time; he had extended the age of the earth from six thousand to many millions of years, though publicly he was content to claim only eighty thousand. To be sure, the Church persuaded him to make a retraction of even those modest calculations, but it was a tactical withdrawal, and no one took it seriously, for it was taken for granted that Buffon was right." Commager, *The Empire of Reason*, 7

the Enlightenment. Its sensibility was not that of the later imperialists or the conquistadors, supported by the Catholic Church, who slaughtered the Aztecs and the Incas. Its new global vision instead challenged both existing religious beliefs and, ironically, what might now be termed "western" prejudices. Enlightenment thinkers knew that history evidenced a plurality of sophisticated exotic cultures and their ideal presentations of them provided utopian images with which to criticize the status quo: China was idolized during the Enlightenment, its repressive characteristics ignored by Voltaire and his friends, while the image of the Persian and the American Indian and the Tropical Islander—unspoiled by western religion and "civilization"—achieved enormous popularity through the writings of various philosophes. Less revealing indeed is the knowledge of these cultures than the interest they aroused and the good will extended to them by Diderot, Leibniz, Voltaire, and the rest: it was assumed that "simplicity, honesty, generosity, and natural morality seemed to be the general character of all the extra-European and non-Christian peoples."[45]

Just as new geographic explorations and scientific investigations contested the prevalent understanding of space, the new interest awakened in nonwestern cultures transformed the sense of time. The archaeological discoveries concerning classical antiquity by figures like Johann Winckelmann helped place feudalism in historical perspective. It fostered both a sense of decline regarding the ancient regime and a desire for rebirth—a feeling for progress—that would prove of ideological significance for the European interest in the American Colonies and their War of Independence. The delight in the discovery of diverse cultures helped create a feeling that things could be different and, in turn, this undermined belief in the divine right of kings and a static aristocratic order whose origins were shrouded in the mists of time. That the world can be changed, and that individuals have the right to change it, is the challenge posed by the idea of progress. It is the minimal prerequisite for any attempt by the victims of modernity—women, religious minorities, people of color, and other oppressed groups—to challenge the restrictions placed upon them. This new perspective on transformation, on progress, is an essential part of the Enlightenment heritage.

Innovation and change became words of praise rather than abuse during the Enlightenment.[46] Their advocates freed history from theological presup-

45. Cobban, *In Search of Humanity*), 50.
46. Gay, *The Enlightenment* 2:3, 56

positions, secularized the notion of causation, and opened new territories of inquiry.[47] Partisans of these ideas may not have been able to reconcile the citizen and the bourgeois in their honest attempt to realize "the good life on earth."[48] But their belief in progress enabled the philosophes to view themselves as reformers intent upon furthering education, fostering a cosmopolitan spirit of civility and toleration, while abolishing censorship, the debtor's prison, the galley, the stake, slavery, torture, and the Inquisition. Wealth, gender, race, and birth might continue to play a role in social life. But the Enlightenment provided a new political framework for attacking these expressions of prejudice and privilege. The constitutions introduced in the United States and elsewhere during the age of democratic revolution—whatever their limitations—left room for revision, for reform, for progress. And that was no small achievement. The Enlightenment generated an ideal of social justice and citizenship that already spoke to an international civil society, contested national prejudices, and the political concerns of exploited classes and groups. Its thinkers basically agreed that the "natural" capacities of the individual were capable of realization only in society. Once differences were understood in sociological rather than religious or racial terms, moreover, they believed it possible to better the lot of the most victimized. Thus, Holbach could write in the idiom of his time:

> The savage man and the civilized, the white man, the red man, the black man; Indian and European, Chinaman and Frenchman, Negro and Lapp have the same nature. The differences between them are only modifications of their common nature, produced by climate, government, education, opinions, and the various causes which operate upon them.[49]

This insight concerning the impact of society on individuals was rendered more concrete by Hegel, who noted that the subject is socialized by the particular interaction of institutions like the family, civil society, and the state as well as a culture primarily defined by religion, art, and philosophy. Interrogating the legitimacy of the traditions associated with each of these spheres, which itself requires the exercise of liberty, alone makes further progress possible. Progress will therefore exhibit itself differently in different

47. Ibid., 1:37
48. Robert Anchor, *The Enlightenment Tradition* (Berkeley: University of California Press, 1967), 10
49. Cited in Gay, *The Enlightenment* 2: 4

realms of theory and practice. Scientific progress, for example, is irreversible: discoveries cannot be retracted and, in the information age, they cannot even remain concealed. Cultural progress or *"civilization"*, by contrast, is reversible: barbarism can obviously follow a period of cultural flowering or democratic development. In the realm of aesthetics, moreover, progress need not exist at all: there is no reason to believe, for example, that Shakespeare is "better" than Sophocles. "Progress" in one arena can be accompanied by regression in another. The lack of fit between different spheres of theory and practice is what renders contingency, or the historical expression of freedom, concrete: history thereby resists the imperatives of both functionalism and reductionism. Nevertheless, this same lack of fit between spheres of activity creates a disharmony within society that, when internalized by the individual, can be understood as alienation.

Progress is nonsynchronous.[50] Equating it with harmony, or some all-encompassing category, militates against its concrete character. Hegel was always aware of that. He identified progress with the ability to differentiate between phenomena and the corresponding ability of the mind to provide an increasingly complex set of categories to make sense of an increasingly complex reality. Each moment of the totality was seen as retaining its own unique dynamic (*Eigendynamik*). Hegel also knew better than anyone that the "end of history," which he identified with a form of "multiplicity in unity," would produce neither peace nor fulfillment. War would remain on the horizon as would solitude, illness, and the contradiction between the finality of individual existence and the infinite character of social development. The great philosopher sensed that the harmonious conclusion of history, the unity of subject and object, would never take place: he knew that the dark cloud of alienation would never dissolve into a bright blue sky.

With the division of labor, the lack of fit between different spheres of social life, history could only be understood as working behind the back of individuals: thus the limit of the enlightenment notion of progress is reached. That the actions of individuals are reconfigured by society, that consequences turn against intentions, was already apparent in the medieval idea of the "hidden hand" which, when not applied to the supposedly nefarious activities of the Jews,[51] was seen as providing the unseen harmony underly-

50. Ernst Bloch, *Erbschaft dieser Zeit* (Frankfurt am Main: Suhrkamp, 1973), 104ff.
51. Stephen Eric Bronner, *A Rumor about the Jews: Anti-Semitism, Conspiracy, and the Protocols of Zion* (New York: Oxford University Press, Paperback Edition, 2003), 33ff.

ing the apparent discord of the world. This view anticipated the famous "invisible hand" of Adam Smith and Mandeville, which seemed to assure market equilibrium between supply and demand, but which actually pointed to the basic moral problem of capitalist society: how can private selfishness be transformed into public virtue?[52] Hegel and Marx provided their own solutions to the problem. Envisioning the proletariat as the subject-object of history, however, was as illusory as pointing to the "cunning of reason" employed by the World Spirit. Harmony will never exist between humanity and its works: the relation between them can only prove asymptotic.

Introducing the "invisible hand" already suggested that the "individual" and unmitigated self-interest, while the starting point for the classical liberal understanding of the market, are insufficient for explaining its actual functioning. The same can be said of "society": introducing social processes, while philosophically excluding the individuals that sustain them, only reinforces alienation from a different perspective. Thus, while romantic thinkers of the counter-enlightenment like Carlyle would focus on the "heroic" individual—who manipulates history through the sheer power of his will—positivists would abolish subjectivity by reducing ideas and lived lives to particular social interests or processes. Will, subjectivity, and particularity thereby squared off against the determinism, objectivity, and universality. In reality, however, they are flip sides of the same coin. Just as rigidly deterministic forms of system building obviate the need for political intervention by real individuals, from the opposite perspective, privileging experiential freedom and the will undermines the importance of thinking about social processes and institutional constraints.

Progress requires situating the individual within a context and fostering the ability to discriminate between those constraints that are necessary and those that are not: the implicit injunction to contest atavistic restraints on personal freedom is precisely what renders progress "political." The question whether judgment and resistance are legitimate helped produce the great divide between the Enlightenment and its critics who bemoaned the hubris of those without cultural "niveau" and the manner in which the organic community and its "fine draperies of life" were being torn asunder. Not the advocates of reason, individualism, and equality, but their critics deserve to be charged with elitism. The philosophes were far less concerned with protecting the cultural inheritance of an aristocratic past than contesting prejudices,

---

52. Anchor, *The Enlightenment Tradition*, 10.

insisting upon reforms, envisioning new institutions, and sometimes even promulgating revolutions.

Traditionalists have tended to understand progress as a linear development in terms of which humanity advances steadily in a definite and desirable direction.[53] That made it easy for them to then identify the Enlightenment with unbounded optimism, teleological determinism, and a utopian belief in human perfectibility. But this is a caricature. It was generally assumed by the philosophes —for without such an assumption any serious notion of either moral development or democracy is impossible—that individuals can act responsibly and employ both "common sense" and critical reflection. But the Enlightenment did not seek to bring about a change in human nature, only in the judgment of human behavior. Its leading intellectuals refused to sanction any institutional attempts to impose belief by fiat or exercise power in an arbitrary fashion. They were concerned with expanding the realm of freedom, the range of choices available for the individual, and it was in order to mitigate the drudgery of existence that they stressed the liberating affects of technology.[54]

Advocates of the Enlightenment knew that they could not redeem the past, the sacrifices made, and the hopes betrayed. Most greeted talk about teleological redemption with cynicism. In *Faust*, it is Mephistopheles who serves as the agent of progress: the force that always negates, who insists it is just that everything that exists is doomed to perish, and who finds his "authenticity" in destruction. Montesquieu warned that "it is an eternal experience that every man possessing power is tempted to abuse it"; Hume placed his greatest thesis in a locked drawer; Kant maintained that the "crooked timber of humanity" could never be made straight; the author of *Candide* was no naïf; and James Madison drew the most appropriate political implications from this general outlook when he wrote in the famous fifty-first essay of *The Federalist Papers* that:

> If men were angels no government would be necessary. If angels were to govern men, neither external nor internal controls on government would be necessary. In framing a government which is to be administered by men over men, the great difficulty lies in this: you must first enable the government to control the governed; and in the next place oblige it to

---

53. Bury, *The Idea of Historical Progress*, 5.
54. Henry Pachter, "The Right to Be Lazy," in *Socialism in History: Political Essays of Henry Pachter* ed. Stephen Eric Bronner (New York: Columbia University Press, 1984),15.

control itself. A dependence on the people is, no doubt, the primary control on the government; but experience has taught mankind the necessity of auxiliary precautions . . . where the constant aim is to divide and arrange the several offices in such a manner as that each may be a check on the other—that the private interest of every individual may be a sentinel over the public rights.

Enlightenment thinkers were not utopians with totalitarian inclinations, but realists who understood the costs of progress. Their optimism was tempered by their pessimism concerning the ability of the powerful to exercise power prudently: this indeed led them to insist upon the separation of powers, checks and balances, institutional accountability, popular sovereignty, and the rule of law. Their concern with furthering human happiness was informed by the difficulty, the intractability, of society with its vested interests. But this very insight enabled them to shift the cause of human misery from the classical notion of fate or the religious notion of original sin to society and the impact of ignorance, prejudice, authoritarianism, and inequality.[55] It also led the most sober among them to reject teleological sophistries and insist upon the need for political actors to offer a plausible connection between means and ends. The Enlightenment was left only with the modest comfort that knowledge of the past—of the way in which power was exercised, the institutions through which it was exercised, and the norms that justified its exercise—would put people in a better position to judge the present. This indeed was what Lord Bolingbroke meant when, anticipating Hegel and Santayana, he wrote that: "history is philosophy teaching by example."

Easy enough to criticize the pretensions of "progress," but without it the prospect for determining any liberating notion of social change vanishes.[56] Walter Benjamin was surely correct when he noted that there is no document of civilization that is not also a document of barbarism. But this only begs the question: what is the degree to which any such document expresses the civilized in contrast to the barbaric and how is it possible to distinguish the one from that of another. Progress enables us to differentiate between ideologies and policies, expose the limits of each, and illuminate the interests they serve. It need not become enmeshed in utopian dogma or condone what

---

55. Cobban, *In Search of Humanity*, 126ff.
56. Cf. Georges Sorel, *Illusions of Progress* trans. John and Charlotte Stanley (Berkeley: University of California Press, 1947), 1–30.

Kierkegaard termed the "teleological suspension of the ethical." But it must reject the romantic yearning for simplicity, the organic, and the traditional. Progress shows its value when confronting the new existential and practical problems that history presents. It receives expression in the refinement of human sentiments: the disgust caused by cruelty to the infirm, to animals, to the weak, and the downtrodden. Progress appears in the growing recognition that there is something wrong with the arbitrary exercise of power and that there is something legitimate about contesting it.

The Enlightenment showed how progress can both foster critique and serve a productive function. That is perhaps its greatest legacy. [57] The Enlightenment idea of progress militated against closure and perfection. It existed as a possibility, never a certainty, and—until Hegel—it lacked ontological foundations. Progress was always coupled with an attack on the refusal to judge change in terms of the freedom it might provide. That change is endless and that freedom can never be fully achieved does not invalidate progress. Quite the contrary: it renders the idea more important than ever.

---

57. Ernst Cassirer, *The Philosophy of the Enlightenment* trans. Fritz C. A. Koelln and James P. Pettegrove (Boston: Beacon Press, 1955), 278.

3

INVENTING LIBERALISM

LIBERALISM WAS THE PHILOSOPHICAL EXPRESSION FOR THE AGE OF democratic revolution and the principal political theory of the Enlightenment. Its method was the critical deployment of "reason" and its goal was bettering the conditions of social life and expanding "freedom."[1] No less than the Enlightenment itself, however, the liberal heritage is both underestimated and taken for granted. Often seen merely as an ideological veil for capitalist exploitation, this new political worldview legitimated the idea of "resistance" against established authority—which was already implicit within the scientific revolution initiated by Sir Francis Bacon, Galileo, and Descartes—and it gave members of what would become the "third estate" a new sense of their rights and their dignity.

Liberalism always posed a threat to religion, not merely because its partisans insisted on the separation of church and state, but also because it suggested that injustices—and their remedies—were products of social action. Enlightenment thinkers, indeed, were the first to recognize the ways in which ideology and exploitation are rooted in social and political institutions. Its advocates were always preoccupied with the injustices suffered by the outsider, who admittedly often then became an insider, and with the rational adjudication of grievances over the use of force. The liberal emphasis upon universal principles, the rule of law, and a reciprocal understanding of the rights and obligations of citizens, also offered a standard for contesting the discriminatory values and practices embedded within existing institutions, laws, and customs. Excluded groups like women and people of color would build upon these values no less than socialists concerned with the rights of working people. And this only makes sense. For, in short, the new liberal theory was intent upon constraining the arbitrary exercise of power.

---

1. Herbert Marcuse, *Reason and Revolution: Hegel and the Rise of Social Theory* (Boston: Beacon, 1960), 9.

It is thus simply misleading to claim: "liberal theory is true as an idea. It contains the image of a society in which irrational anger no longer exists and seeks for outlets. But since the liberal theory assumes that unity among men is already in principle established, it serves as an apologia for existing circumstances."[2]

The new political outlook was embedded in a burgeoning capitalism: this led to an underestimation of the potential for exploitation, an overestimation of the possibilities for reform, and a certain naïve sense that the unqualified pursuit of self-interest would somehow soften the worst passions. But there is something mechanical and impoverished in the belief that liberalism constitutes nothing more than a reflex of economic class interests and just another manipulative expression of bourgeois ideology. The idea of "interest" originally meant something more than economic gain.[3] As the Enlightenment wore on, moreover, many became wary of egoism and its consequences: Adam Smith became concerned with moral sentiments, David Hume embraced tradition, Rousseau sought to introduce the "general will," Voltaire became ever more occupied with the sufferings of ordinary people, while Kant and his friends highlighted the role of moral philosophy. In truth, the general interest was never absent from enlightenment political thinking because it was never the stolid and conservative philosophy of a ruling class, but instead that of a class on the rise in need of coalitional support.[4] An inner tension between the practical imperatives of capitalism and the moral claims of liberalism was there from the beginning. It should therefore not be surprising that concrete economic questions concerning the accumulation of capital were less in the forefront than the political role a new bourgeoisie might play in undermining feudal notions of military

2. Max Horkheimer and Theodor W. Adorno, *Dialectic of Enlightenment* (New York: Herder & Herder, 1972), 169.

3. "When the term "interest in the sense of concerns, aspirations, and advantage gained currency in Western Europe during the late sixteenth century, its meaning was by no means limited to the material aspects of a person's welfare; rather, it comprised the totality of human aspirations, but denoted an element of reflection and calculation with respect to the manner in which these aspirations were to be pursued." Albert O. Hirschman, *The Passions and the Interests: Political Arguments for Capitalism before Its Triumph* (Princeton: Princeton University Press, 1977), 32.

4. "The importance of the middle class and capitalism for eighteenth-century history lies precisely in the fact that they did not yet dominate all aspects of society, but rather were becoming the dominant social and economic forces in a society which was in all other respects still semi-feudal." Robert Anchor, *The Enlightenment Tradition* (Berkeley: University of California Press, 1967), 31.

glory, religious prejudices, and outworn superstitions. Such is the real point behind the famous description of the English stock exchange by Voltaire:

> Take a view of the Royal Exchange in London, a place more venerable than many courts of justice, where the representatives of all nations meet for the benefit of mankind. There the Jew, the Mahometan, and the Christian transact together as though they all professed the same religion, and give the name of Infidel to none but bankrupts. There the Presbyterian confides in the Anabaptist, and the Churchman depends on the Quaker's word. At the breaking up of this pacific and free assembly, some withdraw to the synagogue, and others to take a glass. This man goes and is baptized in a great tub, in the name of the Father, Son, and Holy Ghost: That man has his son's foreskin cut off, whilst a set of Hebrew words (quite unintelligible to him) are mumbled over his child. Others retire to their churches, and there wait for the inspiration of heaven with their hats on, and all are satisfied.[5]

The liberal embrace of the market and a state under the rule of law can both be seen, one less prophetically perhaps than the other, as part of a single attempt to secure an institutional basis for the individual exercise of freedom. Thomas Hobbes and John Locke probably best articulated the basic presuppositions of the new liberal philosophy. They identified the public realm with "political society" or the state and the private realm with the interplay of particular interests and personal property in "civil society." They looked neither to history nor to religious dogma in order to legitimate their views. Instead, they made certain abstract assumptions about human nature, linked them with the interests that might bring individuals together in a political community, and drew the institutional consequences. Hobbes described the hypothetical "state of nature" as a "war of each against all" while Locke conceived of it as a rather poorly ordered existence of relatively well-intentioned persons concerned with garnering a bit of property. The difference would prove decisive for the degree of authority each would give the state and, surely, "it is no exaggeration to say that a man's admiration of absolute government is proportionate to the contempt he feels for those around him."[6]

5. Voltaire, "Letter to Frederick the Great," in *The Portable Enlightenment Reader*, ed. Isaac Kramnick (New York: Viking, 1995), 133.
6. Alexis de Tocqueville, *The Old Regime and the French Revolution*, trans. Stuart Gilbert (New York: Doubleday, 1955), pg. xv.

In any event, Hobbes and Locke were far less concerned with conviction than conduct. The enemy of both was the aristocracy. Sharply opposing the dominant forms of political theory associated with the Middle Ages, unconcerned with gallantry and the courtly virtues, Hobbes and Locke had no use for the inflated emphasis on heroism and sacrifice that would inform the right-wing movements of the nineteenth and the totalitarian movements of the twentieth centuries. Both saw the need for a new political order capable of allowing the pursuit of self-interest and determined by the people themselves under the auspices of a hypothetical social contract. Each provided the state with a new importance in theory around the very time it was codifying laws and becoming the predominant form of political organization in practice.[7]

Capitalism is inconceivable without an "impartial" political form predicated on the consent of citizens and capable of enforcing contracts in a consistent manner. That is possible, however, only by divorcing the state from civil society. Both Hobbes and Locke conceived conceived of the state as a utilitarian device: its primary purpose lay in buttressing law through sanctions and regulating the ruthless competition of the market by self-interested if responsible individuals. The concept of *raison d'état*, which would serve as the foundation for the realist school of politics, was not lacking: it would, in fact, probably receive its finest articulation from within an—albeit continental—liberal framework.[8] Its roots lay in the Treaty of Westphalia (1648) whereby the nation-state gained the right to determine the national religion. Ever more surely, however, the needs of the fledgling state came into conflict with the new liberal emphasis on the individual and the consent of the governed.

Sovereignty gradually became identified with the universal citizenry of indeterminate individuals, stripped of their particular empirical qualities, or "the people." This first was given notice in the work of Hobbes whose more

---

7. "When Voltaire in 1765 declared that the cause of the king in France was also the cause of the *philosophes*, he was expressing a view commonly held in enlightened circles, regarding the nature of the governmental and administrative reforms then underway in so many European states. Briefly stated, that view was that monarchs and ministers everywhere to one degree or another influenced by enlightened ideas, were attempting a revision of the political framework of their states as the prelude to and the enabling act for a sweeping series of reforms that would eliminate the irrationalities and injustices of society. Specifically, there was much pleasure at what appeared to be an attempt to assert monarchical authority against the reactionary intermediate groups, especially the nobility, whose special privileges stood directly in the way of really thorough reform." John G. Gagliardo, *Enlightened Despotism* (Wheeling Illinois: Harlan Davidson, 1967), 61.

8. Friedrich Meinecke, *Die Idee der Staatsraison in der neueren Geschichte* (1924); it was translated into English under the odd title *Machiavellism* (New York: Praeger, 1965).

authoritarian tendencies render his work less an expression of liberalism than a transition to the new philosophy. He recognized that the monarch was no better or worse than his subjects and that political legitimacy could rest neither on God nor blood. Hobbes rejected revelation or prophecy as criteria for justifying claims. And, precisely because neither sufficed, he was willing to privilege the visible arbiter of truth rather than any invisible truth in particular. This led Hobbes to render the state sovereign over religious authorities even as it prevented him from legitimating the monarch through anything more than a "social contract" in which everyone transferred all rights to someone not appreciably different than anyone else. Thus, for all his support of absolutism, *Leviathan* (1651) was condemned precisely because it militated against the "divine right of kings" as well as the inherent superiority of the aristocrat.

Hobbes offers no definition regarding who can participate in the creation of the social contract and, while his ideas centered on the creation of the nation-state, he was far less interested in the character of the nation than in the workings of the state. Though liberalism has often been criticized for its lack of historical foundations, its refusal to privilege any particular public good, and its purely formal understanding of freedom, it alone was willing to deal with themes— inadequately addressed by both the realist tradition deriving from Machiavelli and the communist tradition deriving from Marx and Lenin—concerning the accountability and dynamics of institutions. It is, ironically, liberalism that places politics in command.[9] The sovereign is depersonalized by Hobbes and, anticipating Max Weber, identified with a "mechanism" or institution. Public existence now distinguishes itself, concretely, from private existence. The state stands over and apart from the personal interests defining civil society while law becomes external to the individuals who make up the community.

Alienation is therefore embedded within liberal politics from the very beginning: totalitarian and theocratic attempts to surmount it by abolishing the distinction between public and private or the separation of powers, however, would only make the problem worse. The alienated character of the new political philosophy rendered possible the impartial arbitration of grievances and the recognition of individuals with diverse desires and interests. Retribution is now no longer in the hands of church, family, or some

---

9. An alternative perspective can be found in Sheldon S. Wolin, *Politics and Vision: Continuity and Innovation in Western Political Thought* (Boston: Little, Brown, 1960), 286ff.

gang. Citizens will now, according to Hobbes, surrender the right to punish offenses and to define the law as they arbitrarily see fit.[10] In turn, however, they will receive the security necessary in order to go about their business and preserve their lives from the imminent dangers associated with an ongoing condition of war. It was, for Hobbes, a rational exchange predicated on consent. He saw the citizenry as calculating people who understood their own lives in the horrific state of nature as "nasty, poor, solitary, brutish, and short." It only made sense that they should consider the preservation of their lives, if not their liberty, as their central concern.

The immediate implication of this insight was the demand for obedience from the citizenry and the ability to command it by the state: here, interestingly, is where Hobbes paves the way for the continental liberal tradition with its lack of emphasis upon individual rights and the accountability of the state. Whether the state proved monarchical, aristocratic, or democratic was not the issue. The point for him was sovereignty: he thus considered resistance legitimate only if a person's life was in danger and revolution valid only if the regime in question could no longer guarantee the safety of its citizens. Hobbes thereby set the stage for the "positive" doctrine of law with its refusal to countenance as law what cannot be enforced, and its muted concern with institutional accountability and civil liberties. Anything that weakened the exercise of political power was anathema to Hobbes and he opposed the ability of individuals to make claims against the state, the "division" of sovereignty or the separation of powers, and even the "absolute" right of property.[11] Hobbes surely wished to establish an identity between the sovereign and the source of sovereignty or, in somewhat different terms, the representative of the people and the individuals of the community. But his work provided the impetus for a modern liberal conception of politics through its profound secularism, its separation of a public institution from private interests, its demystification of the monarch, and its—albeit timid—recognition of popular sovereignty and the right to resistance. Hobbes' willingness to contest the tyranny of "experience" and tradition" would, indeed, prepare the way for an immanent criticism that highlights how the virtually unlimited power exercised by the "leviathan" ultimately undercuts the very security it claims to provide and its citizens require.

For John Locke, author of the new liberalism, the question was how to

---

10. Thomas Hobbes, *Leviathan,* ed. C.B. Macpherson (Penguin Books: New York, 1968), 324.
11. Ibid. 228ff, 363ff.

maintain the security of citizens without falling into the absolutism of his predecessor. The answer came by way of the original assumption underpinning the social contract: that people are rational and, therefore, have a material stake in preserving order unless their liberty is aggrieved. The mistake Hobbes made, according to Locke, was in identifying this interest with self-preservation rather than property: *lèse majesté* therefore serves as an unnecessary threat to the freedom of each. Locke believed that, so long as citizenship was based on property, rational individuals would simply go about their business. Such was the assumption on which he based his view that the state should engage in only the most important tasks and essentially leave "civil society" to run its course. It is not necessary for individuals to transfer all their rights to the sovereign. They should retain their right to "life liberty, and property," which would later receive a slightly different articulation in The Declaration of Independence as the right to "life, liberty, and the pursuit of happiness."

Locke understood absolutism as "inconsistent" with "civil society."[12] He saw it interfering with the instrumental pursuit of private interests and, for this reason, the rights of individuals. Thus, liberal theory would no longer remain content merely with noting that sovereignty resides in the people and then, in the manner of Hobbes, moving on to authoritarianism. The new philosophy would instead use the notion of popular sovereignty to highlight the accountability of the sovereign and the "right" of private individuals to make claims against the public authority. That is as much the case when speaking about the "right to work," which was originally raised by the labor movement, or the feminist insistence upon the right to "equal pay for equal work," as with the right to free speech, assembly, and religion. The demand for an equality of life chances became the ultimate prize. It informed what became known as the "clarion call" of the French Revolution. Thus, in his *Marriage of Figaro* (Act V, Scene 3), Beaumarchais had his most famous character declaim against the nobility:

> Monsieur le Comte. Because you are a great nobleman, you think yourself a great genius! Nobility, fortune, rank, position: all these make one so proud! What have you done to win so many advantages? You have taken the trouble to be born, and nothing more! For the rest, you are a

12. John Locke, "The Second Treatise: An Essay Concerning the True Original, Extent, and End of Civil Government," in *The Two Treatises of Government*, ed. Peter Laslett (Cambridge: Cambridge University Press, 1960), 326.

man ordinary enough! While, as for me, lost in the obscure crowd, I have had to use more knowledge and planning merely to exist than have been expended over the last hundred years in governing all of Spain.

Everything else flows from this single idea: "right"—from what I can see—ultimately refers to nothing more than the demand for reciprocity and the ability to contest its denial. Whether this constitutes an adequate philosophical "grounding" or not is, really, beside the point: Jeremy Bentham could note that the idea of "right" was nothing more than "nonsense on stilts" though, in spite of his belief in utility and the exercise of self-interest, he certainly made use of its implications. In any event, moral rather than utilitarian decisions have usually generated a concern with rights: animal rights is a dramatic case in point. Liberty cannot be understood in meaningful terms without recourse to this moral understanding of rights predicated on reciprocity: history has shown what occurs when it is denied. This may—again—not provide an absolute foundation, or ultimate justification, for the liberal understanding of freedom. But it offers more than a mere opinion in its behalf. Locke, indeed, put it well when he wrote:

> Freedom of Men under Government, is, to have a standing Rule to live by, common to everyone of that Society, and made by the Legislative Power erected in it; A Liberty to follow my own will in all things where the Rule prescribes not; and not to be subject to the inconstant, uncertain, unknown, Arbitrary will of another Man.[13]

The liberal rule of law can now contest the imperatives of the leviathan because it couples a common law, which all must obey, with the freedom of the individual to do whatever the law does not prohibit; a word like "vice," imprecise and arbitrary, thus cannot be employed to punish an individual for doing what no law has forbidden.[14] Because few sanctions are possible against an all-powerful centralized authority, however, Locke could emphasize the role of the legislature as well as the importance of a constitution wherein the various rights and duties of citizens are delineated. Equality under the law, the formal recognition of reciprocity, becomes the prerequisite for a genuinely liberal order. Each can make the same claims upon the state.

13. Ibid., pg. 284.
14. Peter Gay, *The Enlightenment* 2 vols. (New York: Norton, 1969) 2: 444

The democratic universalism underpinning the liberal rule of law anchors the particular, protects the exercise of "difference," rather than serves as the justification for squashing it. From the beginning

> . . . however it may be mistaken, the end of Law is not to abolish or re-strain, but to preserve and enlarge freedom: for in all states of created be-ings capable of Laws, where there is no Law, there is no freedom. For lib-erty is to be free from restraint and violence from others which cannot be, where there is not law: but freedom is not, as we are told, a liberty for every man to do what he lists: (for who could be free, when every other Man's humor might domineer over him?) but a liberty to dispose, and or-der, as he lists, his person, actions, possessions, and his whole property, within the allowance of those laws under which he is; and therein not to be subject to the arbitrary Will of another, but freely his own.[15]

Women, people of color, Catholics, atheists, and those without proper-ty[16]—for very different reasons—had no place in the original liberal vision. But this was the product less of some inherent defect of *liberalism* than the unwillingness of *liberals* to confront existing prejudices with the logic of their principles. Institutionalizing the universal may not have immediately resulted in recognizing the legitimacy of the outsider, or the "other," but it served as the precondition for doing so. If patriarchy is now seen as having been ignored in the universal social contract,[17] for example, the oversight was actually recognized at the time.[18] Women would, in any case, not have attempted to further their interests by using the arguments of "anti-philosophes" like Justus Moser, who authored "On the Diminished Disgrace

---

15. Locke, *The Second Treatise*, 306.
16. "The right of property was, of course, taken for granted: it was to be embodied in the French Declaration of Rights as 'sacred and inviolable;' but it was generally recognized that the laws of property were civil and not natural laws, the result of convention, and therefore liable to be changed if the interests of society so required." Alfred Cobban, *In Search of Humanity: The Role of the Enlightenment in Modern History* (New York: George Braziller, 1960), 131.
17. See the important study by Carole Pateman, *The Sexual Contract* (Cambridge: Polity, 1988).
18. Few have recognized "the degree to which enemies of the Enlightenment attacked the *philosophes* as patriarchy's greatest scourge, men responsible for weakening, not em-powering, the authority of fathers and the prerogatives of men in public life." Darrin McMahon, *Enemies of the Enlightenment: The French Counter-Enlightenment and the Making of Modernity* (Oxford: Oxford University Press, 2001), 137.

of Whores and Their Children in Our Day" (1772), or Louis Bonald, who thundered against divorce. Olympe de Gouges in *The Rights of Woman* (1791), and Mary Wollstonecraft in her *Vindication of the Rights of Women* (1792) instead referred to the original liberal values of the Enlightenment in criticizing the French Revolution for not realizing its universal commitments with respect to women: in the process, both radicalized the purely formal implications of equality under the law.

Their undertaking is both related to yet different from that of the young Marx in *On the Jewish Question* and *The Holy Family*. These writings highlighted the contradiction between the political commitment of the bourgeois state to liberty, equality, and fraternity on the level of the state—that is freedom from the exercise of arbitrary power, equality before the law, and a concern with the common good—when coupled with the existence of coercion, inequality, and egoism in the economic realm of civil society. In extending democracy from the formal to the substantive, to be sure, he sought the "sublation" (*Aufhebung*) of both the state and civil society with the aim of realizing "human" emancipation. This romantic and utopian vision, however, had far less practical impact than his clarification of the limits of classical liberalism with respect to "social" equality.

What marks the criticisms of classical liberalism launched by feminists like Olympe de Gouges and Wollstonecraft no less than Marx, in any event, is their attempt to extend its implications. This differentiates them from conservative critics like Edmund Burke who, while he may have supported a cause like the American Revolution, also championed by most philosophes, did so more in terms of a newly constituted organic tradition than from the perspective of the *Declaration of Independence*. In the guise of attacking the French Revolution, Burke actually attacked the very idea of universal rights and the possibility of altering the English class structure. His emphasis on community and tradition, indeed, was little more than a façade for opposing the exercise of liberty, the pursuit of equality, and the "sordid darkness of this enlightened age."

Equality derived from what Rousseau termed "the natural equality" of humanity and, in this way, liberal political categories became the tools for dealing with the diverse interests manifested in civil society. Locke's justly famous *Letter on Toleration* (1690), which would influence the entire Enlightenment from Voltaire and Mendelssohn to Tom Paine, went beyond the Treaty of Westphalia by insisting that it was not the state that had the right to select a religion for its citizens, but rather that "the care of each man's soul, and of the things of heaven, which neither does belong to the commonwealth nor can be subjected to it, is left entirely to man's self."[19] Emphasizing tolerance was the only "prudent" course for dealing with the new pluralism born of markets, the sects generated by the Protestant Reformation, and the traditional dogmatism of the Catholic Church. Implicit in the liberal idea is the moral responsibility of the individual for his or her fate, the radical implications of the division between church and state, and the insistence that the grievances of the weak and exploited demand the institutional possibility of redress. Should such redress prove impossible to obtain—when a pattern of political and, in principle, even economic abuses exists—resistance and even revolution becomes legitimate. Thus, Thomas Jefferson could write:

> When forced, therefore, to resort to arms for redress, an appeal to the tribunal of the world was deemed proper for our justification. This was the object of the Declaration of Independence. Not to find out new principles or new arguments never before thought of, not merely to say things which had never been said before, but to place before mankind the common sense of the subject in terms so plain and firm as to command their assent, and to justify ourselves in the independent stand we are compelled to take. [20]

Crucial is that Enlightenment liberalism understood resistance as a permanent right and the need for obedience as inherently provisional.[21] Authority concerning the way the world worked, the nature of God's message, or the structure of political power was—from the first—the enemy of the philosophes. It was not simply the need for resistance or revolution that would prove essential, since that always existed in fact, but rather the new legitimacy they were accorded in theory. Liberalism may thus not have invented the idea of resistance or revolution, but it highlighted their importance—again given a pattern of abuse for which redress is institutionally unavailable—in a way no other philosophy did before. That is, however, too often ignored in the usual way leftists think about the legacy of Hobbes and Locke. They are usually seen simply as representatives of the economic interests of the capitalist class with

19. John Locke, *A Letter Concerning Toleration,* eds. John Horton and Susan Mendus (New York: Routledge, 1991), 44.
20. Thomas Jefferson, *Political Writings: Representative Selections* (Indianapolis: Bobbs-Merrill, 1955), 8.
21. Cobban, *In Search of Humanity,* 94.

philosophical worldviews predicated upon what has been termed "possessive individualism."[22]

Capitalism does rest on behavior guided by utilitarian forms of self-interest. But, though their "possessive individualism" may explain why Hobbes and Locke exerted such a profound influence on the utilitarian philosophy of Hume and Bentham, the category is inadequate for understanding either the politics of the rising bourgeoisie or the economic dynamics of what would become capitalism. It was less Karl Marx than his more "revisionist" and reformist successors like Eduard Bernstein,[23] Fabians such as Sidney Webb, and American "progressives" like Charles Beard, who emphasized the primacy of simple economic interest in understanding political movements: or, to put the matter in a more literary way, it is the sanctimonious petty bourgeois, Mr. Peachum who speaks the famous line "first comes eating and then comes morals" in Bertolt Brecht's *Three-Penny Opera*.

Economic reductionism of this sort highlights the instrumental intentions of individual actors over systemic imperatives. It may help explain the motives requisite for the reproduction of capitalism by individuals but, in fact, it ignores the actual dynamics of capitalist production ranging from the opposition of class interests to the power of the commodity form and the implications of imperfect competition. It is surely the case that the "social contract" introduced by Hobbes dismissed substantive forms of class exploitation, as well as patriarchal relations, in the name of formal equality. But such equality is requisite for addressing substantive inequality and various social grievances. Locke and Smith may have allowed for inequality, and even slavery, but the liberal theory of value and property, identified with the body, highlighted the productivity of every economically active individual, whatever the activity, rather than that of industrial producer.[24]

None of this really has anything to do with "capitalism."[25] The "realism' associated with interpreting liberalism from the standpoint of economic re-

22. Note the classic work by Crawford Brough Macpherson, *The Political Theory of Possessive Individualism, Hobbes to Locke* (Oxford: Clarendon Press, 1969).
23. Note the discussion in Stephen Eric Bronner, "Eduard Bernstein and the Logic of Revisionism," in *Socialism Unbound* 2nd Edition (Boulder, CO: Westview, 2001), 55ff.
24. "Even the model of competition favored by Adam Smith only became a real social force when, a generation later, theorists transformed his vision of harmonious production among producers into a structure of inevitable competition favoring the industrial entrepreneur. "Leonard Krieger, *Kings and Philosophers, 1689–1789* (New York: Norton, 1970), 199–200.
25. Cobban, *In Search of Humanity*, 94.

ductionism is both historically misguided and politically self-defeating: resistance and revolution require solidarity, common goals, and the moral courage to contest the existing political and religious order—even if this undertaking occurs in the name of individualism—rather than mere instrumental calculations of self-interest. It is not the material interests influencing Hobbes and Locke, let alone other famous figures of the Enlightenment that make them salient for understanding the liberal revolutions of 1989 and the struggle for contemporary democracy, but rather their emphasis upon the accountability of the state, popular sovereignty, formal equality, constitutionalism, and the right to resist. That is what rendered them important for a bourgeoisie in search of coalitional support from other classes during the "age of democratic revolution."

This was even more the case with Rousseau and his notion of the "general will." Introduced in his "Discourse on Political Economy" (1755), which he wrote for Diderot's *Encyclopedia*, this idea sought to identify the interests of the citizen and community while leaving the individual as "free as before" in the state of nature. The general will appears, quite obviously, when there is unanimity among citizens. But Rousseau was aware of how rarely such unanimity is achieved and that, while respect for majority rule is necessary, the minority can often find itself in the position of representing the common good. The "general will" is a response to this problem even if its description, as the residue sifted from an open discussion among private individuals with their own particular wills, remains abstract. Rousseau demanded complete obedience from the private person once the public decision concerning the "general will" was made. Also, in contrast to Locke, he refused to specify conditions in which individuals could make claims upon the sovereign. But few were as concerned as Rousseau with abolishing the unjustifiable privileges of the rich and the entitled. Thus, in his "Discourse on Political Economy," he could write with biting sarcasm:

> You need me, for I am rich and you are poor. Let us therefore make a contract with one another. I will do you the honor to permit you to serve me under the condition that you give me what little you still have left for the trouble I shall take in commanding you.

Implicitly aware of the alienation generated by bureaucratic institutions, including the organs of parliament, Rousseau embraced the ideal of direct democracy and "le petit Jean-Jacques" was in turn embraced like virtually no other contemporary philosopher by the people—"the simple souls"—

whose desire for participation he articulated. The meaning of the "general will" remains a matter of contention. It is vague as a concept and, worse, it has been used to justify authoritarian rule. But there is a self-evident sense in which resistance to authoritarianism must occur in the name of what Jürgen Habermas termed "generalizable interests." At the same time, any genuinely democratic ordering must protect the public expression of minority sentiments. It is probably better to interpret the "general will" as an ethical guide for making public choices that expand the possibilities for democracy than as a technique for arriving at decisions.

With this perspective in mind, Kant called upon government not to impede the civic use of reason. Perhaps his call for freedom from censorship stands at odds with his emphasis on the need to obey the political dictates of the sovereign. The contradiction is troubling. But it also generates a profound set of insights concerning the responsibilities of government and the practical justification for revolution left unaddressed by Locke and Rousseau. Late in life, such issues preoccupied Kant, who claimed that any genuinely republican order must institutionally recognize the independence of each as a citizen with formal rights equal to those of all others. Even this kind of order, however, cannot force individuals to be happy in the way any single individual or institution conceives of the term; it must allow each to seek his or her "way of happiness" so long as this does not impinge on the ability of others to do the same or the freedom of all under a general law.[26] The emphasis here is on minimizing coercion and Mendelssohn put the matter well when he wrote:

> Hence, one of the state's principal efforts must be to govern men through morals and convictions. Now, there is no other way of improving the convictions, and thereby the morals, of men than through persuasion. Laws do not alter convictions; arbitrary punishments and rewards produce no principles, refine no morals. Fear and hope are not criteria of truth. Knowledge, reasoning, and persuasion alone can bring forth principles which, with the help of authority and example can pass into morals. [27]

26. Immanuel Kant, "On the Common Saying: This May Be True in Theory, But It Does Not Apply in Practice," in *Political Writings* ed. Hans Reiss (Cambridge: Cambridge University Press, 1970), 74.
27. Moses Mendelssohn, *Jerusalem or on Religious Power and Judaism*, trans. Allan Arkush (Hanover, NH: 1983), 43.

Fostering the "autonomy" of the individual,[28] however, requires certain material resources and, to that extent, the aims of enlightenment call into question any purely formal understanding of freedom. This importance of social justice for democracy was evident long before Jürgen Habermas and John Rawls sought to use Kant for the purposes of furthering distributive equity in their particular versions of "democratic theory." Attempts to radicalize Kant, to use his work as a justification for social reform and radical democracy, had already been undertaken by socialists like Eduard Bernstein and Jean Jaurès, various representatives of Austro-Marxism, and even anarchists like Augustin Souchy. T. H. Green was willing to admit that material inequality truncates the idea of freedom, and that the state must "hinder the hindrances to the good life," while Carlo Rosselli, the anti-fascist martyr and philosopher of liberal socialism, put the matter nicely when he noted that for such a project "liberalism is the ideal force of inspiration, and socialism is the practical force of realization." Any worthwhile understanding of socialism, indeed, is predicated on bringing liberty into the lives of poor and working people.

Both liberalism and socialism retain a utilitarian moment. Hume had already stressed the notion of "utility" even before the articulation of utilitarianism as a self-sufficient theory in Jeremy Bentham's *Fragment on Government* (1776). Though this new approach would break with natural law and call "rights" into question it, nevertheless, retained a moral impetus. The argument by Cesare Beccaria for abolishing the death penalty, for example, was predicated on the claim that life imprisonment is actually a greater deterrent against crime and it less contradicts than complements the moral argument of Benjamin Rush who maintained that it is "murder to punish murder by death." Enlightenment thinkers never rigidly sought to separate principle and interest, passion and reason, the good of the whole and the good of the individual. And this was true of the utilitarian philosophers as well. Since all pleasures were considered equal and interests could be objectively articulated, after all, a principle of equality took shape in which all individuals could be seen as capable of having moral convictions and acting in the public sphere. Because self-interest was built into the general interest of the community, moreover, utilitarianism would highlight the role of law in society and thereby concern itself with both the security and civil liberty of the individual.[29]

---

28. Kant, "An Answer to the Question: What is Enlightenment," in *Political Writings*, 54.
29. Krieger, *Kings and Philosophers*, 181–87.

Claiming that utilitarianism is "amoral" and somehow latently totalitarian is absurd: Hitler and Stalin did not realize their worst genocidal fantasies out of utilitarian motivations. Montesquieu and Beccaria, furthermore, both recognized that a connection exists between the rule of law and the ability of individuals to calculate the consequences of their actions. The implication is clear: only conduct specifically prohibited by law can be punished and, in turn, this produces a constraint on the arbitrary exercise of power by the state.[30] The larger the number of those who understand the laws, or so Beccaria argued, the more rare crimes will become; it is impossible to ignore the connection between this belief and Bentham's famous notion of the "greatest good for the greatest number." Then too, insofar as the aim of society is the happiness of its citizens, the door opens for philosophy to become a practical vehicle for both social justice and political democracy. The struggle for civil liberties took place in the context of the broader struggle for a new "public sphere" intent upon constraining the excesses of authoritarian monarchs and invigorating a burgeoning set of republican institutions during the golden age of liberal theory.

Embracing such a perspective meant balancing fact and value, system and experience, reason and emotion, and—perhaps above all—principle and interest. Such is the sense in which philosophy became political during the Enlightenment as it journeyed from its beginnings in England to its mature phase in France. That emphasis upon the political, by the same token, declined to the same degree that this delicate balancing of opposites gave way before an exaggerated emphasis either upon system or experience, reason or emotion, object or subject, society or individual, determinism or freedom, idealism or materialism. The highest point of this balancing act indeed appears in the idea of a constitution capable, as Kant put the matter in his Universal History, of "allowing the greatest possible human freedom in accordance with laws by which the freedom of each is made to be consistent with that of all others."

Not merely Hume and Bentham, but also Kant, paved the way for the great essay, "On Liberty," by John Stuart Mill. In fact, not the utilitarian, but the "right" accorded resistance is what raises questions about how revolutionary actions are to be judged in moral terms. This became the central concern of an entire generation of nineteenth-century intellectuals and it, of course, resurfaced in the twentieth century with the Russian Revolution and

30. Gay, *The Enlightenment* 2:441–4

the various struggles for national self-determination. Merely invoking the "will" or the needs of the oppressed, or the specter of retribution against oppression, soon was recognized as insufficient. Reactionary movements ranging from the *Vendée*, which fought against the armies of the French Revolution, to modern forms of fascism and totalitarianism also sought legitimacy by pointing to the suffering of their constituencies. Many of these movements would also target the evils of capitalism, the betrayal of national ideals, and sometimes even the imperialist ambitions of their opponents. Kant, for his part, supported the French Revolution of 1789 and retracted his support when the terror began, and the ability to argue and criticize was suspended. He understood that without freedom of expression the possibility of insisting upon a plausible relation between means and ends would vanish.

Voltaire directed his great slogan, *écrasez l'infame*,[31] against the Catholic Church, but only insofar as it served as the most visible institutional expression of fanaticism. No less than Marx, he was aware that part of the ruling class must *choose to* break off and join the oppressed before any radical change could take place. Voltaire recognized that numerous liberal and unorthodox clerics were playing an important role in disseminating Enlightenment ideas. Many of them like the Abbé Sieyes—author of *What is the Third Estate?*— and the historian Raynal were even on the far left of the Enlightenment. Anticipating Julien Sorel, the main character of *The Red and the Black* by Stendhal, they saw the value of the church more for the help it provided them in making a career than as a vehicle for their salvation. But it is also true that Voltaire and most of his comrades understood religious faith as a matter for the individual. They insisted upon the right of others to believe differently, castigated those who used religious dogma to constrain the extension of knowledge, and never sought to coerce what Moses Mendelssohn termed "inner conviction." This speaks to a fundamental issue for understanding democracy: that it is concerned not merely, or even primarily, with the will of the majority but rather with the protection of the minority. Thus, Jefferson could state that:

> though the will of the majority is in all cases to prevail that will, to be rightful, must be reasonable; that the minority possess their equal rights, which equal laws must protect, and to violate which would be oppres-

---

31. Gay, *Voltaire's Politics*, 239ff.

sion. . . . And let us reflect that, having banished from our land that religious intolerance under which mankind so long bled and suffered, we have yet gained little if we countenance a political intolerance as despotic, wicked, and capable of as bitter and bloody persecutions.[32]

Enlightenment thinkers were mostly deists not atheists; some of them believed in the practical importance of religion for social purposes; others in the comfort it provided for the "simple souls." Few of the philosophes were actually intent upon abolishing religion. All of them, however, fought for the separation of church and state, attacked the fanatic intent upon imposing his faith on the community, and understood the pursuit of knowledge as a public endeavor rather than the intuitive possession of priests, alchemists and nobles. Criticism of the ruling elites was always identified with the will of the majority. As far as a theory of political rule was concerned, however, Enlightenment thinkers tended to privilege the rights of the minority. Without the institutional guarantee of such rights, which becomes evident in the case even of populist dictatorships, it is unclear whether the will of the majority is ever actually being represented. There is subsequently something legitimate about claiming that unqualified democracy, stripped of institutional referents that protect the individual, is a potential inspiration for authoritarianism and worse.[33] The utilitarian impulse takes a backseat when Beccarria writes that "if my upholding the rights of man and unconquerable truth, should contribute to saving, from the spasms and agonies of death, some miserable victim of tyranny or of equally fatal ignorance, the thanks and tears of one innocent man in his transports of joy would console me for the disdain of all mankind."[34]

The Greeks conceived of democracy as a type of regime and as a constituent of mixed governments while the Romans understood democracy as a legal concept associated with popular sovereignty. It was also linked—probably from the time of Spartacus—to the idea of resistance against the prevailing authority. It was by fusing all three positions—and privileging the third—that the Enlightenment developed its uniquely modern understanding of democracy: it is equivalent with no single institutional form; it derives political legitimacy from popular sovereignty; and it considers dissent as necessary for its proper functioning. Olympe de Gouges could note in her

32. Jefferson, *Political Writings*, 43.
33. Cobban, *In Search of Humanity*, 207ff
34. Cited in Gay, *The Enlightenment* 2: 445

Declaration of the Rights of Woman and of the Female Citizen (1791) that "any society in which rights are not guaranteed, or the separation of powers not determined, has no constitution and the constitution is void if the majority of individuals who make up the nation have not played a role in drafting it."

New was not the notion of democracy, but the attempt by advocates of the Enlightenment to identify its mechanics with the aims of politics.[35] There is indeed a way in which its most radical expression becomes less the radical democracy envisioned by Rousseau than the new institutional arrangement introduced in the United States. The new federalism introduced by Madison and his friends in *The Federalist Papers* with its "winner take all," single-member district, form of voting may have resulted in weak parties and strong interest groups. But it blended the liberal individualism of Locke with the civic republicanism of Rousseau. Its constitutional structure created a disincentive for a politics with strong ideological claims; its fragmentation of power made radical reform particularly cumbersome and, of course, women and people of color only began to reap the benefits of reform during the middle of the twentieth century. For all that, however, this new experiment in federalism differed from all previous forms of mixed governments or governments that employed the separation of powers insofar as all political institutions, whatever their powers and purposes, were understood as derivative of a single authority: the citizenry of the United States.[36]

The liberal republic has lost a good deal of its radical cachet. Much of the left intelligentsia now criticizes the state and institutional politics in the name of "radical democracy" and "new social movements." The radical democratic alternative is usually seen in terms of atavistic organizational forms like the town meeting or the workers council. It is also usually forgotten that these movements have always presupposed the existence of a state with liberal norms and that their success has been largely dependent upon their ability to use the courts and pressure for legislation. The liberal state remains the point of reference for movements committed to social change and for those interested in the protection of civil liberties. Talk about introducing what Richard Rorty has called a "new language" for the left has been going on now for more than twenty-five years. Especially with the introduction of provincial notions like "ethno-solidarity" and the refusal to employ liber-

35. Krieger, *Kings and Philosophers*, 193
36. Henry Steele Commager, *The Empire of Reason: How Europe Imagined and America Realized the Enlightenment* (London: Phoenix, 1977), 209–10.

al values outside the liberal context, however, the promise of a new language turns into the reality of a new jargon.

It is ultimately not a matter of the *language* anyway, but what the left has to *say*: what aims it projects, what values it embraces, and whether it can render meaningful judgments on its enemies and itself. There is hardly a single ideal of the left that does not derive from the Enlightenment. That is surely the case for a view of socialism in which class action against the market requires a coherent relation between means and ends and seeks to bring about a situation in which "the free development of each is the condition for the free development of all." It is the same across the board. Political theory cannot help but distinguish left from right: the fashionable rejection of this distinction goes nowhere. It was the liberal political theory of the Enlightenment, indeed, which generated the division between left and right in the first place.

4

THE GREAT DIVIDE:
ENLIGHTENMENT, COUNTER-ENLIGHTENMENT,
AND THE PUBLIC SPHERE

THE ENLIGHTENMENT CELEBRATED THE INTELLECT AND ITS representatives provided a new understanding of the intellectual. In earlier times, of course, intellectuals questioned the strictures of religious and political tradition. Some of them even served as the conscience of their epochs. But the self-perception of the intellectual as both the critic and the reformer of society, as committed to a communal project of social change, is the legacy of what the philosophe Pierre Bayle first called the "republic of letters." Its citizens would endeavor to address popular audiences in addition to academic ones. They fervently believed that "the most fundamental ideas were necessarily applicable, communicable, effective, and socially relevant, and that there existed no valid pure idea to be thought or separable basic reality to be analyzed."[1]

Only in the more backward nations of Central Europe would the university serve as a primary site for Enlightenment intellectuals. The vanguard of the scientific revolution of the seventeenth century, the forerunners of the Enlightenment, began by attempting to liberate themselves from universities infused with Catholic dogma and dominated by the study of theology. They championed instead what soon became a growing set of independent institutions of secular orientation such as the Royal Society in London, the Academy of Science of Paris, the Academia della Scienza in Naples, and the Collegium Curosive in Germany. These societies made possible the exchange of ideas and they were gradually complemented by Masonic lodges, salons, taverns, coffeehouses, town meetings, public lectures, theatres, rudimentary libraries. This new amalgam created the context for the exercise of equality, discourse, tolerance, and "common sense." It constituted a "bourgeois public sphere" that would serve as the infrastructure for the democratic revolutions.[2]

---

1. Leonard Krieger, *Kings and Philosophers, 1689–1789* (New York: Norton, 1970), 153.
2. Jürgen Habermas, *The Structural Transformation of the Public Sphere*, trans. Tom Burger (Cambridge: MIT Press, 1989).

This bourgeois public sphere did not emerge *ex nihilo*: it derived instead from a variety of traditions associated with the broader anthropology of enlightenment including the democratic legacy of the medieval free towns, the humanitarian trends inherited from the Renaissance, and the excitement of the scientific revolution generated by Galileo, Bacon, Descartes, and—above all Newton. Their insights made visible the invisible and provided the possibility for new investigations into nature through their discovery of its universal laws. These helped shape the secular belief in universal rights.[3] Beliefs of this sort were contested from the very beginning, however, by conservatives like Sir Robert Filmer. Such thinkers challenged the emerging liberalism of Hobbes and Locke in the name of the divine right of kings, ecclesiastical power, and the primacy of custom over reason. Raising this is important because it prevents identifying the new "civil society" of the seventeenth and eighteenth with the incipient radicalism of the bourgeois public sphere. The Enlightenment was, from the first, contested by a Counter-Enlightenment whose "anti-philosophes"—militant members of the clergy, half-educated aristocrats, traditionalist bourgeois, state censors, conservative parliamentarians, and street journalists—had fought the philosophes since the middle of the eighteenth century and "they burned with envy, anger, and incomprehension."[4]

All movements of the right ultimately are grounded in a politics of *reaction*, and the Counter-Enlightenment was no different. Its anti-philosophes advocated an organic sense of nation, patriarchal authority, and what Edmund Burke termed "the spirit of religion" that rejected the ideal of humanity, the accountability of institutions, and the skepticism associated with science. Controversy fueled by divergent interests and ideologies undermined any consensus in this new sphere hovering between the state and the market. Not to recognize the existence of fundamental ideological and material conflicts reifies both the public sphere and civil society. Better to suggest that:

> Liberal and democratic movements were to be a part, not the whole, of the civil society spawned by the Enlightenment public sphere. Nineteenth century civil society would give birth to liberal, democratic, even socialist

3. Micheline Ishay, *Internationalism and Its Betrayal* (Minneapolis: University of Minnesota Press, 1995), 5–10.
4. Darrin M. McMahon, *Enemies of the Enlightenment: The French Counter-Enlightenment and the Making of Modernity* (Oxford: Oxford University Press, 2001), 6.

and feminist movements and associations, but it also produced nationalist, racialist and militaristic ones, foreshadowings of which were already
visible in the precociously developed political public sphere of eighteenth-
century England. From, say, Imperial Germany where right-wing populist
associations like the Pan-German League and the Navy League produced
a steady stream of chauvinistic and imperialistic propaganda, to the anti-
Semitic diatribes of anti-Dreyfus newspapers and associations under the
French Third Republic, it was obvious that the public sphere of nineteenth
century civil society could take forms that were anything but liberal.[5]

Using the category of the "bourgeois" public sphere fruitfully calls for understanding it in relation to the political struggle between Enlightenment intellectuals and their reactionary opponents. Neither the philosophes nor
their enemies were what the Germans still call "disciplinary idiots," with
brains dulled by specialization. They were instead men of letters interested
in philosophy, curious about the natural world, and ready to change society. The attempts on both sides to provide coherence, meaning, and logical
justification were neither mechanical nor shallow. More was also involved
than sophisticated forms of manipulating power. The philosophes were intent upon fostering engagement rather than lauding "ambiguity." But they
were not driven by "legislative" and "totalizing" ambitions in some dictatorial sense. That was far more the case with the Counter-Enlightenment and
its most important representatives like J. G. Hamann and Joseph de Maistre
whom Isaiah Berlin correctly labeled "the Voltaire of the reaction."[6]

Viewing Enlightenment intellectuals as latent or manifest authoritarians
reflects the political self-doubt plaguing contemporary progressive intellectuals, and coming to terms with this identity crisis thus calls for taking a new
look at the "republic of letters." Institutions were lacking, of course, but it
evidenced a unique form of sovereignty. The republic of letters provided a
response both to a burgeoning nationalism and to a church that may have
been "catholic" in name but whose intolerance for those with unorthodox
or competing beliefs was legendary. The republic of letters inhabited by the

5. James Van Horn Melton, *The Rise of the Public in Enlightenment Europe* (Cambridge:
   Cambridge University Press, 2001), 273.
6. Isaiah Berlin, *The Magus of the North: J.G. Hamann and the Origins of Modern Irrationalism*, ed. Henry Hardy (London: John Murray, 1993); Isaiah Berlin, "Joseph de
   Maistre and the Origins of Fascism," in *The Crooked Timber of Humanity: Chapters in
   the History of Ideas*, ed. Henry Hardy (New York: Vintage, 1992), 91ff; Isaiah Berlin, *The
   Hedgehog and the Fox* (New York: Mentor, 1957), 116.

philosophe*s*, in contrast, anticipated what is rapidly becoming an international civil society of progressive activists and intellectuals. There was no electronic mail and there were no computers, travel and communication were far more difficult, while censorship and costs and lack of libraries made books hard to come by. The "republic of letters" was an ideal, but it gained a measure of reality and its spirit reflected the great motto of the Enlightenment coined by Kant, *Sapere aude!*, or "have the courage to use your own reason."

A cosmopolitan community created the Enlightenment. It should not be identified with France, which is still often the case, since the first stirrings occurred in more economically developed states like England and the Netherlands, or in those with more radical democratic traditions like Scotland, while many of its principles were best realized—albeit in rudimentary forms—in the United States. It therefore only makes sense that the preoccupations of the Enlightenment and the role of the engaged intellectual have changed over time. Where it was originally a matter of providing scientific and metaphysical foundations for a new brand of liberal politics in the seventeenth century, which was so apparent in the thinking of Thomas Hobbes and Spinoza, it soon involved commitment to a more anti-foundationalist and interventionist spirit. But the transition occurred smoothly: it was, in fact, hardly noticeable except in retrospect. The new worldview also spread quickly. David Hume and Adam Smith fostered it in Scotland, Beccaria in Italy, and Jefferson, Franklin, and Thomas Paine in the United States. Lessing and Mendelssohn, Kant and Hegel, Schiller and Goethe embraced it in Germany. Even Spain, shrouded in the darkness of a feudal absolutism, experienced it through the remarkable group of intellectuals gathered around the philosopher-politician Olivares and the painter Goya. The new thinking extended to what was considered the "periphery" of Europe: its Eastern territories, Greece, and the Balkans.[7] It also crossed the Atlantic informing the struggle of Simon Bolivar and Jose de San Martin in Latin America and inspiring the uprising against slavery led by Toussaint L'Ouverture in Haiti.[8]

Fighting against a world dominated by monsters and saints, witches and gods, myths and prejudices, misery and privilege, custom and laziness, demanded a mixture of courage and clarity. The assault on metaphysics intro-

---

7. Franco Venturi, *The End of the Old Regime in Europe, 1768–1776: The First Crisis* (Princeton: Princeton University Press, 1989).
8. C. L. R. James, *Black Jacobins: Toussaint L'Ouverture and the San Domingo Revolution* 2nd Edition (New York: Vintage, 1963).

duced by the authors of *The Spectator*, Joseph Addison and Richard Steele, prepared the way for the new egalitarian emphasis upon "common sense" offered by Thomas Paine. Utilitarianism, so boring in its shopkeeper mentality, nonetheless gave the individual a measure of respect by making clear that each was capable of discerning his or her interest and that social welfare was the primary aim of government. Lessing, Montesquieu, and Goethe challenged the church injunction against suicide. Most partisans of the Enlightenment were repulsed by slavery and the subordination of women plays a role in many of their works. Their privileging of persuasion over coercion, their vision of the fully formed personality, their interest in matters outside their immediate expertise and experience, their emphasis upon tolerance, all project an eradication of what is brutal and unjust in the name of a better society with a new set of human relations. Resistance undertaken in the name of progressive, liberal, and ultimately socialist ideals served to separate critical from affirmative intellectuals and place some thinkers often associated with the Enlightenment, such as Samuel Johnson and Edmund Burke, outside the tradition that they might otherwise seem to espouse. The result was what might be termed a *great divide* that separated intellectuals of the Enlightenment from those of the Counter-Enlightenment.

Enlightenment intellectuals were not pillars of political correctness. Organizations condemning slavery were formed. Salons may have accorded women a new public presence,[9] and the grosser expressions of anti-Semitism and even anti-Muslim attitudes were generally looked down upon. But the Enlightenment was still primarily a male, white, straight, and Christian world. In the United States, moreover, slavery was embedded in the national legislative process: Jefferson supported the idea that a slave is three-fifths of a person for purposes of representation, which won him the election of 1800, and Washington placed the national capital in slave territory. Admittedly, for such individuals, support for measures of this sort probably had less to do with their personal approval of slavery than with its political use to protect the economic base of the South: it remained the case into the twentieth century that no serious political career was open to Southerners

9. Dena Goodman, *The Republic of Letters: A Cultural History of the French Enlightenment* (Ithaca: Cornell University Press, 1994). Also note the fine discussion by Dorindra Outram, *The Enlightenment* (Cambridge: Cambridge University Press, 1995), 80ff.

10. Note the excellent article by Garry Wills, "The Negro President" in *The New York Review of Books* (November 6, 2003), 45; it sets the stage for his book *Negro President: Jefferson and the Slave Power* (New York; Houghton Mifflin, 2004).

opposed to slavery or supportive of civil rights.[10] But that doesn't change the reality: it was what it was.

Still, it would be misleading to lump the philosophes together with their adversaries. The principles underpinning the critique of slavery, sexism, and exclusion of the other derived from the Enlightenment. Then, too, the political stance of its advocates on such issues was generally qualitatively different from those of the Counter-Enlightenment. It is instructive, for example, to consider the views on women and divorce expressed by arch-reactionaries like Justus Moeser or Bonald; the views on prejudice offered by Burke; the irrationalism of Hamann; the unyielding Christianity of De Maistre; the brutal anti-Semitism of the Abbé Bruelle; and the alternatives offered to cosmopolitanism, constitutionalism, and social equality by the rest of the reaction. It is also easy to forget the witch trials that cost thousands upon thousands of women their lives;[11] the slaughters attendant upon the Crusades;[12] the Inquisition, and the constant pogroms. Michel Foucault may be correct in his assertions that the Enlightenment in its time had little sympathy for the "unreasonable": the beggars, the petty criminals, and the insane.[13] In practical terms, however, the more progressive programs for improving the conditions of these groups were again inspired by Enlightenment principles and intellectuals of the Counter-Enlightenment would historically show even less interest in these groups and the reforms capable of bettering their lot.

Above all, however, it wrong to suggest that the prejudices of the philosophes somehow invalidate the ideals associated with their republic of letters. The logic of the Enlightenment suggested that citizenship should be open to everyone with a pen and an argument to make in the name of freedom. Sex, race, religion, property, and class, should—in principle—play no role in determining the ability of individuals to participate in the public realm and they should be able to pursue their private interests as they see fit. Kant's notion concerning the formal equality of all subjects, in fact, made possible a criticism of any such barriers to the public exercise of reason while the principles underpinning the liberal rule of law enabled suffragettes and

11. Norman Cohn, *Europe's Inner Demons* (New York: Meridian, 1975), 206ff.
12. Note the telling criticism by Francis Bacon, "An Advertisement Touching A Holy War" (1622–23) reprinted in *Logos* 1, no.2 (Spring, 2002).
13. Michel Foucault, *Madness and Civilization: A History of Insanity in the Age of Reason,* trans. Richard Howard (New York: Random House, 1965); *Discipline and Punish: The Birth of the Prison,* trans. Alan Sheridan (New York: Vintage, 1979).

civil libertarians as well as advocates of the excluded and insane to contest the existence of positive laws tainted by discrimination and regressive attitudes. It is only fair to note that:

> The Enlightenment public sphere assigned new importance to women as producers and consumers of culture, but often on the basis of values that served to justify their subordination. Its norms of openness and inclusion created new kinds of association, but also new forms of exclusion. For all this ambiguity, however, we continue to invoke the norms of openness and transparency preached by the Enlightenment public sphere even as we criticize its failure to live up to them. For that reason its legacy is more enduring than it seems, whatever its vicissitudes from the Enlightenment to our own day.[14]

"Enlightenment" was initially seen as depending upon the "courage" of the individual to exercise his or her intellect, question rather than obey and, according to the famous formulation, "leave behind his self-imposed immaturity." Contrary to popular opinion, however, Kant did not leave the individual subject hovering in the metaphysical stratosphere. It was clear to him no less than to the rest of the philosophes that summoning such courage becomes easier with the existence of liberal institutions and a "public" animated by civic interests.[15] That is why liberating the "public" not merely from dogma, but from the institutions and conditions that promote it, became the primary goal of Enlightenment intellectuals. The philosophes understood that the right to criticism is the precondition for the exercise of autonomy and, if not the pursuit of absolute truth, then the rectification of error. Thus, in contrast to thinkers of the Counter-Enlightenment like Burke and De Maistre, Kant and Paine would insist that no age can commit the future to a condition in which it would be impossible to extend knowledge or correct errors. [16]

Where the Enlightenment valued liberty, discursive persuasion, and the critical exercise of reason, the Counter-Enlightenment stood for obedience, coercive authority, and tradition. The former renders the future open and the latter closes it down. The rejection of closure underpinned the idea that

---

14. Melton, *The Rise of the Public in Enlightenment Europe*, 275.
15. Immanuel Kant, "An Answer to the Question: What is Enlightenment?" in *Political Writings*, 55.
16. Ibid., 57–58.

freedom of speech is the precondition for all other freedoms. This makes it legitimate to interpret Kant in such a way that "the moment to rebel is the moment in which freedom of opinion is abolished."[17] When freedom of opinion is curtailed then correcting errors from the past and raising grievances in the present becomes impossible. Freedom of assembly and worship are also compromised once this basic freedom is violated. It is consequently no accident that partisans of the revolutionary bourgeoisie should have seen these freedoms as interconnected. The republic of letters rendered everything subject to criticism; nothing was sacred, least of all sacred things. It was this, perhaps above all, that placed the Enlightenment at odds with the Counter-Enlightenment whose thinkers, from the start, privileged obedience to traditional authorities. Thus, suggesting that the assault on orthodoxy by the philosophes was itself a form of orthodoxy "is largely a play on words: their toleration was not complete, but their commitment to the inquiring mind which knew no boundaries made their most self-confident pronouncements open to correction."[18]

Enlightenment intellectuals subordinated national customs and prejudices to the universal assumptions underpinning the critical exercise of the intellect and this the Counter-Enlightenment could not forgive. Its assault on the status quo would, indeed, take two very different forms. The term "intelligentsia" was coined amid the Decembrist Revolt in Russia of 1825,[19] though it became popular in Europe only during the 1860s and 1870s, while the term "intellectual" arose during the Dreyfus Affair about two decades later. The Enlightenment inspired both, but they are not interchangeable: the "intelligentsia" would have a more romantic, nationalistic, and radical vanguard connotation than the liberal, rational, and reform-minded notion of the "intellectual." This difference provides a point of entry for understanding the difference between communists and socialists as well as, in a different way, between revolutionaries and reformists. The Counter-Enlightenment, of course, never really made much of a distinction between them: it would, however, evidence its own internal conflict between fascists and conservatives, apocalyptics and establishmentarians.

17. Hannah Arendt, *Lectures on Kant's Political Philosophy*, ed. Ronald Beiner (Chicago: University of Chicago Press: 1982), 48ff.
18. Peter Gay, *The Enlightenment* 2 vols. (New York: Norton, 1977) 1: 86
19. Marc Raeff, *Origins of the Russian Intelligentsia: The Eighteenth Century Nobility* (New York: Harcourt Brace, 1966), 148ff; Philip Pomper, *The Russian Revolutionary Intelligentsia* (Arlington, Illinois: Harlan Davidson, 1970), 40ff.

The Counter-Enlightenment was defined by what it opposed: it, too, was formed through an informal alliance of commentators living in any number of cities and in any number of nations that dealt with crucial "public" issues ranging from women's rights to capital punishment and penal reform, to censorship and poor laws. The quarreling that took place on either side of the barricades is less germane to what was at stake than academics might believe: quarrels occur in every family. Important is that both the philosophes and their adversaries saw themselves as families.[20] Both groups closed ranks when they felt under attack in the face of some *cause célèbre*,[21] such as the Calas Affair, which dealt with religious dogmatism and the legality of torture, or the attempt to censor Diderot's *Encyclopedia* in 1786. Both movements would also generate intellectual frameworks for their political successors among future generations.[22] The solidarity existing among supporters of the Enlightenment was no greater than among their opponents and intellectuals on one side were not necessarily "smarter" than those on the other. The "public intellectual," in short, emerged simultaneously on both sides of the barricades: crucial is not that this intellectual was attached to some special social stratum, or knew certain texts, or took an "objective" stance, but rather his or her particular *engagement* with the pressing issues of the day and embrace of a distinctive political project.

Sapere Aude! The question was whether to follow one's intelligence, wherever it might lead, or not: the critical confronted the affirmative intellectual. The difference between them has existential as well as material sources. The point is not merely that the critical intellectual stands for civil liberties, the mitigation of economic injustice, and cosmopolitan ideals while his affirmative counterpart embraces authority, tradition, and myth. It is also a matter of whether the intellectual will experiment with the new or remain content with things as they are. The affirmative intellectual can also

20. Gay, *The Enlightenment* 1:6
21. Sarah Maza, *Private Lives and Public Affairs: The Causes Célèbres of Prerevolutionary France* (Berkeley: University of California Press, 1993), 19ff.
22. The famous essays on the intellectual history of the "Counter-Enlightenment" by Sir Isaiah Berlin remain as profitable now as at the time when they were written. But the elective affinity between counter-enlightenment ideas and right-wing political movements is radically underplayed in most of them, which helps explain Berlin's concern with rehabilitating—simply on the level of ideas—figures like Hamann and de Maistre. Useful as a corrective is the study by McMahon, *Enemies of the Enlightenment*, and the anthology by Jean-Jacques Langendorf, *Pamphletisten und Theoretiker der Gegenrevolution 1789–1799* (München: Matthes & Seitz, 1989).

embrace civil liberties, economic reforms, and cosmopolitan claims. But that will be the case only once they have already become customary: thus, the revolting spectacle of conservatives posturing about racial or gender equality when it was their predecessors who sought to maintain existing prejudices. What distinguishes the critical from the affirmative intellectual is the belief in the possibility of reform and the commitment to progress. The former in keeping with the spirit of the Enlightenment, becomes their advocate while the latter, at best, resigns himself to them.

Enlightenment intellectuals therefore looked at history in a new way. They sympathized with the victims of witch trials, religious wars, and the Inquisition. More important, in contrast to their enemies, they highlighted the ways in which the past had failed the present Existence for the bulk of humanity seemed no different than the state of nature so pitilessly described by Hobbes. None of the philosophes was astonished when Rousseau noted in the *Emile* that only half of all children would reach the age of adolescence. The pedagogic character of their enterprise was clear to them: they knew that most considered poverty and backbreaking labor the result of fate or the expulsion from paradise. Most surely would have agreed with Voltaire when in 1771, with a mixture of disgust and compassion, he wrote that "more than half the habitable world is still populated by two-footed animals who live in a horrible condition approximating the state of nature, with hardly enough to live on and clothe themselves, barely enjoying the gift of speech, barely aware that they are miserable, living and dying practically without knowing it."[23]

Transforming this vale of tears—not through prayer but through politics, not through reliance on experience but through innovation, not through received authority but the power of the intellect—provided the rationale for the Enlightenment. Its universal understanding of the citizen and the producer, which had such different implications, were both rooted in the burgeoning world of the commodity. If its partisans were often unaware of the genuinely radical implications of their thinking, however, this evidenced nothing more than the limits imposed by the historical context. The contempt of the philosophes for the *ancien régime* always broke through their willingness to work with it. Still, they weren't revolutionaries. Hardly anyone other than Jefferson spoke about revolution with relish. Only later, once the star of the Enlightenment had started to dim, did figures like Restif de la

---

23. Cited in J. B. Bury, *The Idea of Progress: An Inquiry into Its Origin and Growth* (New York: Dover, 1978), 167.

Bretonne and Sebastian Mercier bring what they considered its revolutionary message to the masses who then made Rousseau their hero.[24] Outside the United States, where the unleashing of revolutionary energies was dampened almost immediately,[25] few philosophes sought political power. They were mostly pragmatic reformers, utilitarians concerned with highlighting self-interest and determining the "greatest happiness for the greatest number;" or moralists committed to educating the sentiments, eradicating prejudice, and lifting what Karl Marx later termed the "material level of culture."

Critical intellectuals assuredly exuded an air of elitism and arrogance as they trumpeted their doubts about popular traditions and their possession of scientific truths. If not many of them then much of their public belonged to the middle class of lawyers and office holders, the educated striving to make their reputation in literary academies and cultural circles. It was the position of this fluid middle class within the existing totality of social relations that provided the philosophes with their independence and sense of universal purpose. This was particularly the case in France where the connection of the middle class with other classes of superior and inferior status was simultaneously more organic and more problematic than elsewhere in Europe. A growing bureaucracy and the willingness of the crown to sell offices bound the middle class to the court while the emergence of a "nobility of the robe," based on the purchase of titles, connected it with the aristocracy and the court. In addition, the emergence of free professionals and merchants from the peasantry, artisans, and traders tied the middle class to what might be termed the "masses." Especially French intellectuals, insofar as they were products of this middle-class milieu, could thus view themselves as representative of universal interests in a fragmented society. They were neither professors like in Germany or clergymen relatively free from religious strictures like in England. Their very lack of an official status or particular social function, in fact, enabled the French to view themselves as free-lance intellectuals committed to the improvement of humanity.[26]

But this sense of purpose ultimately spread beyond France. Enlighten-

24. Roy Porter, *The Enlightenment* 2nd Edition (London: Palgrave, 2001), 44.
25. "What the royal charters and the loyal attachment of the colonies to king and Parliament in England had done for the people in America was to provide their power with the additional weight of authority; so that the chief problem of the American Revolution, once this source of authority had been severed from the colonial body politic in the New World, turned out to be the establishment and foundation not of power but authority." Hannah Arendt, *On Revolution* (Middlesex: Penguin, 1964), 178.
26. Krieger, *Kings and Philosophers,* 174.

ment intellectuals saw themselves as an international vanguard—though not in the sense of a political party unaccountable to the masses—intent upon creating the intellectual and practical conditions by which the individual might emerge from his "immaturity" and humanity from its degradation and barbarism. There was nothing soppy or sentimental in speaking about "humanity" or what would later be understood as its fulfillment in the notion of "fraternity." Such ideals evidence themselves in dark times. Each of them, as Hannah Arendt noted in her lovely essay on Lessing, "has its natural place among the repressed and persecuted, the exploited and humiliated, whom the eighteenth century called the unfortunates, *les malheureux*, and the nineteenth century the wretched, *les miserables*."[27]

Enlightenment intellectuals sought to link their ideals with a practical assault on the privileges and prejudices of the *ancien régime*. All of them searched for the connections between fact and value, system and experience, reason and emotion; Rousseau would indeed consider the attempt to link principle and interest as a primary concern of *The Social Contract*. It became a matter of balancing the needs of the individual with those of society and, as this concern became more pronounced, the Enlightenment became more political as it journeyed from its beginnings in England to its mature phase in France.[28] Flexibility was thus the mark of Enlightenment politics.

Few of the philosophes were consistent in the regimes to which they extended support: but all were consistent in the values that they advocated within those regimes. Rousseau could project the vision of direct democracy, but also warn against the introduction of radical measures in the Kingdom of Poland. Kant envisioned an international federation of republics even as he insisted upon obeying the dictates of monarchs. Voltaire adapted his ideas on civil liberties, tolerance, and anti-clericalism to the changing political situations though his general concern with constraining the exercise of arbitrary power remained constant. And this was the case whether he was in Prussia dealing with the Frederick the Great, confronting the parochial asceticism of Rousseau in his attack on theater, or turning against his own bourgeois supporters in the name of the disenfranchised and excluded of Geneva.[29] The political practices of Voltaire and his comrades may have

---

27. Hannah Arendt, "Humanity in Dark Times: Thoughts about Lessing," in *Men in Dark Times* (Middlesex: Penguin, 1973), 20–21
28. Krieger, *Kings and Philosophers*, 153.
29. Peter Gay, *Voltaire's Politics: The Poet as Realist* (New Haven: Yale University Press, 1988), 185–238.

been opportunistic, but their ideals were unambiguous. Enlightenment intellectuals were, for the most part, guided by a form of pragmatic idealism in addressing the issues of the day.

Authenticity during the Enlightenment may not have demanded the self-conscious *engagement* required by modern existentialists, but the philosophes were engaged in spite of themselves: they were apostles of resistance. Pursuing scientific truth pitted them against religious institutions, exploring the economic logic of an emerging capitalism pitted them against the aristocracy, castigating public prejudices pitted them against the "masses," and seeking to constrain arbitrary authority pitted them against all the forces of the *ancien régime*. Especially their preoccupation with the latter, which translated into compassion for the least fortunate and a belief in humanity, makes it ridiculous to suggest that the Enlightenment and its use of scientific reason somehow inherently fulfills itself in the thinking of the Marquis de Sade.[30]

He, too, may have refused to grant the validity of anything that cannot be rationally proved in the character of Juliette,[31] and —in keeping with various philosophes—this may have produced an unrelenting attack on metaphysics. But his reduction of people to instruments of appetite in works like *The 120 Days of Sodom* had far less to do with scientific rationality than with privileging an unconstrained egoism and what—in terms far cruder than Nietzsche—might be termed "the will to power." Sade's point was that, precisely because nothing moral existed in nature, all morality must be understood as hypocritical. But Kant, Vico, and Voltaire could all share the same initial assumption about nature and arrive at completely different conclusions about morality. Sade's emphasis upon "reason" and "science" was always a pose. The reduction of people to things is a political choice, not some prescribed implication of reason or science. Decisive instead was his belief that without God there is only license: not simply the outrageous sexual transgressions depicted in his writings, but his insistence that without an absolute there is only moral chaos is what made Sade a figure of such interest to contemporary postmodernists. The self-serving character of his argument is obvious in his case and, in philosophical terms, no better example exists

---

30. Max Horkheimer and Theodor Adorno, *Dialectic of Enlightenment*, trans. John Cumming (New York: Herder & Herder, 1972), 94ff.

31. " . . . for all the pretentious philosophizing the Marquis de Sade injected into his novels, he was never more than a caricature of the Enlightenment whose heir he claimed to be." Gay, *The Enlightenment* 1:25

of being defined by what one nominally opposes. The importance of Sade's pseudo-philosophical pornography derives less from its iron logic than its arbitrary equation of freedom with license. His celebration of the coercive, the cruel, and the solipsistic runs counter to every value associated with the theory and practice of the Enlightenment. His work indeed reflects a situation in which:

> The growing doubt of human autonomy and reason has created a state of moral confusion where man is left without the guidance of either revelation or reason. The result is the acceptance of a relativistic position which proposes that value judgments and ethical norms are exclusively matters of taste or arbitrary preference and that no objectively valid statement can be made in this realm. But since man cannot live without values and norms, this relativism makes him an easy prey for irrational value-systems.[32]

Enlightenment thinking runs directly counter to that of Sade. All of the most important philosophes distinguished between pluralism and relativism. They sensed that, where the former requires an institutional framework with which to constrain power, the latter was merely the flip side of absolutism: it would serve the interests of the powerful and leave criticism unable to privilege freedom over intolerance.[33] Enlightenment intellectuals, in this regard, never believed that everyone must embrace the same goals as they, let alone that everyone must somehow reach these goals by the same logical means. Such an interpretation is possible only when the Enlightenment is identified with some rigid and uniform rationalist philosophy. It was instead inspired by a belief in the need for shared principles that underpin the liberal rule of law and enable redress of grievances without resorting to violence.

This was certainly not the position of the Counter-Enlightenment. The philosophes may have been elitist but their elitism was social rather than political and, if it can be put this way, of an anti-authoritarian rather than an authoritarian sort. Intellectuals can be chastised as a social stratum removed

---

32. Erich Fromm, *Man for Himself: An Inquiry into the Psychology of Ethics* (New York, 1947), 4–5.

33. "Relativism, no matter how progressive its bearing, has at all times been linked with moments of reaction, beginning with the sophists' availability to the more powerful interests. To intervene by criticizing relativism is the paradigm of definite negation." Theodor W. Adorno, *Negative Dialectics*, trans. E. B. Ashton (New York, Continuum, 1973), 37.

from the masses. But there is a something contradictory in speaking about an "organic" intellectual.[34] Not since the time of Socrates have intellectuals ever stood in a genuinely "organic" connection to the community. Populist criticism of this sort was common in the labor movement, and later many of the new social movements, but its modern formulation was originally provided by proto-fascist groups of the 1880s. And it is basically true. Critical intellectuals read books, debate, and value research. Those engaged in progressive causes seek to dispel prejudices and contest popular beliefs or, to paraphrase Walter Benjamin, "rub society against the grain." There is no way around it: insofar as intellectuals abandon this endeavor they surrender their critical function while, insofar as they embrace it, their "organic" character becomes problematic.

Enlightenment intellectuals reflected the concerns of an era in which "society discovered that its fate was in its own hands" and "people began to trust in the power of the will with an optimism born of the triumph of intelligence, and they began to live and talk and look at things in new ways that questioned the whole of existence."[35] This atmosphere surely inspired intellectuals as varied as Benjamin Franklin, Rousseau, Thomas Paine, and Goethe to laud the "common sense" of everyday people. But the connection between intellectuals and the broader public should not be seen in mechanical terms. Enlightenment thinkers recognized that intellectuals can serve the masses with integrity only insofar as they resist compromising the knowledge they offer.

Self-styled demagogues of both the left and the right have always sought to exploit know-nothing populism and resentment at the exercise of the intellect. More telling, however, is the thinker who, through rational argument, seeks to privilege intuition or emotion in evaluating claims and rendering judgments—that is, the anti-intellectual intellectual. Such an intellectual usually has an affinity for the Counter-Enlightenment: its im-

34. Bound to the working class through both job and lifestyle, according to the great Italian theorist Antonio Gramsci, this new intellectual would foster "counter-hegemonic" values among the oppressed and exploited. That effort would build consciousness, overcome fragmentation, and perhaps even lead to the introduction of new institutions like soviets capable of making a vanguard party unnecessary. But forgotten is usually that the connection between the "organic" intellectual and the masses is mediated by the party and, while the attack on "hegemonic" ideas can take place with an eye on the interests of the exploited, Gramsci had little to say about the "organic" character of the intellectual when criticism of the exploited or their party would be demanded by conscience. Antonio Gramsci, *Selections from the Prison Notebooks* ed. and trans. Quinton Hoare and Geoffrey Knowles-Smith (New York: International Publishers: New York, 1971), 3–24.

35. Daniel Roche, *France in the Enlightenment*, trans. Arthur Goldhammer (Cambridge: Harvard University Press, 1998), 487.

pressive array of thinkers ranges from Edmund Burke to Michael Oakeshott and, further on the right, from Joseph de Maistre to Martin Heidegger. Enormous differences exist between them. All believe, however, in the primacy of intuition over reason and experience over speculative critique. The local takes precedence over the cosmopolitan and the particular over the universal. Any judgment incapable of making reference to the community is considered "abstract" by definition. The opinion of the "outsider" is always suspect since the value of an argument rests on the "authenticity" with which it is delivered and the "rootedness" of its author in a given group or tradition. Thus, putting it crudely, the task of the anti-intellectual involves a critique of the intellect and a derision of the "intellectual."

Contempt was already directed against the "intellectual" when Maurice Barrès first introduced the term in damning his liberal and socialist opponents during the Dreyfus Affair.[36] Intellectuals like Emile Zola and Jean Jaurès could decry the injustice accorded Dreyfus—the Jew—because, in keeping with the general tenor of the Enlightenment, they chose to place reason above experience, evidentiary truth above tradition, and a more universal sense of justice above the "honor" of the army and the supposed exigencies of the national "community." Barrès and his friends, Paul Bourget and Charles Maurras, by way of contrast, embraced the tradition of the Counter-Enlightenment. Their argument was simple enough. Their rejection of universal reason in favor of intuition and the logic of the particular supposedly enabled them to remain "rooted" in their community and stand in a more genuine experiential, or "organic," relation to the "people" than their adversaries. But there should no mistake: many on both sides of the barricades were indeed intellectuals. Those with reactionary views actually stood in no closer relation to the "people" than their Dreyfusard opponents on the left—and, arguably, less so. Nevertheless, by packaging their message in a populist rhetoric, an elitist stigma soon became attached to the critical "intellectual."

There is something to be said for the belief that intellectuals connected "empirically" with particular social movements might be best placed to build the need for solidarity with other groups.[37] But this should be construed less

36. The term 'intellectual' appears to originate from the pen of Clemenceau in an article in *L'Aurore* of January 23, 1898, as a collective description of the most prominent Dreyfusards. The new term was promptly taken up in a pejorative sense of unscrupulousness and irresponsible disloyalty to the nation by Maurice Barrès in *Scenes et doctrines du nationalism* (Paris, 1902), pg. 46 (where incidentally even the un-French quality of the word itself becomes part of the accusation)." J. P. Nettl, "Ideas, Intellectuals, and the Structures of Dissent," in *On Intellectuals,* ed. Philip Rieff (New York, 1969), 87.

as a matter of principles than tactics. The Counter-Enlightenment showed the danger of reducing intellectual work to the symbolic or existential gesture of the "person" whose own "I" is in the postmodern era, moreover, always fundamentally in doubt. Judgment can then rest only on the immediate "experience" of reality. Critical reflection will become subordinated to some intuition of reality privileged by the race, gender, or ethnic background of the individual. Fixed and stable categories of "identity" are basically affirmative: they militate against new concerns with hybridity first raised by "postcolonial" thinkers; they offer nothing other than tactical possibilities for solidarity between groups, and they ignore how the ability to choose an "identity" with some degree of safety depends upon the existence of liberal institutions with liberal norms. These institutions and norms have their source within the Enlightenment. Many a postmodern or and communitarian intellectual obsessed with privileging "experience" in the world of today is not far removed from the anti-intellectual intellectual of yesterday.

The critical intellectual from the time of the Abbé Galiani to Jean-Paul Sartre has always been willing to "meddle in what is not his business."[38] Intellectuals like Albert Einstein, Linus Pauling, and Noam Chomsky stand in this tradition. They have used the prestige they gained in highly specialized fields of inquiry to intervene positively in debates over crucial political matters often, in the process, illuminating hidden normative and material interests embedded within elite forms of decision-making in striking ways. The Enlightenment intellectual knew that it takes no particular experience or expertise to recognize injustice and Edward Said was insightful in noting the connection between the intellectual and the "amateur." Therein one finds the legacy of Voltaire and the critics of the *ancien régime*, of the Dreyfusards, and the students who went to protest segregation in the American South or the atrocities of the Vietnam War. These people were neither necessarily intimately associated with the oppression they witnessed nor experts in legal or military affairs. They could engage themselves precisely because they felt unrestricted by their particular "experiences" or fields of expertise.

But praise for the amateur also has its limits. To ignore the need for critical disciplinary intellectuals with various forms of scientific expertise is to

37. Michel Foucalt, "Intellectuals and Power" in *Language, Counter-Memory, Practice,* ed. Donald F. Bouchard (Ithaca: Cornell University Press, 1977); 205ff; also "Truth and Power," in *The Foucault Reader,* ed. Paul Rabinow (New York: Pantheon, 1984), 68ff..

38. Jean-Paul Sartre, "A Plea for Intellectuals" in *Between Existentialism and Marxism* trans. John Matthews (London, 1974), 230.

abdicate responsibility for a host of issues involving knowledge of fields ranging from physics and genetics to electronics and even environmentalism. There is surely an overabundance of jargon and mystification and, as has been mentioned before, the need exists for a new sensitivity to the vernacular.[39] But it is also the case that complex issues sometimes require complex language and, often for good reasons, fields generate their own vocabularies. A judgment is undoubtedly necessary with respect to whether the language employed in a work is necessary for illuminating the issue under investigation: that judgment, however, can never be made in advance. There must be a place for the technocrat with a political conscience as surely as for the humanist with a particular specialty. The battle against oppression requires a multi-frontal strategy. Best to consider the words of Primo Levi who understood the critical intellectual as a "person educated beyond his daily trade, whose culture is alive insofar as it makes an effort to renew itself, and keep up to date, and who does not react with indifference or irritation when confronted by any branch of knowledge, even though, obviously, he cannot cultivate all of them."[40]

But the historical trajectory of modernity appears to have plotted a different course: what began in the age of democratic revolution as the attempt by Enlightenment intellectuals to offer a "practical program" for the liberation of the individual from the dogma of "throne and altar" seemingly created a world dominated by specialists and a bureaucratic, if not always totalitarian, society marked by the "dull indifference and apathy of the individual towards destiny and to what comes from above."[41] Critical theory had always been skeptical about claims concerning the autonomy of philosophy, but its partisans nevertheless sought to explain this development through the supposedly immanent dynamics of Enlightenment philosophy. In so doing, however, they produced a reified understanding of "reason" that fit an equally reified understanding of reality. Conflicts of ideological interest fell by the wayside—the wars of words and bullets, and the great moments of political decision as well. Seeking to deal with the unintended consequences produced by Enlightenment thought, in keeping

39. Russell Jacoby, *The Last Intellectuals: American Culture in the Age of Academe* (New York: Basic Books, 1987).

40. Primo Levi, *The Drowned and the Saved*, trans. Raymond Rosenthal (New York: Vintage, 1988), 132.

41. Max Horkheimer, "The Social Function of Philosophy," in *Critical Theory: Selected Essays*, trans. Matthew J. O'Connell et. al (New York: Continuum, 1982), 271.

with its idealist heritage, critical theory felt it sufficient to illuminate a new version of what Hegel termed "the cunning of reason."

The myth still exists that the Enlightenment intellectual is the source of modern totalitarianism. It is spread on both the left and the right. Some argue that the erosion of authority through critique opened the floodgates of revolution:[42] as if it would have been better to leave the authoritarian institutions, the economic misery, and the cultural prejudices of the *ancien régime* intact. Others suggest that the problem involved the belief of Enlightenment intellectuals that they retained a "privileged" insight into truth, justice, and progress.[43] Taking any position or "standpoint" necessarily involves privileging it. But the philosophes were generally skeptical about ontological claims, they debated openly with one another, and their primary battle was against dogmatism. The philosophes inspired antifascist movements while their enemies paved the way for Mussolini, Franco, and Hitler. Critics of the Enlightenment intellectual rarely take this into account because they usually show only contempt for political history and political engagement.

Arguments claiming that contemporary intellectuals—in contrast to their predecessors—should remain content to "interpret" misunderstandings between groups, rather than attempt to "legislate" conclusions,[44] exhibit the same political irresponsibility and simply rehash the myths of a warmed over populism. They over-estimate the power of intellectuals in the same way others overestimated the hegemony of Enlightenment values. Smugly they ask why "sophisticated" and worldly Enlightenment intellectuals, who prided themselves on their tolerance, should have grown "apoplectic" or "descended into sarcasm and smut" when dealing with "priests and creeds." They forget that a political battle was in progress against repressive institutions and customs with which priests and their churches were—correctly—associated in their minds.[45]

A dictatorship of the intellectuals is, of course, an appalling notion. But when did Enlightenment intellectuals ever hold power? The philosopher-

42. R. J. White, The Anti-Philosophers: A Study of the Philosophes in Eighteenth Century France (London: Macmillan, 1970);

43. Karlis Racekvis, *Postmodernism and the Search for Enlightenment* (Charlottesville: University Press of Virginia, 1995).

44. Zygmunt Bauman, *Legislators and Interpretors: On Modernity, Post-modernity, and Intellectuals* (Ithaca: Cornell University Press, 1987), 5ff and *passim*.

45. Porter, *The Enlightenment*, 31

king has always been little more than a useful fiction. Enlightenment intellectuals lacked a catechism of orthodoxy, an articulated program, and a political party: if there was a problem with their political vision, from a revolutionary perspective, it had less to do with their hidden authoritarianism or intolerance than their inability to envision the prospect of a counterrevolution or what it might take to deal with it. The philosophical justification for revolutionary terror was, other than a few famous phrases like that of forcing people to be free, precisely what the philosophes did not provide. The best that can be said historically is that the absence became the presence. Intellectuals did not rule in 1793 and, long before the purges of the 1930s, Stalin had displaced Lenin's self-appointed vanguard party of "professional revolutionary intellectuals" with his own thugs under the slogan "gangway for talent." Various important intellectuals extended their support to Stalin and Hitler. In doing so, however, they obviously compromised their "critical" role and the political principles of the Enlightenment.[46] In any event, the idea that intellectuals somehow held sway over the Nazi and Communist regimes is ludicrous.

Enlightenment intellectuals were always held in contempt by totalitarians on both sides of the political spectrum. And that is because they were, historically, committed to curbing state power and contesting dogma. Talk about their "legislative" ambitions under such circumstances becomes just another mode of populist posturing: as if reaching conclusions on matters of policy or organization were somehow better left to non-intellectuals or that for the intellectual in the totally administered society, there is nothing self-serving in the claim that "inviolable isolation is now the only way of showing some measure of solidarity."[47] Enlightenment intellectuals engaged in politics were always a threat to the authoritarian establishment. Their skepticism and their humanism made them suspect. In fact, such intellectuals fostered precisely what is most fundamental to undermining the appeal of totalitarianism: the will to know.

---

46. "If there was a uniquely German phenomenon that prepared the ground for Nazism, it was not the spread of anti-Semitism among the population in general but its spread among the intellectual elites. . . . In the 1920s the Nazis attracted an important section— the teachers and students especially, because the universities had become a hotbed of extremist right-wing ideas decades before." Yehuda Bauer, *Rethinking the Holocaust* (New Haven: Yale University Press, 2001), 33.

47. Theodor W. Adorno, *Minima Moralia: Reflections of Damaged Life*, trans.E.F.N. Jephcott (London: New Left Books, 1974), 26.

5

ABOLISHING THE GHETTO
ANTI-SEMITISM, RACISM, AND THE OTHER

VOLTAIRE ONCE NOTED IN A JUSTLY FAMOUS QUIP THAT IF GOD DID not exist it would have been necessary to invent Him. It is the same with the Jews and the Enlightenment: if the "accursed race" did not invent it then they should have. Times have changed since the totalitarian attempt to annihilate the Jews—the *other* of western civilization since its inception—seemed to justify the belief that progress had culminated in the most radical form of reification: the number tattooed on an inmate's arm. While this stance left *Dialectic of Enlightenment* locked into identifying the *absolute* evil with the holocaust, with little to say about other atrocities, the Jew is no longer the innocent victim. Anti-Semitic slogans are still scrawled on walls; cemeteries are sacked; synagogues set ablaze; fringe groups of neo-Nazis molest Jews in the streets; a half-wit prime minister of Malaysia, who opposes the introduction of democracy into the non-western world, rants about the power of world Jewry. But this is all very different both in terms of the quantity and quality of anti-Semitism than in times past. Outside the Middle East, where hatred of Jews is fueled by the imperialist policies of the Israeli state, anti-Semitism has become detached from any party or mass movement genuinely competing for political power. Gone are the uniforms and insignia, the pogroms and riots, the coordinated propaganda and the academically reinforced dogma, the paramilitary organizations and fascist parties, the discriminatory laws and the concentration camps. Over the last fifty years, moreover, other victims have taken center stage: people of color, women, gays, and inhabitants of colonized territories. Nevertheless, the historical experience of the Jews provides an excellent illustration of the misunderstandings associated with the critique of Enlightenment and the salience of its values for the struggles of the subaltern and the *other*.

Critical theory began with the belief that scientific rationalism had somehow undermined civilized behavior and inhibited the exercise of individual conscience. This allowed for the unleashing of instinctual resentments against those carriers of modern capitalism in the sphere of "circulation," the Jews,[1] and provided evidence for the way in which progress had "objectively" transformed the Enlightenment into "delusion" and anti-Semitism into the boundary, or the "limit," that reason cannot transgress.[2] The vaunted pessimism of the Frankfurt School thereby reached its apex. Absolute evil was attained: there is no poetry after Auschwitz. Hope now really does exist only for the hopeless. Even education won't help: Enlightenment projects fascism, reason withers in the face of paranoia, and—thus—the distorted perception of "the Jew," the *other*, cannot be cured.[3]

This argument informed the thinking of Theodor Herzl, who became disillusioned with liberalism, cosmopolitanism, and assimilation during the Dreyfus Affair. It also supports the defense of "Jewish" identity against the heritage of the Enlightenment. Modern anti-Semitism will then be traced back over the French Revolution to the philosophes.[4] Their writings will be combed for anti-Semitic sentiments to demonstrate their similarities with the rest of the *goyim*.[5] It will then become apparent that the assimilation of Jews was championed by many of those who considered them a "plague on the nation." Without drawing a distinction between the Enlightenment and the Counter-Enlightenment, however, moralizing about the ubiquity of anti-Semitism easily turns into a substitute for political judgment. The issue is not whether the Enlightenment was intent on preserving Jewish identity, but whether its values or those of the Counter-Enlightenment best enable the Jew—or the particular member of any subaltern group—to live as a citizen among other citizens and choose, most freely, what kind of private life he or she might wish to lead.

Medieval society was not kind to the Jews. The great majority of them

1. "Anti-Semitic behavior is generated in situations where blinded men robbed of their subjectivity are set loose as subjects. . . . They demonstrate the impotence of sense, significance, and ultimately of truth—which might hold them within bounds." Max Horkheimer and Theodor W. Adorno, *Dialectic of Enlightenment* (New York: Herder & Herder, 1972), 171.
2. Ibid., 204.
3. Ibid., 193, 197.
4. Cf. Arthur Hertzberg, *The French Enlightenment and the Jews* (New York, 1968)
5. Cf. Leon Poliakov, *The History of Antisemitism: From Voltaire to Wagner*, trans. Miriam Kochan (New York: Vanguard Press, 1975). A modern and somewhat more esoteric version of this approach, which offers the same result, is provided by Michael Mack, *German Idealism and the Jew: the Inner Anti-Semitism of Philosophy* (Chicago: University of Chicago, 2003).

were dirt poor, lived in overcrowded ghettoes,[6] and suffered under the social power of half-educated authoritarian rabbis.[7] Traditional debates were esoteric: free thinkers like Uriel da Casta were either driven to suicide (1640) or, like Spinoza (1656), excommunicated. Jews also bore the brunt of various myths spread by gentiles. Accusations abounded concerning how Jews purposely spread disease, poisoned wells, secretly amassed great wealth, worshipped the devil, engaged in an ongoing conspiracy against Christian civilization, and used the blood of Christian children for their *matza* on Passover. Romantics preoccupied with the organic community would view Jews as a nation within the nation or what Fichte termed a "state within the state." It is true that for certain periods, and in certain nations, Jews lived on relatively friendly terms with their gentile neighbors: viewing them simply as "victims" would be a mistake. But this relationship was open to change at any moment. Pogroms always loomed, Jews were still perceived as killers of Christ and, in a sense, they were kept in reserve as a scapegoat. The feudal subordination of law to the Christian religion put Jews at an obvious disadvantage: most of them lived under a theocratic order in which—as St. Ambrose put the matter—"civil law must bow before religious devotion."

This made it only logical for Jews to identify with the new monarchical state whose centralized legal system provided the foundations for modern liberal democracies,[8] and whose "enlightened despots," like Joseph II of Austria-Hungary, attempted to abolish the legacy of prejudice inherited from the feudal past. As for the philosophes, they too mostly supported the new centralized regimes. But they were less concerned with the particular

---

6. "Certainly the Jewish quarters of Europe, such as, for example, the one in Venice from which all got their name, were much more crowded, poorer in living space and facilities, and more inescapable than even our worst slums of today. To use some random examples: the Jewish ghetto in Cologne was the narrowest street in town: it was even called the 'Narrow Street.' In the Frankfort ghetto 4,000 persons lived in one short gloomy street, twelve feet wide, where the roofs of the small houses met at the top, making for gloomy darkness all day. In some cities the brothels were placed in the one small street in which Jews were permitted to live, to add to their ill repute. In the infamous Roman ghetto, at times as many as 10,000 inhabitants were herded into a space smaller than one square kilometer. In nearly all ghettos several families often had to occupy the same room." Bruno Bettelheim, "Mental Health and Urban Design," in *Surviving and Other Essays* (New York: Alfred Knopf, 1979), 217.

7. Exposing the stultifying character of religious life in Poland, and demystifying the "rabbi," are important themes in Salmon Maimon, *An Autobiography*, trans. J. Clark Murray (Urbana and Chicago: University of Illinois Press, 2001), 155ff.

8. Blandine Kriegel, *The State and the Rule of Law*, trans. Marc A. LePain and Jeffrey C. Cohen (Princeton: Princeton University Press, 1994), 11ff and passim.

conditions of the Jews than with the universal principles underpinning the liberal polity. Locke put the matter succinctly in his *Letter on Toleration* when he wrote that: "neither Pagan nor Mahometan, nor Jew, ought to be excluded from the civil rights or the commonwealth because of his religion."

Such is the Enlightenment response to anti-Semitism, and its logic holds for other subaltern groups. Montesquieu stood in the forefront of the battle against anti-Semitism in France, William Penn and Roger Williams led the struggle for religious liberty in the United States, while Lessing and Wilhelm Dohm pled the case of the Jews in Germany. Others may have been less altruistic but, from the beginning, the central issue revolved around whether to embrace the vision of a Christian community or a universal understanding of the citizen stripped of any particular empirical attributes. The charge of fostering a conspiracy against an organic Christian community, often levied against Voltaire and the philosophes by the Abbé Barruel and other reactionaries, intensified the traditional xenophobic fears directed against Jews and Freemasons. This linkage of Jews and Freemasons with the Enlightenment—as conspiratorial agents of modernity and bourgeois revolution—would carry over into the thinking of twentieth-century racists and reactionaries. But there is also a way in which this linkage—if not the conspiracy—makes sense. Voltaire and many philosophes were freemasons, whose lodges were havens of toleration, and emancipating the Jews was, indeed, part of a more general political assault on the *ancien régime*.

The crowning achievements of this enterprise were the three great democratic revolutions that occurred in England (1688), the United States (1776) and France (1789). All of them were predicated on the vision of a new constitutional order in which equal citizens of diverse background and different interests might determine their fate together peacefully under the liberal rule of law. Constitutionalism and suffrage rejected—*in principle*—the idea of individuals living without explicit human rights in a "community" bound together by land and custom. The principle, of course, did not instantly translate into fact and, thus, there began the long struggle for suffrage by excluded groups whose most important representatives, from Mary Wollstonecraft to Martin Luther King, Jr., pointed to the contradiction between universal ideals and the prejudiced society that denied them. It only makes sense that the formation of a liberal and secular order should have been welcomed not only by those Jews seeking entry into gentile society, but—what is so often forgotten—also by those seeking freedom from the theocracy of the provincial ghetto. Eighteenth-century constitutional revolutions tore down the walls of the ghetto, opened society, and—finally—enabled Jews to claim their rights as equal citizens. The failings of these revolutions with respect to implementing equality among citizens, it should be noted, were due less to the inadequacies of their Enlightenment supporters than the unrelenting assault upon their most basic political values by the heirs of the Counter-Enlightenment.

The mechanistic, rationalistic, individualistic, and egalitarian assumptions underpinning this constitutional political vision were contested not merely by anti-Semites but also by orthodox Jewish traditionalists and members of the newly formed *hasidim*, who sought to liberate the spirit by rendering holy the affairs of everyday life, as well as self-interested conservatives with a stake in the status quo, and small-minded provincials who sought their safety in the ghetto. They opposed the modernizing spirit of the *haskalah*, or "Jewish Enlightenment," and their thinking often mirrored that of reactionary advocates of an organic society and the cultural conservatism of Counter-Enlightenment thinkers like Burke, DeMaistre, and Hamann. The situation is not much different with the young Gershom Scholem, who advocated a radical separatism, or Franz Rosenzweig, who called for a mystical inner renewal and the "blood" bond of the Jews. Nonsense like this has again become fashionable: it seems to fascinate even postmodernist and progressive intellectuals. But few have much use any longer for Mendelssohn or his gentile friend Gotthold Ephraim Lessing, author of the celebrated plays *The Jews* and *Nathan the Wise*, though they stood in the vanguard of those who would lead the assault against both the anti-Semitic prejudices of gentile society and the provincialism of established Jewry. Leaders of the *haskalah* called upon Jews to enter society and public life. Mendelssohn himself was observant of religious custom. Nevertheless, he and his followers made easier the abandonment of religious tradition through their emphasis upon secular values and participation in the wider world of the burgeoning nation-state.

Taking advantage of the new possibilities offered by liberal society had a negative impact on the traditional sense of identity: Jews became secular, moved out of the ghetto, increased their contact with gentiles, and sought advancement. Many among the ambitious and educated became baptized like the great composer Felix Mendelssohn-Bartholdy, Heinrich Heine, and the fascinating Rahel Varnhagen whose salon served as the home of many leading intellectuals of the period. Many made their choice on practical grounds like Eduard Gans, the teacher of Karl Marx, who converted in order to secure his chair of philosophy at the University of Berlin. But others felt what Heine called the "betrayal complex" or, like Varnhagen, remained obsessed with their Jewishness until their death. The trend toward baptism, and the exodus from the ghetto, would increasingly cause the anti-Semite to begin identifying "the Jew" less by religion than by pseudo-biological attributes. Neither the motivations nor the methods of these anti-Semites had anything to do with the Enlightenment. The problems associated with the "betrayal complex" and the dangers associated with the new pseudo-science of racism were foisted on Jews not by the Enlightenment, but by its enemies.

During the nineteenth and much of the twentieth centuries, the Enlightenment was still embraced only by a minority in Europe. It was precisely where liberal traditions and institutions were strongest, however, that the pursuit of Jewish "identity" was best protected. The "Jewish question" *became a question* only in nations where a burgeoning constitutional liberalism and capitalism confronted powerful reactionary social forces committed to the hierarchical and "Christian" vision of a feudal past. Emancipation was not an issue of any practical importance in the United States while, in Imperial Russia, it was not even a topic for discussion. To be sure: economic crisis brings out anti-Semitic sentiments but, with respect to the issue of "emancipation," this should not be considered the primary issue: England, the United States, and the Netherlands also suffered from the "Great Depression" without experiencing the same racist consequences as Germany. In western nations with liberal institutions and liberal traditions, indeed, "emancipation" was basically successful.[9] A sense of identity, meanwhile, did not help the Jews in Poland and Eastern Europe from the Nazis. It makes as little sense to speak about the "failure" of Jewish emancipation in nations lacking liberal institutions and deeply rooted liberal traditions as it does to speak about the "failure" of Marxism in economically underdeveloped nations where proletarian revolutions were undertaken without a proletariat.

Critics of "emancipation" have noted how, during the French Revolution, Clermont Tonnerre emphasized that the aim of the new society was to liberate individual Jews rather than Jewry.[10] But this criticism misunderstands the nature of constitutional liberalism. It offered individuals freedom from the arbitrary interference of the state in their private lives, and equali-

---

9. For a somewhat different view, see Leonard Dinnerstein, *Antisemitism in America* (Oxford University Press, New York, 1994).

10. Reinhard Rürup, "Judenemanzipation und bürgerliche Gesellschaft in Deutschland," in *Vorurteil und Völkermord: Entwicklungslinien des Antisemitismus* hrsg. Wolfgang Benz und Werner Bergmann (Freiburg: Herder, 1997), 138

ty under the law; it did not offer "group rights." It sought to turn each individual into a capitalist, not to abolish capitalism; it offered formal equality under the law, not substantive equality in the realm of civil society; it projected fraternity in terms of the national interest and the primacy of self-interest in economic matters. Marx indeed saw these defects as warranting the move beyond "political emancipation" and toward "human emancipation" in his early work, "On the Jewish Question" (1843),[11] which employs anti-Semitic terminology and retains anti-Semitic overtones.

Written prior to what would become his famous analysis of capitalism, lacking the categories he would later employ in *Das Kapital*, Marx associated the new economic system with Jewish attributes: he built on an economic motivation for anti-Semitism inherited from the Middle Ages when, following the Third Lateran Council of 1179, Christians were prohibited from charging interest and Jews were placed in the position of serving as moneylenders in an agrarian society. The anti-Semitic characterizations used by Marx were common among intellectuals of the period. More striking was the lack of any institutional referent for "human emancipation" against the idea of "political emancipation" predicated on the existence of a republic. This same inadequacy is apparent in the thinking of those seeking the "emancipation of Jewry." Their abstraction from political history is noteworthy since everywhere the success of the struggle for Jewish emancipation ran parallel with the fortunes of constitutional liberalism.[12] Often, initially, only Christian males with property were granted full citizenship and the right to vote. Since constitutional liberalism was predicated on universal principles of formal equality and reciprocity, however, it became possible to contest discriminatory laws and practices. That is precisely what anti-Semites and reactionaries hated about the new order introduced by the democratic revolutions, articulated by the Enlightenment, and unevenly spread throughout Europe by Napoleon.

Emancipation not in the abstract, but into the broader society, was the hope of the Jews. Organizing themselves in terms of their "identity" was nowhere a viable political option: Zionism was itself a "post-emancipation" phenomenon with little intellectual or mass support before the last quarter

---

11. Note the seminal study by Henry Pachter, "Marx and the Jews," in *Socialism in History: Political Essays of Henry Pachter*, ed. Stephen Eric Bronner (New York: Columbia University Press, 1984), 219–255.
12. Paul W. Massing, *Rehearsal for Destruction: A Study of Political Antisemitism in Imperial Germany* (New York: Howard Fertig, 1967), 3ff and *passim*.

of the nineteenth century. The liberal vision of emancipation offered the sole serious possibility for bettering the lives of Jews in the historical context of the eighteenth and nineteenth centuries. The Jews knew it and proponents of the anti-Semitic reaction knew it as well. The champions of liberal democracy fought for it and the counter-revolutionary enemies of liberal democracy fought against it. Jewish critics of emancipation thus focus on the wrong target. The primary problem was—again—not the proponents of emancipation who recognized "the Jew as a person, but not as a Jew." It was, instead, the opponents of emancipation who refused to recognize the Jew as a human being endowed with rights under the law. It was they who saw this "outsider" as a threat to their atavistic vision of an organic and homogeneous "community." [13]

The years following the Napoleonic Wars were dominated by attempts to introduce a "restoration" of precisely such a community. Stendhal appropriately called the period, stretching from 1815–1848, a "swamp"; it was dominated by the army and the church or, using the title of his most famous work, "the red and the black." Anti-Semitism and the romantic ideology of this self-proclaimed "counterrevolution" shared a profound and transparent connection. Both were directed against everything associated with the Enlightenment and the French Revolution. Experience and intuition were given primacy over reason. Christianity was resurrected, so to speak, in order to contest the earlier trend toward secularism.[14] Authoritarian demands for obedience, adherence to tradition, and a romantic assault on modernity became the responses to republicanism and "freedom of conscience."

Integral nationalism and messianic visions of a Christian destiny have always intoxicated the advocates of both racism and the Counter-Enlightenment. But Jews too, especially those who worry most about the erosion of their identity, can evidence the qualities of their persecutors. The strengthening of prejudice became the underside of the struggle for liberty. With the republican ideal of the citizen came the attack on the rights of the *other*. Rejection of natural rights and human dignity, which the Enlightenment inherited from the Renaissance, was the motor for

13. A different perspective, which highlights how Jewish distinctness became the prism for reflecting upon German culture, is presented in the intelligent study by Jonathan M. Hess, *Germans, Jews, and the Claims of Modernity* (New Haven: Yale University Press, 2002).

14. Eva G. Reichmann, *Hostages of Civilisation: The Sources of National Socialist Antisemitism* (Westport, CT: Greenwood Press, 1949), 83ff.

transforming hatred of the Jew into a distinctly social prejudice during the early nineteenth century. This ongoing battle of differing value systems was—again—generated less by some "dialectic" inherent within the Enlightenment than the political vision of its representatives as against those of the Counter-Enlightenment.

Concern with race reaches back to the "purity of blood" statutes introduced during the fifteenth century in Spain: it was, clearly, directed against Jews who had converted to Christianity (*conversoes*) as well as those who secretly continued to follow their original religion (*marranos*). Francois Bernier was probably the first to use the term "race" as a way of demarcating groups through physical attributes in 1684 and Voltaire employed the category in *The Philosophy of History* to counter the idea that all people are commonly descended from Adam. Kant wrote about "race," though he juxtaposed it against the idea of the "species," in "Of the Different Human Races" (1775). Whatever the misguided prejudices of these thinkers, however, the crucial point is that none of them viewed race—or religion—as an organizing category for action. Their concerns with race were mostly academic and, especially for Voltaire and Kant, had little bearing upon their activism or their general theories.

Romantic advocates of German nationalism introduced the first political program based on "purity of race." Their motivation was not simply to establish hierarchical relations of superiority and inferiority, or even to create perverse stereotypes, but to oppose the opening of the ghettos. Angered by the success of Jews who entered public life, their racism consciously opposed the universal principles of Enlightenment political theory. It instead served to justify their *rishes*, or anti-Semitic "resentment," and provide reasons why Jews could not assimilate into the nation. The point was to show why Jews were not people like other people and why they were incapable of participating equally in Christian society: indeed, precisely because Jews were seen as constituting an organic "race" or "nation," it followed that non-Jews must begin identifying themselves in the same way. Only through an explicitly racial consciousness would it be possible to recognize the Jewish threat. And so, depending upon the context, "the Jew" would be pitted against "the French" or "the German," or "the Aryan." Those who ignored this ineradicable conflict between Jews and gentiles were obviously traitors to their nation and their race.

Anti-Semitism evidences pre-modern longings for provincialism, authoritarianism, and hierarchy that resist cosmopolitan, liberal, and socialist values. The connection between these values was solidified—again—during the

Dreyfus Affair.[15] Movements like the *Action française* and the various fascist *ligues* no less than the Nazis exhibited an almost pathological fear of any attempt to fragment society and uproot the old myths associated with social rank and national virtue. The French Revolution undertaken against a monarchy rooted in ancient traditions—if not according to Edmund Burke then according to those more extreme in their conservative views—could only have been the work of "outsiders" intent upon manipulating simple-minded people with dreams of equality and democracy. Again, the quest for uniformity and the willingness to impose it upon the community has its roots not in the Enlightenment, but the Counter-Enlightenment.

Such thinking was in already prevalent in Germany when, just as the debates over Jewish emancipation were taking place, the "Hep-Hep" pogroms broke out in 1819.[16] They spread throughout southern and eastern Germany, causing loss of property and lives, fueled by what demagogues called the "anger of the people." A new form of Counter-Enlightenment protest was crystallizing. It would simmer in the next three decades following the pogroms: the old aristocratic reaction remained dominant. But then it burst forth in the decades following the revolutions of 1848 that, essentially, sought to establish republican institutions and social justice. The ensuing reaction ultimately brought figures like Napoleon III and Bismarck to power even as it generated a new commitment to integral nationalism and the organic community. Counter-Enlightenment ideas of this sort inspired the rise of populist movements led by powerful figures like Karl Lueger, who would become the longstanding mayor of Vienna, and Adolf Stoecker the court chaplain of Kaiser Wilhelm I in Berlin. Literary figures in France like Maurice Barrès worried about their nation becoming "deracinated" while in Austria during the last quarter of the nineteenth century Georg Ritter von Schoener-er—among the leaders of the staunchly authoritarian and anti-Semitic

15. "As a universal weapon, anti-Semitism targeted the Republic (Jewish in origin and nature) and defended Catholicism (attacked by Jewish Freemasonry) and the people against capitalism (Jewish usurers, Jewish Banking). The Dreyfus affair appears to have been decisive in France, however: in the end, anti-Semitism became fixed on the right and the socialist movement seems to have purged itself of its last anti-Jewish relics." Michael Winock, *Nationalism, Anti-Semitism, and Fascism in France*, trans. Jane Marie Todd (Stanford: Stanford University Press, 1998), 101–2.

16. "Hep-hep" was an anti-Semitic cry, or the slogan, which tended to accompany anti-Semitic actions. Its roots are unclear although the best guess is that it goes back to the time of ancient Rome when the Temple fell and the Romans yelled *"Hierosolyma est perdita"* ("Jersualem is lost"). Detlev Claussen, *Vom Judenhass zu Antisemitismus: Materialien einer verleugneten Geschichte* (Darmstadt: Luchterhand, 1987), 74ff.

German-national movement and an idol of the young Hitler—was already
successfully employing the slogan: "Germany for the Germans" and "From
Purity to Unity."[17]

Behind the seemingly endless array of mutually exclusive interests—
bourgeois and proletarian, universal and particular, pacifist and imperialist—a unifying force, these reactionaries believed, must exist. It was necessary to find a way of explaining the seeming triumph of the Enlightenment,
the revolution, and the dire consequences both held for Christian society.
Employing racism as an explanation for the dynamics of history was the
point behind popular works of anti-Semitism like *The Jewish Question as a
Racial, Moral, and Cultural Question* (1881) by Eugen Dühring, *Jewish
France* (1886) by Edmund Drumont, and *The Foundations of the Nineteenth
Century* (1899) by Houston Stewart Chamberlain. The use of race by these
avowedly Counter-Enlightenment thinkers enabled anti-Semites to fuse
the multiplicity of liberalizing and secularizing modern forces into a single
enemy, the Jew, and the extent to which this enemy could be identified
with *all* enemies of the organic community proved the extent to which
anti-Semitism dominated the thinking of the political right in any particular nation. It increasingly became an article of faith among the forces of reaction that the republic was an alien system imposed by an alien entity
upon the "people's community" and, everywhere in Europe, the attempt
was made to translate the attack on "the Jew" into an attack upon "the Jew
republic" –whether the Third Republic in France or the Weimar Republic
in Germany.

Contempt for the masses or "the crowd," which Gustav LeBon originally
identified with the social democratic labor movement, *by the masses and the
"crowd"* was the key to the new anti-Semitic perspective on politics in the
modern era. Since only they can really understand the urgency of the situation given the supposed Jewish control over public life, anti-Semites longed
for an authoritarian state in which they might press their message without
criticism or opposition. The connection between antidemocratic and anti-
Semitic politics occurs from the very onset of modernity. Anti-Semites always—correctly—saw liberal democracy as hampering their ability to deal
with the Jewish conspiracy: its civil liberties, reliance on common sense, and
democratic discourse left them ham-strung in attempting to persuade the
more gullible gentiles of the threat posed by the "Jewish" conspiracy. That

17. Brigitte Hamann, *Hitlers Wien: Lehrjahre eines Diktators* (München: Piper Verlag, 1998),
    337ff.

idea would, indeed, fit nicely with the thinking of a Counter-Enlightenment obsessed with the ways in which the "crowd" was being misled by the forces of modernity.

Nowhere does this become clearer than in the infamous forgery known as the *Protocols of the Learned Elders of Zion.*[18] Its anti-Semitism, explicitly directed against the political legacy of the Enlightenment, was justified by the supposed existence of a Jewish world conspiracy against Christian civilization. The tract responds not merely to economic or political conditions, but to existential needs as well. It expresses the usual paranoia, projects conspiratorial violence on the Jew, and constantly employs negative stereotypes. Hatred of Jews appears as an irrefutable lived experience through which, in Sartre's great phrase, the bigot "turns himself into stone." The anti-Semite cannot defend his position for that would place him in existential jeopardy: intuition thus supplants reason as the primary basis for making an argument. Or, better, anti-Semitism becomes an article of faith: the overwhelming power of the Jews, and the invisibility of the conspiratorial threat they present, is simply assumed.

Discursive justification or empirical verification is unnecessary. Arguments become legitimate only insofar as they support the claims of a faith, or an experience, uncontaminated by critical reflection. Reason is, after all, universal: it can be employed by anyone at anytime and it privileges no "place." No wonder then that the anti-Semite sees reason as the tool of the "rootless cosmopolitan" Jew, who lacks a fixed "place" in the world, or that the intellect should be seen as lacking appeal for the uncomplicated Christian, who is guided by intuition, formed by experience, and aware of his position in an imaginary society. The lack of feeling for any "place" combined with the rejection of healthy intuition is what supposedly enables the Jew to manipulate events; it explains to the anti-Semite why the Christian—loyal to his "experience" and his "place"—is always outwitted and why both the Jew and the need for anti-Semitism have persisted in various forms from the beginning of time. It is important to consider, however, that the Jew can embrace a similar complex of paranoid epistemological assumptions that in moments of crisis can prove not merely self-defeating, but a self-fulfilling prophecy. Indeed, with paranoid views of the non-Jewish world, the result for Jews can only be isolation from the rest of global society.

---

18. A fuller exposition of the arguments derived here can be found in Stephen Eric Bronner, *A Rumor about the Jews: Anti-Semitism, Conspiracy, and the* Protocols of Zion (Paperback Edition: New York: Oxford University Press, 2003).

Not every traditional anti-Semite was a fascist and not every fascist was an anti-Semite, but the two positions reinforced one another. The fascist ideology seemed a way of reinvigorating the more traditional politics of anti-Semitism by infusing it with a new missionary, almost religious, fervor. The enemies of fascism were, moreover, generally the same as those of more established elites whose views derived from the Counter-Enlightenment. Such traditionalists were generally driven to panic by the Reds and their "Jewish" leaders. They were just as committed to a homogeneous "people's community," and most were just as critical of the cultural "decadence" and liberal spirit associated with the Enlightenment, as the partisans of the more extreme right. Remnants of the past were carried over into modernity: pre-capitalist classes struggled against the new capitalist system; aristocrats and the petit bourgeoisie battled first the monarchical nation-state and then its republican incarnation; and, finally, religious institutions fought the Enlightenment legacy. There is nothing pure about progress: even its proponents were often scarred with outworn prejudices. The anti-modern reaction was built into modernity from the very beginning and helped shape its development. Older forms of anti-Semitism thereby became reconfigured in the new liberal context: their supporters were increasingly thrown on the defensive.

The history of anti-Semitism attests to the superiority of Anglo-American over a continental liberalism that was far less individualistic and far more inclined toward an exclusivist, inflexible, and emotive form of nationalism. Its advocates retained a certain romantic commitment to the idea of a homogeneous "people's state" (*Volksstaat*) and they often aligned themselves with authoritarian state builders like Bismarck. Some like Fichte deified the German *Volk* and considered nationalism as the equivalent of revealed religion. Continental liberals dominated the famous "anti-Semitism controversy" (*Antisemitismusstreit*) of 1879 between Heinrich von Treitschke and Theodor Mommsen in which the former stressed the undue influence of Jews on German society, called upon Jews to beome more "German," and introduced the phrase that would become a popular slogan under the Nazis: "The Jews are our misfortune!" (*Die Juden sind unser Unglück!*). Such views, contradict the spirit and the premises of constitutional liberalism. Indeed, they attest to the lack of a genuinely liberal tradition in Germany and other nations where anti-Semitism played an important political role.

In the shadow of the holocaust and amid lingering memories of the failed Weimar Republic, which Hitler trampled on the road to power, postwar scholars showed themselves increasingly skeptical about liberal solutions to the "Jewish question": they looked to Germany in order to explain the "failure" of emancipation.[19] But, in fact, it proved emblematic only of those nations in which the liberal "emancipation" of Jews was attempted without indigenously rooted liberal institutions and traditions. Emancipation was undertaken gradually in Germany, step by legislative step, with varying degrees of success in a mosaic of mostly reactionary principalities where radically different numbers of Jews lived. Germany was not even a nation in the beginning of the nineteenth century and the lateness of its emergence as a state generated what would remain an assorted set of existential problems associated with its national identity.[20] The liberal assumptions embraced by supporters of "emancipation," in short, cannot be judged by the results more than a century later in what was still notably an "illiberal society."[21]

Anti-Semitism like racism and hatred of the *other* has always been embedded in a Counter-Enlightenment marked by the anxiety of provincials, the traditionalism of conservatives, and the brutal irrationalism of fascists. Anti-Semitism not only remains "the socialism of fools," but the philosophy of those who choose to think with their gut. Its claims rest on *faith*: the point is not whether they are true, but whether the anti-Semite *believes* them to be true. The power of bigotry, indeed, has always stood in inverse relation to the support for Enlightenment ideals. That is still the case: recognizing the dignity of the *other* is the line in the sand marking the great divide of political life.

19. Reichmann, *Hostages of Civilisation*, 20ff and passim.
20. Helmuth Plessner, *Die Verspätete Nation* (Stuttgart: W. Kohlhammer, 1959).
21. Fritz Stern, *The Failure of Illiberalism: Essays on the Political Culture of Modern Germany* (Chicago: University of Chicago Press, 1955), 3ff.

6

THE ILLUSORY DIALECTIC:
FROM ENLIGHTENMENT TO TOTALITARIANISM

"Enlightenment is totalitarian."
—MAX HORKHEIMER AND THEODOR ADORNO[1]

THE SPECTER OF TOTALITARIANISM STILL HOVERED OVER THE political landscape when *Dialectic of Enlightenment* was published in 1947. Nazism had conquered Europe and it nearly won the war. But the state structure of the Soviet Union, its secret police, military style, propaganda, and "cult of the personality" were roughly the same as that of its fascist enemy while its anti-fascist ally the United States, whatever of its formal commitment to democracy, was tainted by racism, imperialist ambitions, and the looming specter of McCarthyism. Max Horkheimer and Theodor Adorno saw the future appearing as present: and it was not the future that the Enlightenment had foretold. Its promises of cosmopolitanism, autonomy, and moral progress already seemed to have been betrayed by a "totally administered society." The bureaucratic imperatives of modernity were seen as everywhere putting the eradication of conscience and reflection on the agenda.[2] Thus, it seemed logical to claim that "resistance" can no longer be based upon the old ideals of liberalism, socialism, and the good society: critical theory should instead throw the individual a life-preserver or, better, toss a bottle with a new metaphysical message of freedom into the ocean since "in the age of the individual's liquidation, the question of individuality must be raised anew."[3]

It would probably have been impossible for anyone who had lived through the 1920s and 1930s, especially thinkers schooled in Hegel and Marx,

---

1. Max Horkheimer and Theodor W. Adorno, *Dialectic of Enlightenment*, trans. John Cumming (New York: Herder & Herder, 1972), 6.
2. "The idea that after this war life will continue 'normally' or even that culture might be 'rebuilt'—as if the rebuilding of culture were not already its negation—is idiotic. Millions of Jews have been murdered, and this is to be seen as an interlude and not the catastrophe itself. What more is this culture waiting for?" Theodor W. Adorno, *Minima Moralia: Reflections from Damaged Life*, trans. E. F. N. Jephcott (London: New Left Books, 1974), 55.
3. Ibid., 129

not to think that modernity was implicated in the creation of totalitarianism. But Horkheimer and Adorno believed the source of this development derived from the Enlightenment. Liberal politics had apparently engendered its opposite: the liberal "provisional government" of February 1917 had made way for communism; Italian liberals folded in the face of Mussolini's "black shirts;" and Nazism emerged from the Weimar Republic. Progress seemed to have resulted in regression. Science and technology had not alleviated misery but instead made possible "total war"; *Bildung* was now tainted by propaganda; the manifold personality envisioned by Goethe and the philosophes had retreated in the face of "the mass man."[4] Socialism was shot. Discrete insights of this sort, however, only touch the surface. It became a matter of showing not merely the internal connection between totalitarianism and the Enlightenment, but how the germs of barbarism existed in western civilization from the beginning.

Given its epistemological influences and premises, critical theory was uniquely poised to make such an argument. Dialectics rests on the concept of immanence and in its idealist variant, which exhibited such a profound influence upon critical theory,[5] ideas retain their own dynamic; intentions generate unforeseen consequences; complexity becomes the sign of progress; mutually exclusive phenomena turn into contradictory manifestations of an organic whole; and philosophy changes in order to express the new meaning of a new epoch. These premises made it possible to understand the attack on religious myth orchestrated by the Enlightenment as merely the prelude for a war of "pure reason" on everything associated with "practical reason," including the exercise of conscience and the value of autonomy. Others would argue, by contrast, it was originally the attempt by Kant and Hegel to delimit the sphere of science by allowing for a realm "outside the space of representation"—knowledge of which might even grasp the absolute—that helped philosophically fuel totalitarianism.[6] The ideal of the new totalizing philosophies was a fixed and finished utopia in which a "perfectly transparent language" would name all things with perfect clarity. From the first, however, totalitarianism was notorious for its perversion of language and its

4. Jose Ortega y Gasset, *The Revolt of the Masses* (New York: Norton, 1932), 54ff.
5. Stephen Eric Bronner, "Sketching the Lineage: The Critical Method and the Idealist Tradition," in *Of Critical Theory and Its Theorists* 2nd Edition (New York: Routledge, 2002), 11ff.
6. Michel Foucault, *The Order of Things* (New York: Vintage, 1973), 242ff.

rejection of linguistic rigor.[7] Better then to show how progressive intentions produced unintended reactionary results and qualitative differences between regimes dissolved in favor of their common reliance on bureaucracy and instrumental rationality. Thus, the dogmatic claim of Hegel that the "whole is true" was transformed into the even more dramatic yet equally dogmatic assertion that "the whole is false."[8]

In the shadow of Auschwitz and Hiroshima, critical theory insisted that the cost of progress was too high. Utopian visions of harmony between the individual and society had only increased reification. Best then to emphasize the "non-identity" between subject and object and an explicitly "negative" understanding of dialectics intent upon preserving the individual from the incursions of a reified world. This new perspective in critical theory turned the tradition of Hegel and Marx upside down. It subordinated history to anthropology, politics to metaphysics, and any institutional concern with securing liberty to an indeterminate freedom experienced by the individual. In highlighting the unintentional transformation of the Enlightenment into totalitarianism, moreover, critical theory severed the connection between theory and practice. Modernity lost its specificity; its regimes lost their institutional determinations; and, with the communist betrayal of the revolutionary proletarian mission, organized politics ceased to serve as an avenue of change. Resistance instead would now require an aesthetic-philosophical assertion of subjectivity, an anti-political form of politics, directed against a world ever more akin to a huge "business office in which the employees have created cliques that attempt to dominate one another though the situation has the flavor of Kafka since it has become questionable whether an employer actually

---

7. "Totalitarian propaganda is a form of violence. . . . Its argument is imposition; its counter-argument is intimidation. . . . Even the grammar of the fascist propagandist reflect his confused state of mind. In terms like *Gebürtenschlacht* (battle of birth), *Opfer an der Idee* (sacrifice unto the idea) and *battaglia del grano,* and similar highpressure slogans, and in many sentences written in "Nazi German," subject and object are interchangeable. . . . It is typical of this language that nouns take the place of verbs as if human action were contained in a bureaucratic ukase. . . . In the Nazi meeting the speaker is a "drummer" not an advocate [and as for the language itself] what matters here is not the insane content of the message but the pseudo-revolutionary dynamism of its tenor—that particular blend of motion where no one moves, with freedom where everyone is obedient." Henry Pachter, "Fascist Propaganda and the Conquest of Power," in *Socialism in History: Political Essays of Henry Pachter* ed. Stephen Eric Bronner (New York: Columbia University Press, 1984), 110ff.

8. Adorno, *Minima Moralia,* 50.

exists: it appears that the nasty, brutal, exploitative character of the system already exists in the competing groups waiting in the wings."[9]

Moving forward calls for bringing critical theory out of the metaphysical mist and the night in which all cows are black. It involves recognizing that the finest critics of reification might themselves have "reified" totalitarianism: extrapolating their historical experience into the future, ignoring movements and institutions, they would use totalitarianism to understand very different non-totalitarian circumstances. New forms of critical theory must begin asking whether the "individual" really is in danger of vanishing, and whether "instrumental reason" poses an inherent threat to subjectivity. They might start with seeking historical justifications rather than metaphysical assertions for claims that the Enlightenment "dialectically" turned into its totalitarian opposite. New forms of critical theory should also reflect on whether the connection between totalitarianism and modernity is simply misguided. There are reasons why fascism should have found its mass base not in modern classes like the bourgeoisie and the proletariat but in precapitalist classes like the aristocracy, the petty-bourgeoisie, and the peasantry. In the same vein, it is crucial to consider whether the fascist assault on civilization may have been orchestrated less by individuals robbed of conscience and choice than men and women who consciously made the choice to join authoritarian movements with dogmatic ideologies indebted to the Counter-Enlightenment. Considering such a set of possibilities, however, means placing primacy on political history rather than metaphysics.

Enlightenment thought was deeply influenced by the values of a burgeoning capitalism with its emphasis upon self-interest, secularism, utility, innovation, experimentation, and a form of instrumental or scientific rationality that had little patience for scholastic speculations. Locke and Hume, Mandeville and Voltaire, Kant and Lessing, Jefferson and Madison, and most other citizens in the "republic of letters" called for a weak state—though admittedly one with checks and balances, an independent judiciary, and the capacity to preserve civil liberties. But that is only half the story. Most philosophes were also reformers and innovators seeking to link self-interest with the welfare of the community, the market with concern for the lowly and the insulted, and the liberal state with a commitment to social change. Liberals in the United States fused these two strands of the Enlightenment into a philosophy capable of gripping the masses first in the form of Progressivism during the beginning of

---

9. Max Horkheimer, "Letter to Theodor Adorno (13/11/1944)," in *Gesammelte Werke* 17: 604.

the twentieth century, then in the New Deal of Franklin Delano Roosevelt, next in the Civil Rights Movement, and finally in the Poor People's Movement. Given the democratic character and egalitarian aims of these movements—whatever their inadequacies—no historical or political justification exists for claiming that Anglo-American liberalism turned into its totalitarian opposite.

Admittedly, things were different in Europe. Seeking to forestall any repeat of the terror unleashed during French Revolution, Benjamin Constant and Madame de Stael highlighted the need for the separation of powers, the rule of law, and a constitutional order. But the defeat of the Revolutions of 1848 by reactionary forces, fighting against republicanism and socialism in the name of values inherited from the Counter-Enlightenment,[10] led continental liberalism to surrender its radical impulse. European liberals wound up exchanging the original cosmopolitanism associated with the Enlightenment for new imperialist aspirations, the old emphasis upon republicanism and civil liberties for support of existing monarchical regimes—and, in the case of Italian thinkers like Croce and Gentile, for a brief flirtation with fascism—and the spirit of social reform for an almost unqualified belief in the market. Thus, in contrast to its Anglo-American variant, continental liberalism ultimately served as little more than the political philosophy of the bourgeois gentlemen. Its advocates throughout the latter half of the nineteenth century, and well into the twentieth century, would essentially act as brokers between the authoritarian movements of the right and the socialist movements of the left. Until the anti-communist rebellions of 1989, in fact, continental liberal parties were never able to secure a mass base for their worldview—and, even today, they still have their problems. .

None of this is explicable by making reference to the erosion of the individual or the increasing hegemony of instrumental rationality: feudal social relations continued in most of Europe until the end of the First World War, a democratic institutional heritage was lacking; and—crudely speaking—the Counter-Enlightenment was successful in preventing its opponent from achieving ideological hegemony. For all that, however, Enlightenment ideals maintained their mass appeal. The socialist labor movement soon entered the breach and, during the last quarter of the nineteenth century, wound up shouldering a "dual burden:"[11] its working class became intent upon realizing the universal liberal political values inherited from the bourgeoisie while, si-

---

10. Note the fine study by Joseph V. Femia, *Against the Masses: Varieties of Anti-Democratic Thought Since the French Revolution* (New York: Oxford University Press, 2001).

11. Stephen Eric Bronner, *Socialism Unbound* 2nd Edition (Boulder, CO: Westview, 2001), 1ff.

multaneously, furthering its own particular economic interests. Or, to put it another way, social democrats attempted to link what today we call "negative liberty" with "positive rights."

Enlightenment traditions were pivotal in shaping the social democratic worldview. Secularism, science, cosmopolitanism, contempt for class privilege, republican commitments, and a preoccupation with social reform influenced the most important intellectuals of the labor movement. Karl Kautsky, Eduard Bernstein, and Rosa Luxemburg in Germany; Rudolf Hilferding and Viktor Adler in Austria; Georgii Plekhanov and Julius Martov in Russia, as well as Jean Jaurès and Léon Blum in France, were forthright in drawing the theoretical connections between Enlightenment political theory and socialism. Most were adherents of "orthodox Marxism" or influenced by it and, interestingly, social democracy was most successful under monarchies undergoing rapid industrialization in which the working class could champion republicanism.[12] It only made sense that the social democratic labor movement should have been the most consistent opponent of totalitarianism.[13]

Social democratic parties may have sent mixed signals by using revolutionary theory to foster the practice of reform in the early years of the twentieth century. They supported their nation-states in World War I.[14] They opposed the revolutionary movements that arose in the aftermath of the conflict; they often vacillated in moments of crisis. They also indulged in what might be termed an "ideology of compromise." But their tradition is still, for the most part, honorable: social democracy maintained the loyalty of the great majority of the working class throughout the twentieth century; it introduced the first democratic parties to Europe; and, still officially clinging to the ideology of "orthodox Marxism," it served as the mass base for all the republics that emerged in the 1920s.

---

12. Note the important work by John H. Kautsky, *Social Democracy and the Aristocracy: Why Socialist Labor Movements Developed in some Industrial Countries and Not in Others* (New Brunswick: Transaction, 2002).

13. See the fine studies by William David Jones, *The Lost Debate: German Socialist Intellectuals and Totalitarianism* (Urbana: University of Illinois Press, 1999); Gerd-Rainer Horn, *European Socialists Respond to Fascism: Ideology, Activism and Contingency in the 1930s* (New York: Oxford University Press, 1996).

14. That decision was more complex than many might care to think: it involved not merely the spontaneous eruption of nationalist sentiments by the working class but also fear of repression and the existence of genuine constraints. Note the discussion in Stephen Eric Bronner, "In the Cradle of Modernity: The Labor Movement and the First World War," in *Moments of Decision: Political History and the Crises of Radicalism* (New York: Routledge, 1992), 13ff.

Social democratic thinkers also offered the first, the most incisive, and the most prophetic criticisms of communism:[15] Karl Kautsky warned of the dire political consequences attendant upon attempting to realize a socialist revolution in an economically undeveloped nation; Rosa Luxemburg prophesized that the use of terror would take on its own dynamic; and Léon Blum complained about the "moral incompatibility" between communists and socialists. The humanitarianism of the philosophes was not transformed into the dull positivism of social democrats supposedly lacking in political purpose and stripped of moral conscience. Such a view is simply inaccurate. With respect to the left, indeed, critical theory chose the wrong philosophical enemy: not the advocates of economic determinism, scientific rationality, and the mechanical stage theory of history but those committed to "voluntarism," preoccupied with "agency" and "consciousness," emphatic about the role of the "vanguard," insistent upon the power of *the will* to overcome all objective constraints, and inclined toward the "permanent revolution," were most susceptible to the totalitarian temptation.

Mussolini and Hitler always expressed admiration for Lenin and Stalin. All of them were voluntarists and embraced a politics of the will. All of them also explicitly opposed—albeit for different reasons—social democracy and the liberal political legacy of the Enlightenment. Communism first gained its political identity, in fact, when Lenin sought to differentiate his movement, with its new commitment to a party dictatorship, from social democracy with its republican ideals. By the early 1920s, moreover, the Communist International had already passed resolutions stating its refusal to support parliamentary democracies and Stalin's famous refusal of 1928 to form a common front with the socialists against the Nazis, since they had supposedly become "twin brothers," hurt the anti-fascist cause far more than its enemies. With the same venom, movements of the far right despised liberals and social democrats everywhere in Europe. Germany was only the most notorious instance: its fascists condemned the "traitors" who provided their nation with a "stab in the back" during the First World War as well as the "November criminals" who signed the humiliating Treaty of Versailles and brought about the Weimar Republic. Both communism and fascism embraced a military vision

15. The most famous examples of what constitutes a veritable flood of criticisms—all projecting the authoritarian future—were offered in 1919 by Karl Kautsky, *The Dictatorship of the Proletariat* (Ann Arbor: University of Michigan Press, 1971) and a work written in 1918, but only published in 1922, by Rosa Luxemburg, "The Russian Revolution," in *Rosa Luxemburg Speaks*, ed. Mary-Alice Waters (New York: Pathfinder, 1970),

of the political party, identified their party with the state, relied upon a cult of the personality, and ruled through a mixture of propaganda and terror. Both considered terror a means and an end: both participated in creating what has justly been called a "concentration camp universe." Neither had any use for the liberal heritage of the philosophes or—what is the cornerstone of Enlightenment political theory—the need to curb the arbitrary exercise of power. Nevertheless, communists did evidence a certain admiration for the Enlightenment that fascists did not.

Until 1917, in fact, Lenin had insisted that the revolution must initially introduce a republic and, within three years following the communist seizure of power, he identified socialism with modernization. But the real point is that the political legacy of the Enlightenment never influenced Lenin's organizational vision, his ethical perspective, his authoritarian style, or his political choices. His privileging of the "vanguard party" pitted him first against the liberal "provisional government" led by Alexander Kerensky in February 1917 then against the radically democratic "soviets," which Lenin had originally endorsed on the road to power before crushing them at Kronstadt in 1921,[16] then against the trade unions, and finally against any organization or "faction" capable of undermining the political hegemony of the communist party or its leadership. Conflict over the machinery of power is very different than conflict over philosophical claims, cultural experiments, and social reforms. The parallel between the philosophes and the communist vanguard is ultimately more symbolic than real.

Conservative and postmodern critics can note how both shared a commitment to progress, secularism, modernization, and even utopia. But these terms meant something very different for Communism than for the Enlightenment: Lenin was concerned with preserving the working class from the temptations of reform in the name of revolution while the philosophes opposed revolution and were everywhere intent upon introducing reforms; Lenin's vanguard was guided by the principle of "democratic centralism," which required that disagreements be kept within the confines of the party, while the philosophes constantly and openly battled among themselves; Lenin embraced a moral relativism predicated on class interest for his ethics while Enlightenment thinkers, for the most part, sought to uncover universal rules of moral judgment; Lenin never evidenced any concern with constraining his vanguard party while Enlightenment political theory highlighted the

16. Note the balanced discussion by Paul Avrich, *Kronstadt 1921* (New York: Norton, 1970).

need to check and mitigate the exercise of power. Most important, while Enlightenment thinkers served as the radical expression of a burgeoning modernity, Leninism was always understood, using the language of Marxism,[17] as the political reflection of economic underdevelopment. That is probably why most postmodern and conservative critics have been content with establishing an indirect connection between communism and the Enlightenment mediated by Marx, the Jacobins, and the French Revolution.

Attempting to preserve Marx from authoritarian contamination, by scrupulously determining what he "really" meant, smacks of academic conceit: the communist tradition is obviously indebted to Marx.[18] Just as it is mistaken to view Leninism as the only possible outcome of Marxism, however, so is it equally mistaken to understand 1789 as the only revolution undertaken by the bourgeoisie. Social democracy is as legitimate an heir of Marx as Leninism—perhaps even more so given its belief in a stage theory of history and its explicit rejection of the tactics associated with revolutionary "insurrection"—and many orthodox Marxists, especially outside France, looked with particular admiration at the English Revolution. Karl Kautsky preferred it to the French Revolution, so did Rosa Luxemburg;[19] and Max Weber read with profit a classic work on the topic by Eduard Bernstein.[20] There are important political implications attendant upon this choice of revolution. Further research would probably indicate how—outside France—those socialists committed to republicanism and civil liberties looked across the English Channel while those with more authoritarian tendencies embraced the "legend" of 1793.

Lenin himself bought into that legend and he liked to speak of his communists as "Jacobins connected to the proletariat." In spite of this self-understanding, however, the philosophes were not Jacobins and the Jacobins

---

17. This general view of Karl Kautsky and other orthodox Marxist intellectuals was made particularly clear by Rosa Luxemburg, "Organizational Questions of Social Democracy," in *Rosa Luxemburg Speaks*, 112ff.

18. A particularly incisive political analysis of this connection is provided by Arthur Rosenberg, *Geschichte des Bolschewismus* (Frankfurt am Main: Europäische Verlagsantalt, 1966).

19. Luxemburg could write from her jail cell on August 8, 1917 that: "I am now reading [Francois] Mignet and [Heinrich] Cunow on the French Revolution. What an inexhaustible drama, which grips and entrances one again and again! Yet I still find the English Revolution more powerful, splendid and full of imagination, even though it did run its course in such morose forms of Puritainism." *The Letters of Rosa Luxemburg* ed. Stephen Eric Bronner (2nd Edition: Atlantic Highlands, NJ: Humanities Press, 1993), 226.

20. Eduard Bernstein, *Cromwell and Communism: Socialism and Democracy in the Great English Revolution* , trans. H.J. Stenning (New York: Schocken, 1930).

were not Leninists. Thus, when considering the French Revolution, its dictatorial climax was not a party dictatorship because the Jacobin Club never provided a genuinely disciplined, centralized, and ideologically homogeneous organization to wield power.[21] It was actually in response to the perceived "weaknesses" of Robespierre and his followers that Filip Buonarroti, a survivor of the Babeuf conspiracy, launched the legend that the Jacobins provided the example for an "educational dictatorship."[22] In fact, the Jacobins themselves had no need of doing so since they always held a majority in the Chamber of Deputies. Often forgotten is that democracy never recovered from the Thermidor and the fall of Robespierre. It was suspended in favor first of a new directorate and then Napoleon. There is indeed a sense in which "the revolutionaries were the philosophes' willing executioners."[23]

Even if the idea of a party dictatorship and the modern idea of the "nation" were introduced by Jacobinism, however, neither would be attributable to the Enlightenment. [24] Better to argue that the Enlightenment left Jacobinism in the lurch. Liberalism never seriously entertained the possibility of counter-revolution, or provided any thoughts on how to deal with it, and the Jacobins were the first to experience the consequences of these failings. It was the inability of the republic to wield authority in its defense that Buonarroti sought to overcome with his notion of an educational dictatorship, which then passed over to Blanqui, to Peter Tkachev, and—finally—to Lenin and the Bolsheviks. The original liberal and republican beliefs of Robespierre and the Jacobins, who had initially opposed the death penalty and supported civil liberties in a relatively consistent fashion, degenerated not due to the increasing hegemony of "pure reason" but in the face of political exigencies created by the counter-revolution.

---

21. Richard Lowenthal, *Model or Ally? The Communist Powers and the Developing Countries* (New York: Oxford University Press, 1977), 52.
22. Ibid., 54.
23. Darrin M. McMahon, *Enemies of the Enlightenment: The French Counter-Enlightenment and the Making of Modernity* (Oxford: Oxford University Press, 2001), 97.
24. "The Revolution was many things. It was an attempt to reform the government of France, a revolt against well-known abuses, a struggle to displace the privileged classes, and much more. But it was also, and this is what concerns us here, the embodiment of a great idea, the idea of the sovereignty of the people or nation. For a statement of the meaning of the principle of popular or national sovereignty, we do not have to go to the writings of the Enlightenment, and if we did we should not find it there." Alfred Cobban, *In Search of Humanity: The Role of the Enlightenment in Modern History* (New York: George Braziller, 1960), 189.

As for Babeuf and Buanorrotti, like Lenin, they were never liberals to be-gin with. Both were instead democrats without institutional convictions, unconcerned with civil liberties, and unaware of the dynamics that might lead a revolution, like Saturn, to devour its children. Their romantic no-tions of democracy lacking in safeguards for individual liberty may well have provided an impetus for communism. But this has little to do with the general thrust of Enlightenment political theory or claims that its postulates somehow logically lead to "totalitarian" rather than "liberal" democracy.[25] Even if the oxymoronic notion of "totalitarian democracy" can be traced back to Rousseau,[26] a highly questionable assertion for a man whom Kant termed "the restorer of the rights of humanity," this would only vindicate his alienation from the general liberal political tenor of the Enlightenment and suggest that the treatment of him as an enemy by Voltaire and his friends was justified.

Alexander Herzen, the great liberal revolutionary, hit the mark with his prophetic claim that communism would become little more than the "Russ-ian autocracy turned upside down." Lenin may have opposed the church, the aristocracy, and the other remnants of Russian feudalism with an ideology comprising voluntarism, science, and utopia. But his modernizing ambi-tions, no less than his initial utopian promises of a "soviet" regime, were cou-pled with contempt for the liberal political legacy. Communist leaders like Lenin and Stalin and Mao betrayed the Enlightenment insofar as they cham-pioned a state in which questioning authority became a crime, individualism was rendered illegitimate, civil liberties were ignored, and any attempt to constrain arbitrary power was identified with the "counter-revolution." Dif-ferent policy choices made during the 1920s could have produced something other than a "totalitarian regime in the 1930s. Only the communist party, however, could make those choices. All organizations capable of competing for power, or providing institutional checks upon it, had already been crushed by 1923. This is not the place to deal with matters of historical exi-gency or whether Stalinism was a necessary outcome of Leninism.[27] But it is the place to challenge claims that—setting the stage for totalitarianism—

25. J. L. Talmon, *The Rise of Totalitarian Democracy* (London: Secker and Warburg, 1952).
26. Even if one were to agree "that Rousseau's political thought is totalitarian, this would only serve to show that he had broken with the liberal individualist ideas of the Enlight-enment, and that the *philosophes* were right in regarding him as their greatest enemy." Cobban, *In Search of Humanity*, 184
27. Bronner, "Leninism and Beyond," in *Socialism Unbound*, 78, 100ff.

Enlightenment reformers generated the belief that "reason is planning considered solely as planning," and that "the totalitarian order gives full reign to calculation and abides by science as such."[28] It is also the place to contest the even more misleading suggestion that Stalinism is the "quintessential Enlightenment utopia."[29]

Enlightenment thinkers maintained that the liberal rule of law incarnates the political exercise of reason.[30] This underpinned their belief that freedom lies in the law: "where there is no law there is no freedom" wrote John Locke in his *Second Treatise* and that sentiment was echoed both by Voltaire, who claimed that "freedom lies in living within the law," and Rousseau who put the matter beautifully when he wrote that "A free people obeys, but it does not serve. It has leaders, not masters. It obeys laws, but only laws. And it is by virtue of the law that it does not obey men." Enlightenment reform was, or its notion of "planning" was, intertwined with this view. Notions of planning forwarded by the philosophes presupposed the existence of conditions for debating any "plan," employing scientific criteria to judge its efficacy, calculating the consequences of introducing the plan, and fostering the security and well being of the majority.

Totalitarian forms of planning, no less than the values underpinning them, retain only the most remote association with the Enlightenment. Its goals and the perspectives of its most important representatives were very different. To be sure: if most of the populace was not ready for freedom then they would have to be made ready. All the philosophes knew, however, that this would take time and that it would require a new liberal form of civic and practical education. Indeed:

> Education formed an indispensable part of their reform schemes: peasants needed to be instructed in the use of new implements, merchants and manufacturers to be acquainted with new techniques or products, public servants to be trained to new tasks. But civic education was something else again. After all, like all good education, good civic education aimed at making the educator unnecessary. . . . [31]

---

28. Horkheimer and Adorno, *Dialectic of Enlightenment*, 89, 86.
29. Stephen Kotkin, *Magnetic Mountain: Stalinism as a Civilization* (Berkeley: University of California Press: 1995), 364
30. Peter Gay, *The Enlightenment* 2 vols. (New York: Norton, 1969) 2: 441.
31. Gay, *The Enlightenment*, 2:499.

All this is a far cry from totalitarianism in which the leader or the party or history—not the liberal rule of law—incarnates "reason" or, better, the irrationalist equivalent, "destiny." Under a totalitarian system, individuals *should* not be able to calculate the consequences of social action; efficiency is defined by the needs of the leadership; and there is little concern for the rights or welfare of the individual. Stalinist "planning" was always ideologically driven, erratic, insulated from criticism, and concerned less with efficiency, or even industrial progress, than with securing the position of Stalin himself. Its plan was never based on an integrated program of development, modernization had no connection with meeting consumer needs, and inefficiency was built into it from the beginning.[32] This helped create the basis for a semi-legal black market and, more importantly, justification for the ongoing terror. Structuring the plan in that way, no less than enforcing it as Stalin did was a choice rather than a dialectical "necessity."[33] Whatever polemical usage he might have tried to make of Marxism or the Enlightenment heritage, moreover, Leszek Kolakowski is surely correct when he wrote that:

Marxism under Stalin cannot be defined by any collection of statements, ideas, or concepts; it was not a question of propositions as such but of the fact that there existed an all-powerful authority competent to declare at any given moment what Marxism was and what it was not. "Marxism" meant nothing more or less than the current pronouncement of the authority in question, i.e. Stalin himself.[34]

Teleology and determinism, science and positivism, historical "laws" and "grand narratives," were actually taken seriously not by the communists, who used "science" to excuse every miscalculation and "historical necessity" to justify every crime, but rather by orthodox Marxists and social democrats. Neither Lenin nor Stalin nor Mao nor Pol Pot had much patience with economic determinism or claims concerning the "necessity" of passing through the "bourgeois" stage of history before the "proletarian" revolution could

32. These Stalinist models of planning, "which have given a bad name to socialism, are not the poorly managed samples of a basically sound structure, but monstrosities in their very conception." Pachter, "Three Economic Models," in *Socialism in History*, 43.
33. Bronner, *Socialism Unbound*, 104ff.
34. Leszek Kolakowski, *Main Currents of Marxism* 3 volumes, trans. P. S. Falla (New York, 1978) 3:4.

occur. Whether in terms of the role accorded the vanguard party, the idea of forced industrialization, the indoctrination of propaganda, or the use of terror, the impact of voluntarism, subjectivism, and the politics of the will were far stronger on totalitarianism than teleology and positivism. No wonder that even Antonio Gramsci—a forerunner of critical theory—should have initially viewed the events of 1917 as constituting a "revolution against *Das Kapital*."[35]

Communism may have been the "wind from the East." It may have brought the pre-industrial colonial nations, the vast majority of the world population, into the center of the socialist discourse. It was surely a force in fighting imperialist arrogance and racism. Its proponents were committed to modernization and the elimination of poverty, ignorance, and disease. But the failure of the Russian Revolution ultimately stems from the attempt to create a bourgeois republic without a bourgeoisie in February and the subsequent attempt to produce a proletarian revolution without a proletariat in October. Not modernity but the lack of it, the pre-modern conditions in which the communist revolutions took place, was the source of "left" totalitarianism. Or, to put it another way: Marxism turned totalitarian when its realization was attempted in conditions where a bourgeoisie and a working class, the dominant classes of the modern production process, were absent along with —most importantly for our purposes—indigenous political traditions grounded in the Enlightenment.

With respect to understanding totalitarianism of the left and the right, *Dialectic of Enlightenment* began with the wrong premises and drew the wrong conclusions. Crucial was its claim that the attack on metaphysics by Enlightenment notions of science undermined the exercise of conscience thereby unleashing a savage egoism. In contrast to bourgeois liberalism, however, fascist thinking is marked by the demand for irrational sacrifice for the race or the nation or the class. Thus, it would necessary to make the purely abstract assertion that "in the innermost recesses of humanism, as its very soul, there rages a frantic prisoner who, as a Fascist, turns the world into a prison."[36] The same connection between humanism and the prison would later find expression in the writings of Michel Foucault[37] which, also

35. Antonio Gramsci, "The Revolution against 'Capital'," in *Selections from the Political Writings 1919–1920*, ed. Quintin Hoare (New York: International Publishers, 1977), 34ff.
36. Adorno, *Minima Moralia*, 89.
37. Michel Foucault, *Discipline and Punish: The Birth of the Prison*, trans. Alan Sheridan (New York: Vintage, 1979).

in keeping with the Frankfurt School, noted the exclusion of the mentally ill and children from universalistic worldviews like humanism and liberalism: the terms in which these groups should be treated, of course, are never discussed. There is also no reference to the reflexive element within humanism, its intrinsic belief in the dignity of the individual first raised by Pico della Mirandola, or the relevance of "rights" in addressing the claims of the weak and exploited.[38] Enough to claim that what the Enlightenment sought to destroy will reappear as its own product and that the "turn from the liberal to the total authoritarian state occurs on the basis of one and the same economic order and with regard to the unity of this economic base, we can say that it is liberalism that 'produces' the total-authoritarian state out of itself, as its own consummation at a more advanced stage of development."[39]

This obscures what is unique about totalitarianism: the political. But, then, the real issue for critical theory was always less the actual conflicts generated by capitalism than the metaphysical critique of its production process and how the logic of the commodity form undermines all normative concerns. This lets the discussion shift from "capitalism" to "advanced industrial society" or "modernity." The anthropological merges with the historical critique of Enlightenment. Qualitative differences between regimes vanish and diverse regimes fall under the same rubric. The resulting standpoint is both fatalistic and didactic. What only became apparent at the end is now projected back to the beginning. The issue is no longer how totalitarianism might have been resisted, but how it emerged as the *telos*, the logical projection, of what preceded it.

Philosophy comes too late: the Owl of Minerva yawns at dusk. Enlightenment sets the stage for Weimar and Weimar for Hitler. Everything else is a combination of naïve hopes, ideology, and nostalgia. The image emerges of a society blithely and unwittingly walking into the abyss. The way opens for a library of mid-level novels and films produced by the culture industry that use fascism or Nazism as the backdrop, and that provide the audience with a frisson regarding the horrible result without offering any sense of how it was actually achieved. Political ethics becomes the province of the resigned prophet or simply the scold. Thus it only made sense for *Dialectic of Enlightenment* to claim that humans will "pay for the increase of their power

---

38. Ernst Bloch, *Natural Law and Human Dignity*, trans. Dennis J. Schmidt (Cambridge: MIT Press, 1986).
39. Herbert Marcuse, "The Struggle Against Liberalism in the Totalitarian View of the State," in *Negations*, trans. Jeremy J. Shapiro (Boston: Beacon, 1968), 19.

with alienation from that over which they exercise their power. Enlightenment behaves towards things as a dictator toward men. He knows them insofar as he can manipulate them."[40]

The meta-political and anthropological "dialectic" becomes a replacement for the analysis of political and historical conflicts. Progress will thus generate regression and modernity will inspire barbarism. If the alienation embedded within liberalism and the logic of science reaffirm illiberal forms of authority and the power of myth then fascism can be seen as an expression of what it opposed: the Enlightenment. This indeed makes it possible to interpret totalitarianism in terms of "the conditions that prevailed before its coming to power, not in a negative sense, but rather in terms of their positive continuation."[41] The point for Horkheimer and Adorno no less than their postmodern followers is not simply that fascism grows in liberal societies, but that totalitarianism is both the culmination of the anthropological enlightenment and the—albeit unintentional—product of the historical Enlightenment. In this way, though its lessons were actually quite limited, the Weimar Republic would become a "parable" for the fragile character of liberal democracy in general.

This prejudice is sometimes seen as hindering the Frankfurt School from making differentiated political judgments in the aftermath of World War II.[42] There is also something to this claim. Members of the Frankfurt School, however, were often capable of discerning differences within the "totally administered society" in terms of everyday politics: Herbert Marcuse, for example, called upon American students to support George McGovern against Richard Nixon in the presidential elections of 1972. Horkheimer and Adorno were also aware that, in spite of their previous equation of "mass enlightenment" with "mass deception," education might mitigate threats to liberal norms.[43] The question is whether such pronouncements logically derive from the theory or rather are insights whose determinations were essentially *ad hoc*. They cer-

40. Horkheimer and Adorno, *Dialectic of Enlightenment*, 9, 87.

41. Helmut Dubiel, *Theory and Politics: Studies in the Development of Critical Theory*, trans. Benjamin Gregg (Cambridge: MIT Press, 1985), 71.

42. Richard Wolin, *The Terms of Cultural Criticism: The Frankfurt School, Existentialism, Poststructuralism* (New York: Columbia University Press, 1992), 59

43. Regarding prejudice, it became possible to note that: "an aroused conscience is not enough if it does not stimulate a systematic search for an answer. . . . Our aim is not merely to describe prejudice but to explain it in order to help in its eradication. That is the challenge we would meet. Education means re-education, scientifically planned on the basis of understanding scientifically arrived at." Theodor W. Adorno et. Al, *The Authoritarian Personality* (New York: Norton, 1950), v, ii..

tainly never received sustained political, philosophical, or anthropological justification. This would indeed have been difficult to provide: for, while it might still have been possible to claim that the "the whole is false," parts of the whole would now apparently need to be considered more or less "false" than others and in the same vein, if "wrong life cannot be lived rightly,"[44] the question arises whether in drawing such distinctions the fundamental principle of "negative dialectics" is being betrayed. These are crucial matters since only upon the assumption that the Enlightenment and totalitarianism are integrally related elements of "modernity" is it possible to speak about a "totally administered society" in which the metaphysical—or, better, philosophical-aesthetic—assertion of subjectivity must supplant explicitly political forms of resistance.

Totalitarianism did free the instincts from what is commonly called conscience and Horkheimer and Adorno were correct in their claim that "anti-Semitic behavior is generated in situations where blinded men robbed of their subjectivity are set loose as subjects and action becomes an autonomous end in itself and disguises its own purposelessness."[45] Linking this philosophical perspective with the Enlightenment, however, is possible only by broadening it to include its greatest and most self-conscious critics: Sade, Schopenhauer, Bergson, and Nietzsche.[46] With any of them it can be said— though not for any of the major philosophes—that action becomes its own end and disguises its lack of purpose. It was again less either rationalism or positivism than voluntarism, though admittedly of a vitalist sort, which influenced the thinking of right-wing totalitarians. Henry Pachter was surely correct when he wrote that:

> The common denominator of all these undercurrents of European civilization was the new feeling that "life" had been slighted. It expressed itself in a vitalistic philosophy, which the Nazis bowdlerized into a murderous racism, the Fascists into a swaggering nationalism. Transposed onto

---

44. Adorno, *Minima Moralia*, 39.
45. Horkheimer and Adorno, *Dialectic of Enlightenment*, 171.
46. Horkheimer would later term Nietzsche "the most radical enlightenment figure in all of philosophy." And in the general indeterminate way in which Horkheimer used the term "enlightenment" that might even be true. In terms of the values and political ideas deriving from the actual movement, however, such a claim is nonsense. Here, the unfortunate consequences of using one term in two different ways becomes apparent. Horkheimer, "Die Aufklärung," in *Gesammelte Schriften* 20 Bde (Frankfurt am Main: S. Fischer, 1989) 13:574.

the political scene—where it did not belong—this pseudo-rebellion appeared as sadism, clothed in the glitter of heroism.[47]

Neither Sade, Schopenhauer, Bergson, nor Nietzsche had the least identification with the principles of enlightenment political theory or the practices associated with it. They were anti-liberal, anti-socialist, anti-democratic and anti-egalitarian, anti-rationalist and anti-historical: enough of them and their followers, moreover, prized the very exercise of arbitrary power that enlightenment political theory sought to curb. There is something provocative about the later insistence of Adorno that "not least among the tasks now confronting thought is that of placing all the reactionary arguments against Western culture in the service of progressive enlightenment."[48] But the "progressive" character of this imperative was left hanging in the abstract. Thus, while important insights can obviously be gained from conservative political thinkers, the potential contradictions generated by the attempt to merge right-wing ideology with left-wing practice were never taken into account.

Whatever the theoretical sweep of the argument advanced by *Dialectic of Enlightenment*, from the standpoint of history and politics, it was predicated on false concreteness and misplaced causality. Instrumental reason did not bring about Nazism or destroy the ability of individuals to make normative judgments: it is indeed time to move beyond this abstract and indeterminate perspective. Instrumental reason and bureaucracy may have been the necessary, but they were not even the remotely sufficient condition for totalitarianism: all twentieth-century western movements have been bureaucratic and, by definition, modern.[49] The question is why fascism emerged victorious in some instances and failed in others and why totalitarianism arose in some dictatorial circumstances and not in others.

Demands for historical specification explode metaphysical and anthropological forms of argumentation. The Nazi victory was the historical product of a political clash between real movements inspired by divergent intellectual traditions whose members were quite capable of making diverse judgments concerning both their interests and their values. Is it really that difficult to discern the debt to the Enlightenment of those democrats and socialists like Heinrich Mann or Harry Kessler or Rudolf Hilferding who

47. Pachter, "Fascist Propaganda and the Conquest of Power," in *Socialism in History*, 119.
48. Adorno, *Minima Moralia*, pg. 192.
49. Note the criticism of such arguments by Yehuda Bauer, *Rethinking the Holocaust* (New Haven: Yale University Press, 2001), 68–84.

defended the Weimar Republic as against the debt to the Counter-Enlightenment of those who sought to bring it down like Ernst Jünger, Oswald Spengler, and the gang surrounding Hitler?

Fascism was not the product of some philosophical dialectic of enlightenment, but rather a self-conscious response to the Enlightenment and its two progressive political offspring, liberalism and socialism, by the successor to the Counter-Enlightenment. The mass base of the Italian Fascists and German Nazis, again, resided in premodern classes like the peasantry and the petty-bourgeoisie whose "non-synchronous" interests and values were threatened by the dominant classes in the modern production process: the bourgeoisie and the proletariat. [50] In terms of German politics: most of the bourgeoisie identified with an increasingly impotent set of parties embracing a continental variant of liberalism while the majority of the working class voted until the end for their social democratic parties. All these political organizations supported the Weimar Republic and all were avowed enemies of the Nazis who made war on them in word and deed. The attempt to unify qualitatively different phenomena under a single rubric can only produce historical disorientation and political confusion. Better to have drawn the practical implications from *The Gay Science* by Nietzsche, whom Adorno liked to quote for his philosophical insights, that: "to perceive resemblances everywhere, making everything alike, is a sign of weak eyesight."

Weak eyesight is precisely what results from the meta-political and meta-historical form of inquiry embraced by late critical theory and its postmodern acolytes. The reifying character of the approach becomes as total as the anthropological development culminating in the "totally administered society." There is no place for mediations or qualifications. A reactionary pseudo-universalism that is imperialist, racist, coercive, and irrationalist becomes conflated with a genuinely democratic universalism that is liberal, discursive, cosmopolitan, and critical. Each institution suffers equally from the impact of instrumental reason and there is never the genuine recognition that some institutions can expand or inhibit the range of free experience for citizens in ways others cannot. Bureaucracy is the problem, the "commodity form" is the culprit, and modernity is the enemy. The "whole" is what counts

---

50. See in particular the discussion of the practical and ideological role played by "non-synchronous contradictions" carried over into modernity from premodern epochs in an unreconciled state. Ernst Bloch, *Erbschaft dieser Zeit* (Frankfurt am Main: Suhrkamp, 1973), pgs. 45ff.

and no attempt to transform it is ever radical enough since either revolution or reform must, in some degree, make recourse to instrumental rationality.

Real conflicts thus get smothered in all-encompassing abstract categories and, because the "whole is false," distinctions between regimes and movements become purely *ad hoc*. What remains is only an impotent and self-serving "negative dialectic" intent upon preserving the individual from a reified reality, emphasizing the "non-identity" between subject and object, and remaining open for the "totally other." That is not merely inadequate but reactionary in its general formulation. The repressive conditions this form of critique claims to contest are—even in theory—left intact. Solidarity is treated either as an arbitrary sentiment or a demand for conformity while enlightenment collapses into the "mass deception" of the culture industry. Critique has a different fate in store: it retreats into irrelevance. The theory of politics makes way for the politics of theory.[51] Unable to deal with political institutions and social movements, incapable of drawing qualitative distinctions between intellectual phenomena, the critical heir of the Enlightenment ultimately collapses from exhaustion. Thus, it turns into merely another instance of what Thomas Mann called a "power-protected inwardness."

51. Dick Howard, *The Specter of Democracy* (New York: Columbia University Press, 2002), 40.

7

EXPERIENCING REALITY:
THE CULTURE INDUSTRY, SUBJECTIVITY,
AND IDENTITY

THE CULTURE INDUSTRY FIRST CAME UNDER ATTACK WHEN
capitalist society began to experience what Hendrik de Man termed the
"massification" of society: the standardized production of goods and servic-
es in a world of interchangeable individuals stripped of their identity. Few
on the left initially believed that the Enlightenment was the source of the
problem and even fewer believed that "mass education" is the equivalent of
"mass deception." But the interwar period saw the individual subordinated
to the collective, public opinion shaped by propaganda, responsibility identified with obeying orders, tastes structured by the media, sacrifice for the
masses perceived as a good unto itself, and the encounter with death become
the hallmark of authenticity. The universal subject—nation, party, class—
seemed to lend itself to this new form of mass society. That is the reason for
what in the postwar period would become a general artistic and philosophical preoccupation with authentic experience and the "end of the individual." On the left, however, only *Dialectic of Enlightenment* would pit subjectivity against the liberal subject, modernity, and the Enlightenment. The
issue here involves the success of that undertaking.

The new form of critical theory, from the first, retreated from politics. Its
authors had little to say about new issues pertinent to the political legacy of
the Enlightenment such as the struggle for civil rights or national self-
determination or imperialism. Capitalist *culture* was perceived as the problem and the metaphysical response, the assertion of subjectivity, was demanded by the all-encompassing system of reification that it nominally
wished to oppose. In spite of its self-styled radicalism, therefore, this new
stance reflected what Daniel Bell called "the exhaustion of political ideas in
the fifties" and—with an eye cast on the prewar years—the pervasive belief
of the time that any attempt to change society would have to take place
"without me" (*ohne mich*). The point is not that Horkheimer and Adorno
feared rocking the boat, which they did, or that they should ultimately have

distanced themselves from their own radical followers like Hans-Jürgen Krahl and Rudi Dutschke in the 1960s. It was rather their attempt to recast what had been a materialist theory of society, committed to realizing the interests of the exploited and disenfranchised, into pure philosophy. The aesthetic-philosophical intensification of subjectivity became the fulcrum of resistance against the incursion, not only of political or economic forces fostering reification, but especially the "culture industry."[1]

Volumes have already been written about this extraordinary idea. Whether in terms of ripping a work from the context of tradition, thereby eradicating what Walter Benjamin termed the "aura" of an artwork and the unique experience it generated,[2] or subverting the possibility of emancipation supposedly preserved within the aesthetic realm,[3] the "culture industry" was seen as changing public life in advanced industrial society. Modern culture now required its own administrative bureaucracy as its producers sought the largest possible audience, which meant finding the lowest common denominator for each product, and searching less for the next Dostoyevsky than the next bestseller. Cultural production fits into the production and reproduction of the whole and thus, the extent to which a work becomes popular, becomes the extent to which its radicalism—or its ability to affirm the "non-identity" between subject and object—is compromised. The point for Horkheimer and Adorno was never that the culture industry will only present "conservative" works, or even that it mechanically serves only the interests of the ruling elite,[4] but rather that any work it does popularize will become conservative, stripped of its liberating character, and affirmative of the status quo *by definition*.

Looking backwards: all of this was less a problem for philosophes intent upon educating the rabble than for their conservative critics. Even before the Enlightenment, however, certain intellectuals were already drawing a radical

1. Max Horkheimer and Theodor Adorno, "The Culture Industry: Enlightenment as Mass Deception," in *Dialectic of Enlightenment*, trans. John Cumming (New York, Herder & Herder, 1972), 120ff. Note also the useful little collection of supporting essays by Theodor Adorno, *The Culture Industry*, ed. J. M. Bernstein (London: Routledge, 1991).
2. See the ground-breaking essay by Walter Benjamin, "The Work of Art in the Age of Mechanical Reproduction," in *Illuminations* ed. Hannah Arendt and trans. Harry Zohn (New York: Schocken, 1969), 217ff.
3. On the roots of this assumption, see Kai Hammermeister, *The German Aesthetic Tradition* (Cambridge: Cambridge University Press, 2002).
4. Edward S. Herman and Noam Chomsky, *Manufacturing Consent: The Political Economy of the Mass Media* (New York: Pantheon, 2002); Michael Parenti, *Inventing Reality: The Politics of New Media* (New York: St. Martin's, 1993).

distinction between "art" and "popular culture."[5] Where "art" was seen as offering catharsis, genuine experience, education, reflection and a sense of the "beautiful"—even if only as an illusion (*Schein*)—popular culture was believed to provide only spurious gratification, prefabricated experience, regression, emotional identification, and entertainment. The puritanical roots of this distinction are fairly obvious. It revolved around whether culture should amuse or instruct. Pascal held the position that culture must intensify his own version of "pure experience" deriving from Jansenism while Montaigne, the great humanist and skeptic, believed that amusement might offer everyday people some relief from the misery of their lives: it is noteworthy that he should have refused to privilege any particular style let alone some prescribed purpose for art.[6] Another version of the same controversy occurred in the debate between Rousseau and Voltaire over whether a theater should exist in Geneva. Their differing views took on a symbolic character for the different social groups in the city: patricians, bourgeois, and the great host of the disenfranchised.[7] Rousseau maintained that the theater corrupts by its very nature while Voltaire emphasized its enjoyment. There is, however, a political issue of some importance hidden in this ongoing debate over culture.

Montaigne and Voltaire believed that the variety provided by the arts was the antidote to dogmatism. Their critics emphasized, by contrast, the way in which a "deeper" truth was undermined by the plurality of experiences that entertainment or theater might provide and their corrupting influence on public morals and the reigning cultural niveau. Such corruption aided by a burgeoning set of capitalist entrepreneurs was what Goethe and Schiller castigated in their "Schema on Dilettantism" (1799). In contrast to Flaubert who claimed —anticipating much of later critical theory—"the time for beauty is over," these two giants recommended neither resignation nor withdrawal. They did not envision the end of civilization: the assault upon the imagination by the supposedly unthinking masses should only intensify the commitment of the genuine artist to preserve it in public life.

Attempts to establish some deep-seated difference between the collective cultural unconscious of France and Germany reach back to the nationalist response against Napoleon and the *Addresses to the German Nation* by

5. Note the classic essay by Leo Lowenthal, "The Debate over Art and Popular Culture: A Synopsis," in *Literature and Mass Culture* (New Brunswick, NJ: Transaction, 1984), 19ff.
6. Ibid, 22.
7. Peter Gay, *Voltaire's Politics: The Poet as Realist* (New Haven: Yale University Press, 1988), 195–16.

Fichte. It was carried over into the twentieth century by pitting a heavy-handed romantic belief in the profundity and "depth" associated with *Kultur*—the inner torment of the genius, the revelatory quality of truth, the paintings of Casper Friedrich, and the operas of Wagner—against the skeptical lightness and rationalist "superficiality" of *civilisation*: that was associated with the Enlightenment and, in particular, the wit and cosmopolitanism of Voltaire. Both *Kultur* and *civilisation* can, of course, be employed in a stereotypical fashion and manipulated for nationalist aims as was the case during World War I. Its aftermath indeed witnessed the famous battle between Thomas Mann, who justified the German war effort as an unsuccessful attempt to protect *Kultur* from the appeal of *civilisation* in his *Reflections of a Non-Political Man*,[8] and his far more progressive brother, Heinrich Mann, the incarnation of the *Zivilisationsliterat*, who responded with a ringing endorsement of the Enlightenment and its democratic legacy in his *Reflections of a Political Man*.

The author of magnificent works like *Death in Venice* and *The Magic Mountain* never looked worse in print. He trotted out every reactionary cliché about the Enlightenment, portrayed the Dreyfus Affair as little more than a mob spectacle, and barely mentioned the material interests generating the "great war." Thomas Mann was concerned with cultural traditions and attitudes: Schopenhauer, Wagner, and Nietzsche thus confront Rousseau, Zola, and Romain Rolland.[9] The issue in his view was whether the "apolitical" commitment to culture should be compromised by a democratic commitment to politics;[10] whether the "lonely" individual and the intensity of the intuitive moment should be prized over public life and a concern with social reform; whether irony should take precedence over the pursuit of "abstract" ideals;[11] whether traditions rooted in time should be celebrated over the more facile universal and instrumental use of "reason"; whether metaphysical experience should be privileged over and against the material concern with a better life; whether the *Volksstaat*, a state in which the "people" disregard their private interests and essentially want what their cultural "destiny" requires of them,[12] should take precedence over the pursuit of particular interests under the liberal rule of law embodied in the *Rechtsstaat*. [13] There is no

8. Thomas Mann, *Betrachtungen eines Unpolitischen* (Frankfurt: Fischer Verlag, 1988), 160ff
9. Ibid., 94ff
10. Ibid., 21ff
11. Ibid., 14
12. Ibid., 259
13. Ibid., 141ff, 23

need to look further for the cultural foundations of the "sensible republicans" (*Vernunftrepublikaner*) who, enthralled with the "moderate liberalism" of Goethe, were willing to accept the new regime in Weimar but not genuinely embrace its values. Indeed, the debate between Heinrich and Thomas Mann exposes the difference between the cultural vision of the Enlightenment and that of its romantic and neo-romantic critics.

Democracy requires conviction. It also requires *civilisation* with its emphasis upon reflection, recognition of the "other," and what the Enlightenment understood as "progress."[14] *Kultur*, by contrast, speaks to something experientially fixed, ungraspable by the "other," and—by implication—a nationally or ethnically determined form of understanding.[15] The former involves public life, enjoyment, and what Voltaire correctly called a "softening of customs" while the latter is cultivated inwardly against the public. Where *civilisation* is often criticized for its Eurocentric, and elitist connotations, this idea actually projects the possibility of educational reform, seeks the point of intersection between cultures, and elicits the contributions of the "other" non-western societies. *Civilisation* retains a democratic and cosmopolitan quality that is missing in the existential exaltation of a unique and rooted subjectivity by *Kultur*.[16]

Kant would have had no trouble choosing between the two: he understood aesthetic experience as a form of "purposeful purposelessness." Often it has been noted that this view attacked those intent on viewing art as the handmaiden of religion, politics, or community morality: its utopian impulse, however, was to divorce it even from existential self-affirmation. It instead highlights the moment of joy. Moral education can, of course, change what brings enjoyment. It should: people used to enjoy watching a hanging and there is still the bullfight and the cockfight. But, for all that, the great insight of Kant was that aesthetic experience, as against the work that elicits it, is not a matter of ethical judgment. Aesthetic enjoyment, in contrast to matters of morality or science, need follow no rules. "Taste" is relative: its affirmation presupposes tolerance. The experience of Emma Bovary reading her trashy novels is, according to this logic, no less "pure" than the connoisseur reading *Finnegan's Wake*. Kant understood what was at stake: profound love for an artwork is not something one can teach, and it does not need justification,

14. Norbert Elias, *Über den Prozess der Zivilisation* 2 Bde. (Frankfurt am Main: Suhrkamp, 1997), 1:91ff.

15. Thomas Mann, *Betrachtungen eines Unpolitischen*, 23ff.

16. Ibid., 31

while respect for the innovations made by an artist can be taught and might even provide new ways of appreciating his or her creation.

Interesting about most critical writings on the culture industry is the refusal to consider aesthetic distinctions between different traditions of mass culture and the differing importance of different works. Also too often ignored is how the culture industry, while itself often expressive of capitalist interests, provides new experiential opportunities for its audience. Later critical theory, by contrast, preserves genuine aesthetic inquiry only for works capable of intensifying the non-identity between subject and object, and essentially dismisses the need for categories capable of distinguishing between Louis Armstrong and Kenny G, or Charlie Chaplin and the Three Stooges; postmodern theory, for its part, will generally view any work or inquiry as just another form of signification. Critical theorists and postmodernists have evidenced a virtual obsession with how high can turn into popular culture without recognizing what is perhaps even more important: that the reverse is also possible.

According to the *Dialectic of Enlightenment,* in any event, attempts at "mass enlightenment" can now only produce "mass deception." The Enlightenment—as usual—becomes the source of the problem. But little acknowledgement is given to the pedagogic heritage associated with Locke's attack on rote learning, Voltaire's contempt for the authoritarian curriculum, Rousseau's emphasis on the need for practical education, Kant's concern with public debate, and Goethe's insistence upon developing the individual "personality." These ideas remain at the core of any progressive notion of education. But, then, they cannot be implemented anyway what with the corruption of the public sphere by the culture industry and the transformation of "engaged art" into a self-defeating enterprise.[17] No less than for conservatives, therefore, left-wing proponents of later critical theory must also view education as an elite enterprise. Any critique of the establishment and any expression of a utopian possibility, after all, will necessarily be reconfigured by the culture industry to reinforce the "happy consciousness" of the status quo: Herbert Marcuse would term this process "repressive desublimation."[18]

Eliciting the unique experience—whether aesthetic, philosophical, or even religious—becomes the mode of resisting reification. It is not a mat-

17. Theodor W. Adorno, "Engagement," in *Noten zur Literatur* III (Frankfurt am Main: Suhrkamp, 1965), 109ff.
18. Herbert Marcuse, *One-Dimensional Man: Studies in the Ideology of Advanced Industrial Society* (Boston: Beacon:, 1964), 56ff.

ter of preparing the individual for the practical exercise of freedom. Education *should* retreat from the public sphere and, because the possibilities of solidarity have been exhausted, it should project only what might be termed a permanent revolution of subjectivity. Trying to situate this new subjectivist stance politically or in terms of a "new enlightenment" is useless given its indeterminacy and purposeful ambiguity. There is also little sense in speaking about democracy as an "aesthetic form of life" when reference is not made to the articulation of particular interests or the institutions capable of protecting them.[19] The result then is little more than a pale imitation of Schiller's *Letters on the Aesthetic Education of Man* (1795) with its claim that the establishment of political freedom exists when life becomes art and that to solve the problems of politics, the "road of aesthetics" must be pursued."

In contrast to the old stance, however, the new one is usually unconcerned with solidarity: it privileges esoteric and nonrepresentational art and it lacks categories for differentiating between different works and traditions of mass culture. It simply ignores how the culture industry has expanded the knowledge of the average viewer, brought genuine classics to more people, and heightened the demand for "transparency," thereby making institutions and politicians more accountable. Emphasizing any of these themes would have tied the original critique of the culture industry to the legacy of the Enlightenment. As things stand, however, only the terms by which subjectivity is threatened distinguishes this supposedly immanent critique from phenomenological and postmodern rejections of the Enlightenment *tout court*. The attack on the "system" in the name of the individual can occur from the right, by T.S. Eliot, just as easily as from the left. There is no institutional orientation for what Nishida, the great Japanese philosopher of the 1930s, termed the "pure experience."

What results is a new theory justifying an old practice: withdrawal from the embattled world of politics in the name of an inner resistance. Cynics might look back to Luther, the "un-political German," and even the "inner emigration" undertaken during the totalitarian era: Lukács indeed put the matter most dramatically by accusing the Frankfurt School of "watching the demise of civilization from its grand hotel abyss." Its most important representatives certainly developed perspectives that bear a marked affinity with

---

19. Cf. Morton Schoolman, *Reason and Horror: Critical Theory, Democracy, and Aesthetic Individuality* (New York: Routledge, 2001), 230ff.

Kierkegaard, Schopenhauer, Bergson, Nietzsche, Spengler, and—even more ominously—Martin Heidegger.[20] These thinkers, again, have nothing to do with the historical phenomenon or the political values of the Enlightenment: they prize experience without a discursive referent, which allows for the incursion of ideology, and they have little sense of the utility provided by the indeterminate subject for liberal institutions. They also share a sense of the futility in contesting society. Each is clear about the inability of theory to grasp the irrational sources of suffering and the need to supplant history with "historicity," the lived life, of the individual. The crisis of civilization is seen by all of them as having less to do with the disenfranchised masses than with the marginalizing of "authentic" or "pure" experience. Such are the tenets of a tradition, extending from romanticism to the more avant-garde forms of modernism, whose importance for his own project was noted by Max Horkheimer when he wrote:

> To the artists of the *fin de siècle* the goal was not art but truth, which has no end except the refusal to abide by the bad, the lopsided, the untrue. They wanted to say it as it really was, and the 'it' is always the experience that aims at the whole and can claim no legitimacy before the forum of public knowledge.[21]

This tradition would profoundly influence *Dialectic of Enlightenment* in its struggle against the "ontology of false conditions." But the inability to render its concerns communicable within a public forum, whatever the commitment to an endangered subjectivity, rendered suspect the claims that a radicalization of the Enlightenment heritage was actually taking place. Reacting against this ontology would lead Horkheimer and Adorno to reject any "positive"—determinate, institutional, or "objective"—understandings of freedom in favor of the "non-identity" between subject and object, the individual and the world, and the inkling of "what is not." But this sundered the original attempt of Enlightenment thinkers to make the unknown visi-

20. Max Horkheimer, "Die Aktualität Schopenhauers" and "Schopenhauer's Denken," in *Gesammelte Werke 7*: 136ff and 252ff; also note the oddly favorable essay by Theodor W. Adorno, "Spengler after the Decline," in *Prisms*, trans. Samuel and Shierry Weber (Cambridge: MIT Press, 1994), 51ff; with respect to Heidegger, Theodor W. Adorno, *The Jargon of Authenticity*, trans. Knut Tarnowski and Frederic Will (London: Routledge, 1993).
21. Max Horkheimer, "Decline: Notes 1950–69," in *Dawn and Decline*, trans. Michael Shaw (New York: Continuum, 1978), 204.

ble. Thus, the political world falls back into darkness and, stepping back from Hegel, progress loses any institutional referent.

Conceptualizing subjectivity in this way would involve the Frankfurt School in attacks on virtually every major philosophical school. None were left unscathed: not phenomenology with its ontological flattening of the very experience it claimed to valorize; not empiricism with its blindness to the context of oppression; not positivism with its expulsion of normative values; not instrumentalism with its sanctioning of what exists; and not even Hegel or Marx with their teleological commitment, their affirmation of progress, their preoccupations with revolutionary change, and their belief in the "negation of the negation." None of this makes any sense from a standpoint based on the assumption that "the whole is false." Discussion of the preconditions for exercising freedom or the constraints placed upon it becomes irrelevant. It is enough to note that the truth of freedom is found in its ability to escape all historical and institutional determinations.

This is as much the case for Kierkegaard, Nietzsche, Husserl, Heidegger, Buber, or Rosenzweig as for Horkheimer and Adorno. All of them consider the determinate "negation of the negation" insufficient and one-sided.[22] Freedom cannot present itself in positive terms or receive any form of historical determination. Subjectivity must be understood in experiential terms very different from those offered by reason with its technical fetish. It also doesn't help matters to claim that the "the longing for the totally other" highlighted by Horkheimer or the tensioned-filled "force-field" of aesthetic experience articulated by Adorno, which can only appear as "illusion," are somehow *really* determinate because they contest the totality. Both the religious and the aesthetic experience exist outside history. They are both products of an "intentionless" mode of "non-identical" thinking that militates against the hierarchical and linear style of academic philosophy. Such concerns might justify understanding *Dialectic of Enlightenment* as a composition of "fragments," but it does not justify the attack on the "jargon" of all those other major thinkers with whom its authors claimed to have so little in common. To be sure:

> . . . we must not confuse a heartfelt defense of the old order with an apology for disorder: a solicitude for the individual who risked becoming lost

22. In this regard, it might be useful to compare Martin Heidegger, *Hegel's Concept of Experience*, trans. Kenley Royce Dove (New York: Harper & Row, 1970) with Theodor W. Adorno, *Drei Studien zu Hegel* (Frankfurt am Main: Suhrkamp, 1974 ed.)

in a nascent mass society, with a glorification of the superman; mistrust of the new morality of the flock with an acceptance of the morality of the masters; fear of the plebs with a call for a despot; a theory of political class or of the elites with magnification of the aristocracy (indeed, of a bellicose aristocracy); a defense of civilization feared on the brink of disappearing with heralding a new barbarity'[23]

But the battles between the supporters of late critical theory and post-modernism and those of Kierkegaard, Nietzsche, Heidegger, and the rest—when it comes to the subjectivity of the subject—are so esoterically ferocious precisely because they reflect little more than what Freud termed "the narcissism of small differences." Other than for academic pedants, it is immaterial whether subjectivity is secured through a fleeting moment of aesthetic-philosophic experience in resisting the "totally administered society," the experiential moment fueling the "eternal recurrence," the "insight into the essence" of reality, or the feeling of angst in the face of death. Whether the culprit is "herd society" or "mass society" or the inherently mediocre "public" or the "culture industry" is actually far less relevant than academic philosophers make it out to be. Strange is how the left critique of Enlightenment, supposedly undertaken from the standpoint of Enlightenment itself, should wind harboring affinities with the thinking of right-wing irrationalists and neo-romantics.[24] But stranger still is how, using the original willingness of critical theory to lump opposites together, it becomes evident that "the battle against positivism was common to all the various spiritualist currents that put their stamp, positive or negative, on the culture of the time . . . and that criticism of positivism, whether it came from 'noble' culture or lower quarters, was always accompanied by criticism of socialism, democracy, and political radicalism of all varieties."[25]

Too much time has been spent by fashionable philosophy on the evils of neo-positivism and positivism, which is mistakenly identified with the philosophical spirit of Enlightenment, and too little with whether an imperiled subjectivity is indeed the central problem of modernity: this has, in my

23. Norberto Bobbio, *Ideological Profile of Twentieth-Century Italy*, trans. Lydia G. Cochrane (Princeton: Princeton University Press, 1995), 34

24. Jürgen Habermas, *The Philosophical Discourse of Modernity: Twelve Lectures*, trans. Frederick Lawrence (Cambridge: MIT Press, 1987), 106ff.

25. Bobbio, *Ideological Profile of Twentieth Century Italy*, 33.

view, had a disastrous impact on the critical tradition.[26] Plato had already recognized that politics should not attempt to "care for the soul." But that warning was ignored. Even Herbert Marcuse, whose radicalism contradicted the politics of his more cautious friends in the Frankfurt School, showed little awareness of the dangers in privileging subjectivity and the importance of fostering what Karl Popper termed "the open society." This, indeed, is where the genuinely new efforts in radical thinking should begin.

Reinvigorating critical theory calls for asserting its public aims, reconsidering its understanding of subjectivity, and beginning the critique of those romantic and metaphysical preoccupations that seek to present themselves as political.[27] The problem of subjectivity has concretely—that is to say historically and politically—had far less to do with some utopian transcendence of the given order, or the potential integration of reforms, [28] than the demand for including the excluded, extending the rule of law, civil rights, and economic justice to those suffering the arbitrary exercise of power. The disempowered and the disenfranchised wished not to cultivate their subjectivity like a hothouse plant, but exercise it in the public realm. They wished their unheard voices to be heard and their ignored interests to be articulated: the critique of the culture industry should begin where it contributes to the repression of these voices, the misrepresentation of their interests, and the vulgarity of the life they live.

Rendering media more accountable to the public and expanding the range of what is shown or broadening the spectrum of debate, however, never seem to enter into the discussion. It is for the Frankfurt School, as usual, a question of all or nothing: and, as Brecht liked to say, when called upon to make such a choice, the world is always quick to answer—nothing. But that's all right: such a response only justifies the claim that the whole is false.

---

26. A case in point is the introduction to *Rethinking the Frankfurt School: Alternative Legacies of Cultural Critique*, eds. Jeffrey Nealon and Caren Irr (Albany: State University New York Press, 2002), 5.

27. Stephen Eric Bronner, "Points of Departure: Sketches for a Critical Theory with Public Aims" in *Of Critical Theory and Its Theorists* 2nd Edition (Routledge: New York, 2002), 231ff.

28. The possibility that the "whole" or the given order might qualitatively change for the better is always underestimated with claims like "the liberalization of the Establishment's own morality takes place within the framework of effective controls; kept within this framework, the liberalization strengthens the cohesion of the whole." Herbert Marcuse, *An Essay on Liberation* (Boston: Beacon, 1969), 9

There is no need to offer an alternative to television, high-tech movies, sports, and the existing enjoyments of everyday life. Better to remain content with warning that nothing is safe any longer from the clutches of Hollywood and that, in principle, Beethoven or Schoenberg is as susceptible of manipulation as Elvis Presley or Bruce Springsteen. Better to remain a scold and insist only upon the need to read works—such as the poems of Paul Célan or the plays of Samuel Beckett[29]—that require inordinate concentration and that strengthen the tension between the individual and society or the nonidentity between subject and object. It doesn't matter that this stubborn elitism is but the flip side of postmodern aesthetic relativism. The stylistic difficulty of the Frankfurt School has justified itself by the all-encompassing notion of mass culture its philosophy seeks to contest. The difficulty, nonlinear quality, and fragmentary character of its texts enable them to resist integration by the culture industry and, through undercutting the existing communicative networks, serve the cause of freedom. This same logic, in spite of its oblique references to Martin Heidegger, carries over into a postmodern concern with resolving the supposed current "crisis of humanism" through a "crash diet of the subject" that—note the convoluted language—"would allow the subject to listen to the call of a Being that no longer arises in the peremptory tone of the *Grund* or the thought of thought (or absolute spirit), but that dissolves its presence-absence into the network offered by a society increasingly transformed into an extremely sensitive organism of communication."[30]

When considering the culture industry from the standpoint of a functioning democratic polity, it is less the extent to which the "pure" or "authentic" experience is imperiled than the degree to which the audience is exposed to different forms of aesthetic experience and the different purposes and possibilities attendant upon different artworks. Analyzing cultural life from the abstract and indeterminate perspective of "reification," "mass society," "the herd," or the *das Man* of Heidegger undermines the complexity of the culture industry and its usefulness. The real danger posed by the culture industry has less to do with the trivial character of its products, or the way it neutralizes all radical impulses, than its exclusion of important tradi-

29. Note the brilliant article, which provides an entry into the radical aesthetic of postwar critical theory, by Theodor Adorno, "Versuch das *Endspiel zu verstehen*," in *Noten zur Literatur* II (Frankfurt am Main: Suhrkamp, 1961), 188ff.

30. Gianni Vattimo, *The End of Modernity: Nihilism and Hermeneutics in Postmodern Culture*, trans. Jon R. Snyder (Baltimore: Johns Hopkins University Press, 1990), 47.

tions, its parochialism, and its false pluralism. Criticism of mass society should be focused on its narrowing of discourse, its preoccupation with consensus, its inability to depict meaningful forms of solidarity, and its lack of politics. New forms of critical theory should start highlighting the divergent "structures of knowledge production," using a term from Edward Said, in order to focus upon the differentiated political impact of different trends and worldviews generated by the culture industry. That would give radical cultural criticism a new sense of democratic purpose.

The repression of "individuality" and the need for "self-expression" have already become important themes exploited by the culture industry. Advocates of the "authentic" or "pure" experience have, in this sense, missed the boat. More salient is their preoccupation with the dangers posed by the culture industry and modern life to *their* established aesthetic prejudices and metaphysical preoccupations. Their concerns have a long history. Feeling his alienation from modern life, longing for the rebirth of an organic culture, seeking to "re-enchant" the world, and—above all— express his romantic yearning for religious revelation, Novalis identified philosophy with "transcendental homesickness." This view would, indeed, lay the groundwork for confronting both the anonymity and atomization of modern life.

The philosophical search for "authenticity," a form of insight grounded in the lived life of the individual, would only gain in popularity. Nietzsche insisted that the "will to power" was operating in the realm of nature and society; Bergson noted how the *élan vital* escaped the confines of both metaphysical and scientific categories; and Heidegger sought to overcome the divide between subject and object through his category of *Dasein*. It became a matter of recapturing the inner experience of time, what Bergson called (*la durée*), an attempt that would inform not merely the architects of modern critical theory but also thinkers like Heidegger and Rosenzweig, from the incursions of a mechanistic clock-time grounded in an external understanding of space. Or, more simply, in the face of a standardized and mechanized modernity, intensifying experience became an end unto itself.

Critical theory was not the only attempt to walk a path between metaphysics and materialism. This other existential-romantic tradition tried to do the same thing though, in contrast, it sought a new "foundation" existing beyond the limitations of language. Concern with the ability to intuit a more profound reality beyond all contingent socio-historical factors now appeared in the "insight into the essence" of Husserl, the revelatory unveiling of "Being"—as a "Being-unto-death" (*Sein zum Tod*)– by Heidegger and the illumination by Nishida of a "pure experience" inseparable from other empirical experiences and yet irreducible to them. Only through a feeling of such intensity, or so goes the belief, can the individual find himself or herself "rooted" in the world. That there should have been an interchange between this form of primarily German philosophy and the Far East, or that this new perspective somehow mimics the "religiosity" of the believer against the petrifying rituals of his "religion," is not accidental. Christian mystics like Angelus Silesius, Jakob Boehme, and Meister Eckhardt—who would exert such a powerful influence upon modern subjectivism—have more than superficial affinities with the Buddha. A shared philosophical undertaking presented itself between the inheritors of Christian and Asian mysticism in the attempt to overcome the divide between subject and object, "re-enchant" the world, and explore a mysterious "experience" of phenomenal reality beyond the bounds of discourse that would not—necessarily—entail the introduction of God. Georg Lukács indeed appropriately termed this entire modern trend of philosophy "religious atheism."

Logical forms of philosophical persuasion were employed to privilege the primacy of revelation. But there was always a sense in which religious atheism expressed less a concern for provisional, social or historical, "truth" than the quest for authenticity, the longing for certainty, and the faith that—perhaps through the re-enchantment of reality—meaning might finally be found in a meaningless world. Common to the general approach, moreover, is the way in which the structures of social reality collapse into the individual's experience of them. The constitution of reality in its constraints no less than its options—the original concern of modern philosophy—becomes a secondary matter. The suffering experienced in modernity is thus projected upon reason itself and only emotional transcendence can contest the feelings of anonymity and superficiality engendered by modern life. Pure experience, however, is inherently contemplative. The world is what it is: best then to "let it be" and seek recourse in the revelatory aesthetic or religious experience that can occur in any moment and under any circumstances through the encounter with any phenomena.

There is no explaining the "pure" experience. There is only the completely unwarranted presupposition that others should somehow "understand" that it has taken place. But the judgment of whether a "pure" rather than a secondary "experience" has actually occurred can, by definition, only be self-referential. And that would be in order if, simultaneously, there were not the presumption that something objectively meaningful about phenomenal reality had been illuminated. Or, putting it another way, the problem is not what James Joyce termed the "epiphany," the momentary glimpse of meaning experienced by an individual, but rather the refusal to define its existential "place" or recognize its explanatory limits.

Within the existential tradition, Kierkegaard had probably the best appreciation for the paradoxical character of truth associated with the subjectivity of the subject. His rendering of the story about Abraham and Isaac in *Fear and Trembling* makes this clear. Kierkegaard describes how—having inwardly heard the word of God—the father stood ready to sacrifice his son. But intention was apparently enough for the Lord and so, just as Abraham was ready to strike down Isaac, He intervened. A lesser thinker would have left the matter at that. But Kierkegaard had a feeling for the ironic: he wrote for the individual in search of authentic experience and he knew the difficulties involved. But he also implicitly recognized the difference between public and private, and perhaps unintentionally the need for drawing that distinction, when he went on to ask what would have happened had Abraham actually struck down his son. He would then have had to bring the body back to his community, and tell its elders that the Lord had spoken to him and asked for a sacrifice. Here the more concrete experience of "fear and trembling" occurs: what the individual experiences as a "sacrifice" demanded by God can only be understood as "murder" by society. It becomes evident from Kierkegaard's discussion that, no matter what the good faith of the person hearing the divine word, the community cannot simply take the inner experience of the individual at face value. The discursive "truth" required by society is not the intense inner "truth" sought by the experiencing individual.

Insisting upon the absolute character of revelatory truth obviously generates a division between the saved and the damned. There arises the simultaneous desire to abolish blasphemy and bring the heathen into the light. Not every person in quest of the "pure experience," of course, is a religious fanatic or obsessed with issues of identity. Making existential sense of reality through the pure experience, feeling a sense or belonging, is a serious matter and a legitimate undertaking. But the more the preoccupation with the purity of the experience, it only follows, the more fanatical the believer. In political terms, therefore, the problem is less the lack of intensity in the lived life of the individual than the increasing attempts by individuals and groups to insist that their own, particular, deeply felt existential or religious or aesthetic experience should be privileged in the public realm. Indeed, this runs directly counter to the Enlightenment.

Its intellectuals did not insist that all should share the same religious, cultural, and personal interests and goals. Nor did cosmopolitans like Locke,

Voltaire, or Kant offer a single road to truth. Few of the more important philosophes actually believed in the existence of a "truth"—mathematical or otherwise—capable of informing all the different realms of knowledge; but even if Helvetius did harbor such a belief,[31] for example, he surely presupposed the right of others to challenge it. Most philosophes maintained that a diversity of interests and goals would enrich the public discourse and expand the possible range of experiences open to individuals. Agreement was demanded only on the right of each to pursue his or her beliefs or experiences and the need for institutions capable of guaranteeing that right.

Different ideas have a different role in different spheres of social action. Subjectivity has a pivotal role to play in discussing existential or aesthetic experience while the universal subject is necessary for any democratic understanding of citizenship or the rule of law. From such a perspective, indeed, the seemingly irresolvable conflict between subjectivity and the subject becomes illusory: it is instead a matter of which should assume primacy in what realm. When it comes to political power, unfortunately, even the best believers in the "pure experience" are usually blinded by the light while the worst use their trans-historical categories to obscure the workings of social reality. That a tension exists between the experience of the particular, whose specific identity is grounded in empirical attributes and unique historical traditions, and the universal is undeniable: W.E.B. DuBois, for example, spoke of African-Americans retaining a "double consciousness" while Lion Feuchtwanger in his *Josephus* trilogy highlighted the conflict between ethnic loyalty and cosmopolitanism.

From the standpoint of a socially constructed subjectivity, however, only members of the particular group can have the appropriate intuition or "experience," to make judgments about their culture or their politics. That is the sense in which Michel Foucault sought to substitute the "specific" for the "universal" intellectual.[32] This stance now embraced by so many on the left, however, actually derives from arguments generated first by the Counter-Enlightenment and then the radical right during the Dreyfus Affair. These reactionaries, too, claimed that rather than introduce "grand narratives" or "totalizing ambitions" or "universal" ideas of justice, intel-

---

31. Isaiah Berlin, *Freedom and Its Betrayal: Six Enemies of Human Liberty*, ed. Henry Hardy (Princeton: Princeton University Press, 2002), 11ff

32. Michel Foucault, "Intellectuals and Power," in *Language, Counter-Memory, Practice*, ed. Donald F. Bouchard (Ithaca: Cornell University Press, 1977), 205ff; also "Truth and Power," in *The Foucault Reader*, ed. Paul Rabinow (New York: Pantheon, 1984), pg. 68ff.

lectuals should commit themselves to the particular groups with whose unique discourses and experiences they, as individuals, are intimately and existentially familiar. The "pure"—or less contaminated—experience of group members was seen as providing them a privileged insight into a particular form of oppression. Criticism from the "outsider" loses its value and questions concerning the adjudication of differences between groups are never faced.

Maurice Barrès, had already linked what he called the "cult of the self" with a fear of *les déracinés*. He and his comrades saw genuine interaction as taking place less between strangers confronting one another in a public sphere than between "brothers" or "sisters" or any group whose members shared a common background and "destiny." Only those experiencing themselves as members of the French community, for example, were considered capable of fully understanding why Dreyfus must be guilty: his defenders were simply deluded by universal notions of justice that derived— and this is crucial for the present discussion—more from the intellect and the democratic tradition than from the "experience" of being French. "Intellectuals" could now be derided for their critical rationalism and universalistic ambitions and for placing reason above experience, evidentiary truth above tradition, and human rights above the national community. "Authenticity" and cultural "roots"—what a genuine fascist, Mercea Eliade, termed the "ontological thirst" for primordial belonging—thus became the crucial criteria for judgment.

Not every person who believes in the "pure experience"—again—was an anti-Semite or a fascist. But it is interesting how the "pure experience," with its vaunted contempt for the "public" and its social apathy, can be manipulated in the realm of politics. Utopia doesn't appear only in the idea of a former "golden age" located somewhere in the past or the vision of a future paradise. [33] Freedom also shimmers in the "pure experience" whether in the sophisticated critical version offered by Adorno or the revelatory unveiling of Being in the late Heidegger or the experiential insight of Nishida. Each expresses the longing for that moment untainted by the evils of reification or modernity. But history has shown the danger of turning "reason" into an enemy and condemning universal ideals in the name of some parochial sense of "place" rooted in a particular community. Or, put another way,

---

33. Paul Ricoeur, *Lectures on Ideology and Utopia*, ed. George H. Taylor (New York: Columbia University Press, 1986), 309.

where power matters the "pure" experience is never quite so pure and no "place" is sacrosanct. Better to be a bit more modest when confronting social reality and begin the real work of specifying conditions under which each can most freely pursue his or her existential longing and find a place in the sun.

8

PATHWAYS TO FREEDOM:
RIGHTS, RECIPROCITY, AND THE
COSMOPOLITAN SENSIBILITY

HUMAN RIGHTS IS THE GLOBAL EXPRESSION OF A DEMAND FOR civil liberty. Its origins derive from natural law and the European Enlightenment. Opposition to "rights" from the *ancien régime* was fierce, however, and it took a few hundred ideas for the idea to permeate the mainstream discourse. Human rights only gained currency after Auschwitz and Hiroshima and, in fact, it became popular in the United States only during the presidency of Jimmy Carter in the aftermath of the Vietnam War. Once again, using the famous phrase of Hegel, the Owl of Minerva spread its wings only at dusk: the Universal Declaration of Human Rights of 1948 came too late to help the victims of classical totalitarianism. Old habits die hard. Especially nonwestern supporters of human rights are still opposed by religious institutions and atavistic movements with provincial attitudes rooted in the vision of an organic community. The struggle over "rights" indeed remains a political struggle between two very different outlooks grounded in the assumptions of the Enlightenment and the Counter-Enlightenment.

Human rights no less than liberal values are still, admittedly, usually spoken about more than they are practiced. But they continue to inspire resistance because they challenge what—politically, economically, and socially—constrains the ability to learn, the autonomy of the individual, and the accountability of institutions. It doesn't matter whether the cultural context of the society is Christian, Islamic, Hindu, or Jewish; these profoundly secular ideals have taken on an increasingly universal character. More than that:

> Human rights has gone global not because it serves the interests of the powerful but primarily because it has advanced the interests of the powerless. Human rights has gone global by going local, embedding itself in the soil of cultures and worldviews independent of the West, in order to

sustain ordinary people's struggles against unjust states and oppressive social practices.[1]

There is nothing new in the claim that human rights generates demands for entitlement independent of the particular state in which an individual happens to live: natural law was, from its beginnings, identified with universality and unbounded geographically by time or space. It was only during the "age of democratic revolution" and the emergence of Enlightenment political theory, however, that this idea of "right" first received formal embodiment and an institutional referent in the liberal state. To be sure, the bourgeois notion of rights was limited by property, race, and gender. But the critical element within the rights discourse calls such limitations into question. It militates against attempts to ground the idea of "right" in western notions of positive law or utility. This becomes apparent when considering the protests against "widow burning" (*sati*) in India and in Tianammen Square as well as the civil rights movement in the American South or in the Revolutions of 1989. It is both "an intellectual mistake and an affront to those outside the western tradition to look back at any one of these [western] thinkers as the historical point of authority for how we should think about human rights. We should, rather, look at them as illustrating how human rights can be seen from a variety of angles and the problems that arise when we approach the subject from each of these angles."[2]

Rights can take different forms: some are atavistic like the right to bear firearms and others ultimately exploitative like the right to property. Judgment is required of any "right" regarding "the extent to which it embodies concrete liberty and human dignity, upon its ability to provide for the fullest development of human potentialities."[3] Reciprocity is the decisive criterion. Every institution and tradition should become open to critique. But this does not mean that the terms of criticism should be the same in every instance. The democratic must be judged differently than the authoritarian state because the liberal rule of law, in principle if not always in fact, suspends those empirical qualities of individuals—race, gender, religion, back-

1. Michael Ignatieff, *Human Rights as Politics and Idolatry* (Princeton: Princeton University Press, 2001), 7

2. A. Beldon Fields, *Rethinking Human Rights for the New Millennium* (New York: Palgrave, 2003), 21.

3. Franz Neumann, "Types of Natural Law," in *The Democratic and the Authoritarian State: Essays in Political and Legal Theory*, ed. Herbert Marcuse (New York: Free Press, 1957),72.

ground, property—that might prove prejudicial in addressing grievances or the reciprocity of rights and obligations accorded citizens. But there is a catch. This suspension of empirical qualities undermines the idea of a homogeneous community. It introduces distinctions between public and private, political and personal, universal and particular, which express the "alienation" of modernity. Counter-Enlightenment thinkers were therefore correct in maintaining that alienation is embedded within the liberal political theory of the Enlightenment, and their utopian image of a "golden age" located in a heavenly paradise or a mythologized past fueled the assault upon it.

Global capitalism is now affecting the most remote regions of the planet. This does not mean that all nations and regions have been modernized or that they have been modernized to the same degree. But it does mean that the type of insularity from the outside world, which helped define religious institutions or the organic community, is being ineluctably eroded. Modernity threatens to render anachronistic the established customs and religious beliefs of any community and privilege the notion of an individual intent upon knowing more, learning more, earning more, consuming more, and living life as he or she chooses. The foundation has been laid for extending human rights as never before. Yet the ideal loses its radical quality when reference is not made to a cosmopolitan sensibility and a commitment to social justice and international political institutions.

The great Enlightenment thinkers of international law like Hugo Grotius, Kant, and Samuel Pufendorf articulated an early conception of human rights. But the implications of the idea also became concrete in the activities of Beccaria, Lessing, Montesquieu, and Voltaire, who waged practical struggles against torture, slavery, and religious intolerance. They were opposed from the start by the Counter-Enlightenment. If the philosophes invented the language of human rights, however, they also inadvertently taught it to capitalists and imperialists, communists and nonwestern authoritarians, who would betray its content. Both the modern language of resistance and power were born in the cradle of the European Enlightenment.[4] The progressive political elements of human rights and the inhuman consequences of "modernization" are contradictory elements of globalization.[5] Only in

4. Micheline Ishay, "Introduction" to *The History of Human Rights* (Berkeley: University of California Press, 2003).
5. Manfred B. Steger, *Globalism: The New Market Ideology* (Lanham, MD: Rowman & Littlefield, 2002), 6ff.

terms of the former, however, is it possible to contest the latter in a meaningful fashion. Realizing human rights should be seen as the fundamental element of the modernizing process: it is the precondition for the exercise of autonomy.

Autonomy originally implied the right for each to have his or her faith. Such a position, however, necessarily makes it impossible to privilege any particular faith. The quest for some absolute to underpin the polity is therefore undermined. Enlightenment thinking, from the beginning, concerned itself less with the interpretation of particular religious dogmas, or their truth, than with the political implications of embracing an unyielding religious certainty: it ceased dealing with what is believed and concentrated itself on the practical implications of belief.[6] The liberal polity sought to circumscribe the secular ambitions of all religions. Both in the Occident and the Orient, whatever the differences of social context, the battle will therefore still be over whether what is usually a single religion should dominate public life or, instead, whether every religion should be seen as just another private interest with particular political aspirations. Rejecting this latter view is not simply a matter of the Church, the Synagogue, and the Mosque acting in accordance with divine law against the incursions of the profane, although it can be turned into that, but of institutional self-preservation. Indeed, for the faithful, the more dramatic the demand for reciprocity the more fundamental will be the response.

No more than the Counter-Enlightenment is religious fundamentalism a "dialectical" product of the Enlightenment. It is reactionary in the literal meaning of the word. Religious fundamentalists look backward for their inspiration as surely as integral nationalists and supporters of the organic community. All of them privilege authority over liberty, unquestioning faith over critical reflection, the revelatory over the demonstrable, and the community over the individual. Each rejects the separation of church from state and the critique of patriarchal hierarchies. Each insists upon the legitimacy of traditions simply because they exist. Intolerance and dogmatism are built into this mode of thinking if only because discussion is limited by the holy words of an inerrant Bible, an infallible Pope, the Islamic *Shari'a*, or the Jewish *halacha*.

Critique is thereby inhibited from the beginning: religious fundamentalism ultimately rests on rigid distinctions between the saved and the damned, friend and foe, insider and outsider, the religious ideal and the

6. Ernst Cassirer, *The Philosophy of the Enlightenment*, trans. Fritz C. A. Koelln and James P. Pettegrove (Boston: beacon Press, 1951), 136.

profane reality. These distinctions are insurmountable from within the fundamentalist worldview and thus alienation, which it claims to have overcome, continues to exist at its very core. It doesn't matter that just before a plane lands in a theocratic nation like Iran, women will quickly put on scarves and on leaving, as soon as the plane is in the air, take them off. Privileging revelation over common sense makes this easy to ignore. With its suspicions concerning the subversive character of autonomy and reciprocity, inevitably, any meaningful understanding of human rights loses its appeal for fundamentalism.

Religious fundamentalists call for an uncompromising opposition to modernity. But the rigor of this position is impossible to maintain. The "disenchantment of the world"—again using the famous formulation of Max Weber—not only increases the power of scientific rationality and secular institutions but also transforms the sphere of the sacred. Magic as a technique of salvation comes under steady assault and, as a consequence, the realm of the invisible becomes ever more impoverished.[7] The traditional impact of hegemonic religious institutions upon secular politics and social life is turned on its head. The demands of a secular political reality and economic life impinge upon faith and religion: the new religions now advertise, build malls, sponsor television shows. Revelations and miracles are greeted with cynicism, and when they approach such issues as abortion, the sexual misconduct of priests, assisted suicide, or public prayer, they must deal with the pressure of external political forces and social pressures.

Religion has always been political: Machiavelli knew that. But the machinations of the various churches and their leaders were traditionally cloaked in secrecy and that, too, has changed through the rise of mass media and the political insistence from below for a public dialogue with those of different religions and different views. Not merely the technological or the historical but the existential possibility that things can be different creates both anxiety and a sense of disorientation. The word of God gains new significations, and so the "authenticity" of revelation takes a back seat to the need for guidance or the confirmation of what has already been established. Religion turns into a set of stratagems by which meaning and re-enchantment can be infused into a meaningless and disenchanted world.[8]

7. Marcel Gauchat, *The Disenchantment of the World: A Political History of Religion*, trans. Oscar Burge Princeton: Princeton University Press, 1997), pg. 3.

8. Theodor W. Adorno, "Reason and Revelation," in *Critical Models: Interventions and Catchwords*, trans. Henry W. Pickford (New York: Columbia University Press, 1998), 137.

Complex issues are explained by making reference to the "experience" encoded in anachronistic and stereotyped images. Fundamentalists of all sorts can thus make reference to Satan, while the Rev. Jerry Falwell explains the terrible events of "9/11" in terms of religious retribution. Others castigate the savagery of the "Arab" or the global conspiracy of the "Jews." Imperialism becomes justified by what the Old Testament promised Moses while the geographic site of a Hindu Temple, or the 2002 production of a "Miss World" pageant in the Muslim city of Kaduna in Nigeria, turn into issues worth dying for. The workings of modern life become ever more impenetrable, invisible, as religious dogma determines how believers should deal with reality. Only the certainty provided by absolute faith, which in its intolerance is actually quite fragile, seems capable of contesting the growing alienation of modern life. Fundamentalism rejects the possibility for engaging "the other" raised by theologians like Schleiermacher and Kierkegaard and Buber: there is only an ongoing parochial preoccupation with the self. In this sense—whether Christians, Jews, Hindus, Buddhists, or Muslims—all fundamentalists are bigots.

They are also hypocrites. Not in the manner of Elmer Gantry, novelist Sinclair Lewis's great fictional portrayal of a religious preacher, but in a different way. For, no matter how deeply the resentment against modernity runs, its scientific and technological advances are being integrated into the lives even of those who most oppose its imperializing ambitions. Priests employ cell-phones, rabbis use the Internet, and fundamentalists of all stripes work the mass media. The Jewish state, the Islamic Republic, and the Vatican use the same accounting techniques; all are preoccupied with their secular position in the world; all hire scientific experts; all think about the dollar. What V. S. Naipal identifies with Islam, in this respect, is actually true of religious fundamentalism in all its varieties. Its supporters engage in an emotional rejection of modernity even as they embrace its

> . . . machines, goods, medicines, warplanes, the remittances from the emigrants, the hospitals that might have a cure for calcium deficiency. . . . Rejection, therefore is not absolute rejection. It is also, for the community as a whole, a way of ceasing to strive intellectually, It is to be parasitic: parasitism is one of the unacknowledged fruits of fundamentalism.[9]

9. V. S. Naipal, *Among the Believers: An Islamic Journey* (New York: Vintage, 1982), 168.

Cultural traditionalists and religious fundamentalists resist the intrusion of modern life and liberal society into their lives. But their resistance already presupposes an encounter with the "other": through television, film, the computer, the newspaper, and just plain gossip the awareness arises, no matter how vague, that things can be different. Witness the orthodox Jewish woman insisting upon a divorce from an abusive husband, the stretch limousine enjoyed by an Arab businessman dressed in traditional garb, the attempts to combine the shopping mall with the church in many parts of the United States. Religion has become a smorgasbord: it is no longer all or nothing. Questions concerning sex, diet, dress, and personal life have become matters of individual choice and—in principle—citizens living in liberal democracies will have their choices protected by law. The traditionalist now functions in an anti-traditionalist context, in short, and the fundamentalist reaction against modernity has been transformed into a function of modernity itself.[10]

Religious reaction against the liberal society is growing. But it remains a mistake to consider liberal universalism and cultural particularism simply as opposing "discourses": modernity has put the latter on the defensive. Liberal society can be combated either by speaking of rights in purely relative terms or by embracing a religious absolute that need not justify its privileges to its critics. These two seemingly contradictory perspectives are, in fact, symbiotically linked: Hegel would probably have noted how each is defined by what it opposes. Neither, in any event, offers a progressive alternative to the discourse of rights. Each considers the universal the enemy of the particular even as each ignores how only liberal institutions have guaranteed reciprocity or the practical exercise of religious freedom for the self and the other. Thus, the discourse of "rights" throws down a simple challenge to fundamentalism: it asks whether the fundamentalist of one faith will allow fundamentalists of other faiths to practice theirs.

At stake then is not really the right to practice religion, but the right of others to practice it differently or not at all. In this vein, it is opportunistic and politically misguided to stress the "legitimacy" of a peaceful state that "only" discriminates against one group of citizens. It also dulls the blade of critical democratic thinking to substitute the idea of a "decent people," which liberals will find worthy of respect, for the insistence of liberalism that

10. Ulrich Beck, *Die Erfindung des Politischen* (Frankfurt am Main: Suhrkamp, 1993), pgs. 17–18.

all individuals in a state must be free and equal under the law. [11] The United States prior to 1964 for the most part "only" discriminated against people of color and, surely except for them, citizens of other white nations viewed it as a "decent people." Usually where repression of one group is taking place, however, repression of others—including dissidents—exists as well. Just this "thin" view of rights—always in the name of being "reasonable"—undercuts its critical impact. Enlightenment political theory should not have its relevance circumscribed to those nations where the liberal state exists, but instead have its relevance made plain for those living in "illiberal" societies. The salience of rights, in this same vein, should not exist only for those who already enjoy its benefits but for those who do not. This need not involve a commitment to military "intervention": that is always a tactical question and, in general, even democracy cannot simply be imposed *ex nihilo*. From the standpoint of theory, however, support for progressive values requires conviction where the battle for them is being fought. The present intellectual vogue of seeking to provide a philosophical justification for placating the concerns of non-liberals on "pragmatic" grounds or indulging in a form of "strategic essentialism," which withdraws genuine regard for liberal assumptions, is simply appalling.

Liberty is never a problem for the individual or group that possesses it; the problem arises only when freedom is demanded by the disenfranchised, the exploited, the excluded, the other. Enlightenment political theory thus highlighted the need for reciprocity in the allocation of rights and duties to the state. This creates a strange state of affairs: Orthodox Christian, Jewish, or Islamic intellectuals can criticize liberalism but, according to their fundamentalist beliefs, liberal intellectuals dare not criticize them. With respect to reciprocity, in this vein, it is the height of arrogance that members of the ultra-orthodox communities in Israel should be in the forefront of those championing an imperialist policy while simultaneously insisting upon their exemption from military duty—obviously in order better to pray for victory. All of this is predicated on the refusal of fundamentalists to compromise the absolute character of their belief and accept that they should be treated like everyone else. David Hume put the matter well when he wrote in "An Enquiry Concerning the Principles of Morals":

> Fanatics may suppose that dominion is founded on grace and that saints alone inherit the earth; but the civil magistrate very justly puts these sub-

---

11. Cf. John Rawls, *The Law of Peoples* (Cambridge: Harvard University Press, 1999), 75–78, and *passim*.

lime theorists on the same footing with common robbers, and teaches them by the severest discipline, that a rule, which, in speculation, may seem the most advantageous to society, may yet be found in practice, totally pernicious and destructive.[12]

Enlightenment notions of tolerance are predicated on an indifference to existential or religious experience: fundamentalists will therefore see them as denigrating the true faith. But the issue is really not whether one religion or one interpretation of any sacred text is correct against another. Each can find in any holy work whatever he or she seeks to justify his or her interest. The question is whether an institutional arrangement should exist in which each can pursue a particular belief and interpret any given holy scripture in peace. Thus, it is useful to consider the famous remark by Voltaire from his *Letters from England* in which he notes that a state with one religion tends toward despotism, a state with two religions tends toward civil war, while a democratic state with thirty—like England—enables its citizens to pray after their fashion and sleep soundly at night.

Custodians of the established order have always claimed that the liberal indifference to religion, its belief in toleration, is merely a veiled form of intolerance. Most postmodernists would probably agree. But this is simply playing with language: it is the same as suggesting that the attack on imperialist ambitions is merely a different form of imperialism. It is possible, of course, to assume that democratic values and institutions are secondary since an ontological basis for belief exists—a foundational assumption of grace or transcendence or what Karl Jaspers termed the "encompassing"— that underpins all possible beliefs and that is shared by people of the most diverse religious and even secular faiths. There is a sense in which the religious do form a community and the best among them have often been courageous in opposing intolerance, exploitation, and war. It is also possible for academics to envision a liberating "post-secular" or new "mystical society" though, of course, not the sort advocated by Islamic and Christian fundamentalists who actually have a mass base and a political agenda.[13] A

---

12. David Hume, *Political Writings*, ed. Stuart D. Warner and Donald W. Livingston (Indianapolis: Hackett, 1994), 88.
13. Cf. Bill Martin, "Redemption in the Impasse: An Other Communism," in *New Critical Theory: Essays on Liberation*, eds. William S. Wilkerson and Jeffrey Paris (Lanham, MD: Rowman & Litlefield, 2001), 37ff; Philip Wexler, *Mystical Society: An Emerging Social Vision* (Boulder, CO: Westview, 2000).

new world in the making can be seen as having been generated by a soulless technocratic system and brought into existence by some kind of ethically motivated revolution. As usual, however, such thinking winds up in the metaphysical mist: it deals with neither constraints nor agents nor the institutions capable of sustaining the new order.

No responsible political person can afford to assume that the shared experience of religiosity by individuals will overcome the competing ambitions of diverse religions or that everyone will be tolerant and open-minded simply because they say so. There is also as little historical reason for the outsider to trust the insider, or the dissident the establishmentarian, as for the Jew to trust the Christian, or the Black the White. Different communities have different customs and beliefs. But that does not invalidate the importance of making judgments between and also within these diverse communities. Enlightenment thinking did not reject tradition as such, but it did insist that the individual be able to exercise his or her judgment regarding which traditions should be kept and which discarded. This privileging of critical judgment is crucial: it undermines the "organic" understanding of society embraced by conservatives like Edmund Burke, which maintains that traditions are inextricably linked, and attests to the way in which tradition itself has been redefined by modernity. Because tolerance is predicated on the ability to exercise critical judgment, moreover, it cannot simply be tolerant of intolerance: that is the case both politically and ethically. Only from such a perspective is it possible to identify those who resist "authority" in a constructive fashion.

Enlightenment political theory legitimized civil liberties and their exercise against not merely authoritarian regimes but also democratic regimes that act in an authoritarian manner. With respect to nonwestern cultures, therefore, the issue should not be construed as a "clash of civilizations," but as a clash over what is politically acceptable in the pursuit of interests—whether spiritually or materially defined—and what is not. Democrats and socialists embraced the liberal rule of law precisely because, by definition, they stand apart from private interests even as they ensure the possibility of pursuing them. The "common good" was not ignored, but rather conceptualized critically, or negatively, which was why Enlightenment political theory rested less on the commitment to any particular institutional form than on an ethical imperative capable of constraining the exercise of arbitrary power. Thus, in *The Spirit of the Laws* (Book XI: IV), Montesquieu could write:

> Democratic and aristocratic states are not in their own nature free. Political liberty is to be found only in moderate governments; and even in these

it is not always found. It is there only when there is no abuse of power. But constant experience shows us that every man invested with power is apt to abuse it, and to carry his authority as far as it will go. Is it not strange, though true, to say that virtue itself has need of limits? To prevent this abuse it is necessary from the very nature of things that power should be a check to power. A government may be so constituted as no man shall be compelled to do things to which the law does not oblige him, nor forced to abstain from things which the law permits.

But this public realm standing beyond any private interest is not only important for democracy in a heterogeneous community with many religions but for the homogeneous community with a single religion. After all, it cannot be known in advance what issues and which claims citizens will raise. Just as it is impossible to privilege any particular religion while attempting to be impartial with respect to all, so is it impossible to privilege any particular interpretation of a religion while equally respecting the interpretations of others. That is the case both because belief inspires practice and because, for the guardians of orthodoxy, it is not a matter simply of being "right" against others but of being "absolutely" right. The discourse can, under such circumstances, only prove illiberal. Even the most cursory glance at the historical record will produce a loathing for those believers from all faiths who, always in the name of God, again and again plunged their communities into chaos and war not only in order to extirpate other religions but seemingly blasphemous interpretations of the one "true" faith. It was with these fanatics in mind that two thinkers as different as Thomas Hobbes and Voltaire sought to identify religion as a private interest.

Both of them knew that the religious history of Europe should serve less as an example for other civilizations than as a cautionary warning. The idea of civil liberty was the response to an age of civil war inspired by competing religious ideologies. Human rights was, in much the same way, a response to Auschwitz. Both "liberty" and "right" inherently resist the arbitrary exercise of power. They justify expanding the possible experiences and knowledge of the individual. They must therefore both be understood as dynamic concepts: the initial establishment of some rights has consistently bred a concern with securing other liberties. The liberal discourse indeed provides a striking illustration of the quip by Max Weber that ideology is not like a taxicab that one can stop when one wishes. The logic behind the "rights of man" was, for example, immediately employed to justify the rights of women and the abolition of slavery. But the logic did not stop there. The formal rights of individuals to due process and equality under the law, "bourgeois rights," would ultimately generate a concern with substantive rights like the "right to work," the rights of the physically disabled, and even animal rights.

Political rights or civil liberties should not be treated simply as middle-class concerns while economic and social rights are viewed as concerns of the proletariat and the poor. The "right to work" is meaningless, for example, without the right of workers to organize, and speak their minds about the content and character of their labor. Even when they embraced orthodox Marxism, which was critical of a discourse predicated on "rights," the major thinkers of the European labor movement thus almost always defended civil liberties. But the refusal of social democrats to recognize an unqualified "right" to property made them seem like authoritarians in the eyes of their capitalist enemies. In this vein, especially today, it is necessary to recognize that "rights" can conflict: this is as true in the case of the liberal "right" to property and the socialist "right" to decent working conditions as in the contemporary debate that pits a women's "right" to have an abortion against what some consider the "right" of the fetus.

"Rights can, of course, be used to disguise the social power of a particular class or group. Rousseau already recognized this problem in *The Social Contract*: he made clear that a distinction exists between public and reserved rights. But this only begs the question: who will decide whether any given right is public or reserved. His answer would probably have been: the people or, better, the democratically accountable sovereign. It follows, in any event, that the conflict between rights can only be decided politically within a democratic institutional arrangement. It is therefore simply metaphysical indulgence to worry over whether the logic of rights will undermine the proper "ordering" of our lives, whether the subject should occupy the center of the moral universe, or whether the continuing emphasis on rights will exhaust the democratic polity. Such views always avoid articulating how this proper "ordering" should otherwise be determined;[14] that expanding the possibilities of experience is meaningful only for a subject; and that, if the dynamic of rights renders the "idea of right" meaningless, then calling for greater freedom must, logically, render freedom meaningless.

Taking rights and political freedoms for granted is a big mistake. There is a practical foundation for believing in liberal democracy. Naïve faith in the superior qualities of this ideology or that organization is insufficient. This

---

14. Cf. Mary Ann Glendon, *Rights Talk: The Impoverishment of Political Discourse* (New York: Free Press, 1991).

was something Lenin never realized. The supposed master of political realism never thought about institutions to sustain "democratic centralism" within his vanguard party and the results speak for themselves. It was the same with Trotsky and Bukharin. While in power, they were more than willing to suspend the rights of other parties and movements and they condemned any preoccupation with civil liberties and "rights" as bourgeois. When Stalin repressed *them*, however, then bourgeois democratic values suddenly assumed revolutionary importance. Even at the end, ironically, they never recognized that the source of their oppression was an unaccountable party-state buttressed by an authoritarian faith in its ultimately incorruptible character.

Madison, Montesquieu, and Hegel had a far better grasp of the problem. They knew that freedom remains an abstraction without reference to the institutional forms in which it is made manifest. The issue then is not whether the "whole is false" but rather, within given historical and cultural circumstances, what political institutions and programs are most appropriate to constricting the arbitrary exercise of power. Illegitimate authority has traditionally relied on a closed and unaccountable decision-making group that tends to posit a rigorous distinction between "friend" and "enemy" and an ongoing state of crisis, heightened and justified through propaganda that allows its supporters to believe that anything goes: the aim of politics is thus to find windows of opportunity for the pursuit of organizational interests without reference to the costs born by individuals. Enlightenment political theory contested precisely this kind of authority and, in the same vein, human rights insist upon the "transparency" of institutions and the dignity of the individual. It is indeed becoming increasingly evident that any genuine commitment to human rights requires the prior commitment to liberal norms and a liberal state.

Human rights is useful only from the standpoint of critique and resistance. It projects a form of solidarity that is more than legal and extends beyond the limits of class, race, and nation. It implicitly calls for considering together and in common the plight of Israeli soldiers resisting the policies of their country, the person fighting for an independent trade union in China, and the young girl resisting a clitorectomy by a tradition-bound society in Africa. Human rights is a meaningful concept only insofar as similarities are recognized between such different individuals united by nothing more than the willingness to challenge the constraints of tradition and the dictates of arbitrary power. Human rights is predicated on an existential willingness to feel empathy and compassion for the victim, the oppressed, and the disenfranchised. This existential choice, indeed, helps inform what I have elsewhere termed the "cosmopolitan sensibility."[15]

Cosmopolitanism was never reducible to a set of philosophical claims or imperatives: it is also different from internationalism, the support for global institutions, or even a narrowly political form of solidarity with the "other." Kant provided an insight into the character of cosmopolitanism when he identified it with the ability to feel at home everywhere. It, indeed, enters into the style cultivated in very different ways by figures like Benjamin Franklin, Goethe, Hume, and Voltaire. They exhibited a sensibility predicated on a willingness to step outside oneself in order to engage the other in a substantive and meaningful way. This existential element of cosmopolitanism, its sensibility, has generally been neglected, perhaps because it involves something more elusive than the institutional and legal formalism surrounding human rights.[16]

Many thinkers from different parts of the political spectrum have criticized "human rights" for its legalism, its emphasis upon procedure, its abstract individualism, and its refusal to privilege any particular social good. Raising the existential issue concerning cosmopolitanism—understanding it as a sensibility—provides a response to these criticisms. It also points to one of the most pressing problems for contemporary international or transnational organizations. For, where in the past, international peace or working class organizations were short on institutional power and long on a type of "consciousness," today the situation is reversed: new "bourgeois" international and transnational organizations are generating a huge bureaucracy and ever new powers for enforcing programs and laws without, simultaneously, gaining the loyalty of subjects and citizens. That such institutions are the only available options for mitigating planetary problems of immigration, pollution, regional illness like AIDS, and global poverty makes the lack of loyalty they exact from ordinary citizens all the more distressing.

Introducing the cosmopolitan sensibility gives a pedagogic purpose to the internationalist enterprise and an emotional substance to liberal notions of human rights. Books like *Emile* by Rousseau and *Sentimental Education* by Flaubert anticipated what has become a grounding assumption of progres-

15. Stephen Eric Bronner, *Ideas in Action: Political Tradition in the Twentieth Century* (Lanham, MD: Rowman & Littlefield, 1999), pgs. 329ff.
16. Note the otherwise excellent philosophical treatment, which blends cosmopolitanism with human rights and universalism, by Charles Jones, *Global Justice: Defending Cosmopolitanism* (Oxford: Oxford University Press, 1999).

sive pedagogy: namely, that education is not merely confined to the classroom and that it does not only apply to the intellect, but to the emotions or, better, the sensibility of the individual. It is unnecessary to embrace new age mysticism in order to recognize that there is such a thing as emotional intelligence[17] that can be understood dynamically as an increasing sensitivity to the plight of others and a growing moral consciousness.

Objective conditions for a new cosmopolitan pedagogy are already in place: economic development, managerial authority, and class formation are already occurring on a transnational plane; culture industries are evidencing a global reach; expanded possibilities for contact exist between peoples of different nations; a form of international civil society, if not quite a new "republic of letters," is taking shape. National sovereignty is no longer sacrosanct and traditions are eroding. The progressive political response to this situation should not ignore the existential moment while grasping the interdependent character of a new global society. Engaging the universal is possible only from the standpoint of the particular: of political actors with roots in the most divergent cultures. The particular is an ineradicable element of the universal just as the ethnic is of the national and the national is of the international. Nevertheless, the question involves the terms in which the particular should be employed.

An example that I have often used in the past might prove useful: perhaps a Jew born in Prague, with an abusive father, who spent his time in an insurance office, and passed his evenings in bohemian haunts, would have a better intuitive understanding of Kafka than someone from a very different background. In terms of the cosmopolitan sensibility, however, it is just this person from a different background who becomes important. Transcending context and recognizing the ways in which a work offers multiple significations of meaning—for the stranger rather than for those like oneself—should serve as the aim for a new cosmopolitan pedagogy and, in this instance, a new cosmopolitan interpretation of Kafka. That such approaches are not simply embraced, that national and ethnic loyalties still supersede more universal beliefs, says nothing more than that cosmopolitanism is on the defensive, that there is no guarantee that it will flourish, and that fostering it is a matter of ideological struggle.

Cosmopolitanism is more than the sum of national cultures. Making sense of it requires a leap in perspective: Voltaire and his friends already

17. Martha C. Nussbaum, *Upheavals of Thought: The Intelligence of Emotions* (Cambridge: Cambridge University Press, 2003).

looked to the East and interested themselves in the cultures of pre-modern societies while Goethe translated from more than two dozen languages, suggested that he who knows no other language knows not his own, and actually invented the idea of "world literature" (*Weltliteratur*). But there are others to whom one can look in a tradition that extends to Paul Robeson, W.E.B. DuBois, and James Baldwin: the latter indeed gave a profound insight into the existential moment of cosmopolitanism when he noted that the reason white people should learn something about African-Americans is that this will help them learn about themselves. Cosmopolitanism requires engagement and conviction. "Detachment" or "estrangement" actually strips away the radical and critical character of the idea.[18] It also misses the point to talk in postmodern fashion about "cosmopolitanisms," especially when the inability to specify any genuine traditions or emphasize anything more than the indeterminacy of the phenomenon is the cause of robust self-congratulation.[19] That cosmopolitanism is "rooted" in particular experiences is a truism. Views of this sort compromise what is radical before the idea is even articulated. They undermine the need for the global sense of responsibility and ideological commitment to the new transnational movements and institutions that cosmopolitanism should promote.

Such notions of cosmopolitanism wind up, at best, with little more than what the liberalism of Locke and Mendelssohn already provided: a belief in tolerance. More is ultimately required, however, than a lukewarm respect for all cultures or a vision in which the world is turned into a set of competing cultural ghettos. History itself requires reinterpretation. Bossuet already indicated as much when he noted:

> This kind of universal history is to the history of every country and of every people what a world map is to particular maps. In a particular map you see all the details of a kingdom or a province as such. But a general map teaches you to place these parts of the world in their context; you see

---

18. Cf. Amanda Anderson, *The Powers of Distance: Cosmopolitanism and the Cultivation of Detachment* (Princeton: Princeton University Press, 2001), 5ff.

19. "Cosmopolitanism may instead be a project whose conceptual content and pragmatic character are not only as yet unspecified but also must always escape positive and definite specification, precisely because specifying cosmopolitanism positively and definitely is an uncosmopolitan thing to do." Sheldon Pollock et al. "Cosmopolitanisms," in *Public Culture* 12, no. 3 (Fall, 2000), 577.

what Paris or the Ile-de-France is in the kingdom, what the kingdom is in Europe, and what Europe is in the world.[20]

Universal history need not suppress the histories of individual nations, but it must reinterpret them in terms of their contributions to a more general history. Such an approach relegates national or ethnic histories to the sphere of purely provincial or academic interest. Universal history changes the status and meaning of local history as surely as cinema changes the status and meaning of photography or painting. Cosmopolitanism privileges the encounter with different cultures, the integration of their insights, and—above all—the willingness to construct something new. Those interested in the idea have much to learn not merely from the great figures of the Enlightenment, but also from the great artists of modernism—Gauguin, Gide, Hesse, Klee, Malraux, Picasso, Van Gogh, and the rest —who sought inspiration for their new European art in Africa and the Orient and, in the process, produced works that fused the techniques and values of many cultures into something new.

The contempt for cultural provincialism also has pre-modern roots: it existed in Greece and Rome, and in the thinking of those monarchs who employed master craftsman from all over the known world to build their cathedrals, and in the great works of poets like Hafez who was accorded such respect by Goethe. But modernism played the crucial role in forging the cosmopolitan sensibility for our epoch—though this contribution was never really acknowledged by the stalwarts of late critical theory. For them only metaphysics, the experience of non-identity, could contest a world still dominated by nationalism, religious prejudice, and the narrow preoccupation with identity. These critics of the Enlightenment—always from the standpoint of Enlightenment itself—had nothing that might give purpose to what Kant termed the "unwritten code" of constitutional liberalism or provide a substantive underpinning for human rights.

Exploited and disadvantaged nations, understandably, judge the western powers more by their policies than by their values. Just as human rights can be used to justify the interventionist and imperialist interests of powerful nations,[21] perhaps even more easily, cosmopolitanism can become just another form of fodder for the global culture industries. The cosmopolitan

---

20. Cited in Robert Nisbet, *History of the Idea of Progress* (New York: Basic Books, 1979), 142.
21. Biku Parekh, "Non-Ethno-Centric Universalism," in *Human Rights in Global Politics* eds. Tim Dunn and Nicholas Wheeler (Cambridge: Cambridge University Press, 1999), 128–59.

sensibility, if it is to gain any credence, must be interlaced with a commitment to liberal institutions and economic justice. But it is not, again, a simple set of policy proscriptions or the articulation of fixed interpretive rules. The cosmopolitan sensibility must respond to the existential problems of an increasingly planetary age in which the particular, the culturally "authentic," the local, and the ethnic have shown their limits. This is possible only by projecting a new form of cultural radicalism and appropriating the past in ways that speak to the creation of a genuinely global future. Thus, the cosmopolitan sensibility expresses the unrealized legacy of the Enlightenment: its promise gives new meaning to the phrase—first employed by Gramsci—that the old is dying and the new is not yet born.

9

RENEWING THE LEGACY:
SOLIDARITY, NATURE, AND ETHICS

A NEW WORLD PRESENTS ITSELF WITH THE NEW MILLENNIUM: time is obliterating the limitations of space and the boundaries of community. Globalization is spreading the commodity form to the most remote regions of the world; transnational organizations are dwarfing the nation-state; travel is becoming easier; religions are multiplying; intermarriage is on the rise; new communications and information technologies are rendering the world more transparent. But there is no need to be overly optimistic. Numerous parochial religious, ethnic, and nationalist organizations are arrayed—as they always have been—against the assault on traditionalism. Understandable is their fear of the economic inequality generated by global capitalism, the challenge posed by individual conscience to the dictates of custom, the erosion of organic societies, and the disenchantment of the world. Their anger is real: it grows as these forces of reaction are pushed ever more on the defensive. Dealing with them intelligently—at home and abroad—depends upon renewing the Enlightenment heritage. This calls for refashioning its institutional message, recasting its technological inclinations in the face of a mounting environmental crisis, and defending its view of liberty amid the current explosion of fanaticism. Reconfiguring the Enlightenment to deal with the new context stands in accord with its critical spirit. Some brief summary remarks might therefore be useful in provoking further reflection on its understanding of solidarity, its scientific commitment, and its ethical promise.

〜

Enlightenment thinkers wished neither to abolish the state nor to bring about some utopian alternative. Seeking to constrain the institutional use of arbitrary power, they sought to protect the free exercise of subjectivity and promote the free pursuit of scientific knowledge. The state became the anchor for that enterprise; it was seen as the best institution for securing civil liberties and for furthering social justice. That remains the case. Transnational organizations are, to be sure, required in order to contest emerging transnational economic structures. New ways of establishing and expressing the common interest and a more cosmopolitan outlook will also prove necessary not just in the United States or Europe but also in Latin America, Africa, and Asia. Solidarity must surely be reconceived to meet new conditions. But this still does not justify simply dismissing the state or fantasizing about its future disappearance. Confronting an increasingly global society is impossible when indulging in a misplaced romantic nostalgia for the traditional, the organic, and the parochial.

The left must overcome its more naïve populist inclinations. This means looking beyond the polis, the town meeting, and even the workers' council.[1] Their partisans actually share much in common with the religious and traditional advocates of the organic community. Both seem blind to the dangers involved in dismissing "mechanical" notions of representative democracy with its mass parties, interest group pluralism, separation of powers, and checks and balances. Neither seems willing to confront practical questions of economic coordination, the disappearance of a homogenous citizenry or proletariat, and the implications of an increasingly complex division of labor. Rarely does either consider how local politics fosters patronage, provincialism, and corruption. Bureaucracy is despised for the routine and hierarchy it generates; the importance of an independent judiciary for the preservation of civil liberties is ignored, and little time is wasted on how to maintain acceptable investment or reproduce the conditions for participation in the modern world.

Much easier then to condemn the Enlightenment for "severing the organic links that bind humans to their social nature," maintain that all communities should be "left alone," and insist that freedom is not the insight into but rather "the rejection of necessity."[2] Arguments of this sort, of course, retreat from engaging the actual conflicts between real movements that continue to shape our world. They are instead content to rest on the belief that "the whole is false," and that the true pursuit of freedom requires an

---

1. See the debate that began with my article, "Red Dreams and the New Millennium: Remarks on Rosa Luxemburg," in *New Politics* Vol. 8, no. 3 (Summer, 2001), pgs.162–67, and that was carried on in Vol. 8. no. 4 (Winter, 2002), 127–62, Vol. 9, no. 1 (Summer, 2002), 200–35; and Vol. 9, no. 2 (Winter, 2003), 185–88.

2. Cf. Rajani Kannepalli Kanth, *Breaking with the Enlightenment: The Twilight of History and the Rediscovery of Utopia* (Atlantic Highlands, NJ: Humanities Press, 1997), 130 and *passim*.

anti-political politics. It is the same with even with more serious radicals who insist that socialism can be conceived only as a utopian "other" in which alienation has been abolished and a world of direct democracy has been achieved.

Such radicals look to Marx, but not the Marx of *The Communist Manifesto*, who lauded the bourgeoisie for bringing about greater economic and scientific progress in but three hundred years than all the ruling classes in all the preceding millennia taken together. They are inspired instead by the younger Marx who rejected the liberal "political" in the name of "human" emancipation." This Marx was uninterested in "iron laws," institutional constraints, or even the rudimentary organizational forms of class action. Works like "On the Jewish Question" (1843), *The Economic and Philosophic Manuscripts of 1844,* and *The German Ideology* (1845–46) clearly evidence a romantic streak that points beyond the Enlightenment. They call for the abolition of the state, the division of labor, and religion. By the same token, they envision the creation of a new man—or, better, the fulfillment of humanity's "species being." Inspired by a new sense of subjectivity, un-alienated, aware of his powers, without the intrusion of external material interests that might warp his judgment, this new humanity will finally stop history from working behind the back of individuals and subdue what Hegel called "the cunning of reason." Anticipated here is not a revolution in which a new class introduces a new mode of production, a new political system, and a new ideological worldview, but rather an apocalyptic transformation so complete that alienation will be eliminated. The issue here is less whether such ideas crept into Marx's later work than whether revolution can abolish every trace of oppression and solve every existential doubt. Such "anti-political" utopianism, indeed, has little to do with the Enlightenment; it reaches back instead to Thomas Münzer over Novalis and the romantic idea of the apocalypse.[3]

Voltaire and his comrades were more skeptical and more realistic than the young Marx. They were interested less in the anthropological transformation of human nature than in institutional issues still salient today: separating church from state, fostering social reform, denouncing prejudice, decrying superstition, furthering civil liberties, and generally limiting the power of the church. Furthering such aims was possible during the Enlightenment only because the philosophes were willing not merely to build

---

3. Ernst Bloch, *Thomas Münzer als Theologe der Revolution* (Frankfurt am Main: Suhrkamp, 1972 ed.); Georg Lukács, "Zur romantischen Lebensphilosophie" in *Die Seele und die Formen* (Berlin: Luchterhand, 1971 ed.), 64ff.

public opinion outside governmental channels, but also to work through the monarchical or, when possible, constitutional state. This requirement was even more striking for imaginative state civil servants in nations like Germany, where no vibrant bourgeoisie existed; many of them were among the most intelligent supporters of 1776 and 1789. Their concern with expanding individual autonomy and constraining arbitrary power was paramount. That is why they no less than most philosophes championed the cosmopolitan *Rechtsstaat*, with its emphasis upon the liberal rule of law and the moral autonomy of the individual, rather than the traditional and provincial *Volksstaat*.

The radical left has never formulated an adequate substitute for the liberal republic in theory and it has certainly never offered any sustainable institutional alternative in practice. Some still speak about a "socialist democracy" or long for what is usually a romantic image of the Paris Commune and the workers' council. But the idea of a "socialist republic" generated by the Revolutions of 1848 was still to have been predicated on liberal principles rather than their abolition. With the failure of these revolutions, moreover, the great majority of the European working class came to believe that the liberal republic must serve as the precondition for socialism, and not the other way around. As for the Paris Commune, whose understanding of "revolutionary" justice was often as arbitrary as that of the "popular tribunals," which arose in France and Italy in the immediate aftermath of World War II, it had already become anachronistic by 1921 with the passing of "the heroic years" of the Russian Revolution.

Workers' councils and other "secondary associations," which might foster democratic participation, surely have a place in modern political life. But supplanting the state with them is neither a feasible nor a desirable option. Tensions are unavoidable between the imperatives of bureaucracy and public demands for accountability, centralization and decentralization, representation and participation. They cannot be resolved—once and for all—as the radical followers of Rousseau and the young Marx would care to think. The concern with direct democracy stood at the fringes of Enlightenment politics for the same reason that the "workers' council" remained at the fringes of proletarian politics. Both perspectives believe in the repressed desire of everyone to participate all the time and neither provides a trace of what institutional arrangements should be implemented when "the masses" become exhausted and leave the barricades. The philosophes thought about politics in a different way: they generally understood government as less an end unto itself than as a means for securing liberty and making society less miserable.

~

Liberalism remains the focal point of the Enlightenment legacy. Its emphasis upon institutional accountability; its commitment to civil liberties, its belief in toleration, and its universal view of citizenship remain the cornerstones for dealing with the politics of reaction. Increasingly, however, it has become necessary to challenge the inequities of a capitalist system with which liberalism was entangled at birth. It thus becomes a matter of either freezing the Enlightenment, embracing its prejudices concerning the "watchman state" and "*laissez-faire*," or contesting certain of its claims in the light of new events. To put it another way: it is a matter of either preserving the original as a system of beliefs associated with the Enlightenment or employing the critical implications of its unfinished understanding of freedom.

This choice has become particularly pressing in the current political context. Insofar as the best of progressive movements actually sought to realize certain "unfinished" aims of the Enlightenment, which are connected with economic justice and social reform, the stage became set for an alliance between "classical liberals" willing to defend the "free market" and neoconservatives intent upon turning back the clock on the entire range of issues inherited from the 1960s. Many differences exist between these two camps. There is the matter of style and temperament. Classical liberals may, for example, endorse the free pursuit of knowledge while neoconservatives fear the erosion of religion. But the interests of these two groups have, since the middle of the 1970s, converged in attacking those concerned with altering the existing imbalance of economic power and expanding the possibilities of individual experience.

Elites flourish within the liberal state and they benefit from greater control over resources, better possibilities for coordination, and more access to governmental decision-makers. Too much emphasis is placed, however, on the connection between Enlightenment thinking and laissez-faire economics. This criticism has lost its salience. "Laissez-faire" never seems applicable when it comes to the military or the police, the federal reserve, state sponsored defense contracts for business, and "appropriate" forms of scientific research: it is only relevant when dealing with governmental "waste" and welfare programs To understand modern political conflicts in terms of old economic categories is then to miss the boat. The real battle today is no longer between "laissez-faire" and state intervention but instead over which institutions, organizations, and policies deserve state support as against which do not. This creates the need for a perspective on democratic solidarity different than the existential form currently in fashion among dogmatic advocates of identity politics.

Many crucial cultural gains have been made since the decline of the civil rights and the anti-war movements: racism, sexism, homophobia are no longer treated as they once were either legally or in everyday life. At the same time, however, the economic and political power of working people has radically declined. The last decades have witnessed a devastating rollback of redistributive policies and an equally devastating assault on the ideology of the welfare state: one percent of the American population now garners more after-tax dollars than the lowest forty percent, for example, and it has become common to hear that poor people don't pay enough in taxes because they don't work hard enough. One of the reasons for the success of these attacks on the welfare state, though it is perhaps less important than the ferocity with which newly allied "classical liberals" and neoconservatives went on the attack, is the rise of doctrinaire forms of identity politics and their ideological justifications for fragmentation that have generally been accepted by the left in the name of promoting "difference."

Renewing the Enlightenment will assuredly involve radicals in looking beyond the "simple souls" of Rousseau or the proletariat of Marx. It will call for recognizing the legitimate claims of less traditional clienteles discriminated against under liberal regimes whose voices were not recognized by the populist and class politics of the past. The reforms achieved by the new social movements were real. It is absurd to suggest that they have been "absorbed" by an abstract "system" when, in fact, the cultural character of the "system" concerning the expression of difference has obviously been transformed. Different identity movements, indeed, have provided different possibilities for belonging and for expressing the particular interests of women, gays, the disabled, or people of color.

Support for a liberal constitutional state, especially when its welfare programs are under attack, does not deny the need to support diverse movements from below when the possibility exists for more radical reformist efforts. A flexible strategy of this sort only makes sense. Movements organized around rigid understandings of identity, however, have been blind to the striving for autonomy by their own bureaucratically organized interest groups and also to the class divisions within them. This is all the more serious since the power that capital exerts still depends upon the degree of ideological and organizational disunity among working people. So, if the political aim is to contest capital, categories and ways of thinking must be developed capable of identifying what is common to working people within each of the new social movements without privileging any movement in particular. Thus, the importance of the *class ideal*.[4]

This category has nothing to do with some preconstituted "revolutionary" subject or a vanguard organization whose interests are "objectively" identical with those of the proletariat. It also has nothing to do with attempts to squash cultural differences or movements that raise particular grievances and fight unique forms of social oppression, discrimination or exclusion. The class ideal recognizes the need for reciprocity both among citizens and among working people. It is profoundly informed by democratic universalism. But the class ideal also speaks to tempering the whip of the market, which requires linking liberal universal principles with particular class interests. There should be no mistake: the class ideal cannot be imposed on working people from the outside. Nothing is more arrogant than stating from behind a desk that everyone should surrender their particularity and be unified under a "trans-class" or "color-blind" rubric. The class ideal gains life only insofar as concrete proposals emerge for furthering unity by those actually involved in the struggles of the new social movements and progressive organizations of civil society.

Enlightenment thinkers embraced a form of pragmatic idealism. They understood politics as a learning process. Especially in the United States, however, the idealist element has been largely ignored when dealing with organizational responses to reform. Single-issue coalitions have certainly shown their usefulness and—especially in a bureaucratically fragmented nation, built on interest groups rather than political parties[5]— this kind of strategy cannot simply be discarded. New coalitions—sometimes even with religious organizations—will need to be forged. Grand slogans are not substitutes for concrete demands. Coalitions based on a mere convergence of material interests, however, fall apart once the issue is decided. Each participant is concerned only with its particular clientele and, thereby, becomes susceptible to what might be termed the moral economy of the separate deal.

4. Stephen Eric Bronner, *Socialism Unbound* 2nd Edition (Westview: Boulder, 2001), 164–67.
5. Stephen Eric Bronner, "Transforming the State: Reflections on the Structure of Capitalist Democracy" in *Imagining the Possible: Radical Politics for Conservative Times* (New York: Routledge, 2002), 145–60.

But there is no reason why the left should find itself constantly reinventing the wheel with every new problem that arises. It should not simply accept the suspicions and distrust between groups, or ignore the need to invent new forms of solidarity. These might build upon the Poor Peoples' Movement, more than a mechanical coalition of interests groups and less than a party, which was the last great American movement capable of pressuring government with respect to a general program responsive to the interests of working people. Any new movement with class aims must—in the first instance—commit to contesting the ways in which capitalism treats working people as little more than a "cost of production." Such is the concrete meaning of "reification" and fighting it requires a new *political* perspective on class informed by Enlightenment values with constraining the arbitrary exercise of—in this case—*economic* power. Thus, the class ideal projects the mixture of liberalism with socialism.

Renewing the Enlightenment requires more than a fashionable metaphysical emphasis on the "non-identity" between subject and object. It requires instead strengthening the radical legacy of liberal democracy and reinventing socialism as an ongoing—if ultimately asymptotic—struggle against reification. The Enlightenment should not be debated as an abstract body of thought resting on supposedly inflexible philosophical assumptions. Its "unfinished" character, using the phrase of Jurgen Habermas, is actually little more than the "unfinished" struggle for those reforms associated with a cosmopolitan and liberal socialism. This project may not be philosophically dramatic but its concrete implications surely are.

The Enlightenment has always been—historically and politically—a force for securing liberty and fostering resistance against material oppression. These concerns reach back to the age of democratic revolution; they inspired the Revolutions of 1848, the First International, the socialist movement during the nineteenth and early twentieth centuries, the best among the communist revolutionaries of 1917, no less than the mass of anti-communist revolutionaries in 1989. Liberty and resistance against arbitrary authority fueled the struggle for the abolition of slavery, for suffrage, and for the progressive policies undertaken by labor governments in the ill-fated, if remarkably progressive, republics of Europe during the 1920s. These same ideals influenced the New Deal and the Popular Front. They became manifest in the attempt to transform the civil rights into a "poor people's" movement and, even now, in the cosmopolitan sensibility of new anti-war and anti-globalization movements with their concern for international law and human rights.

Enlightenment ideals contested the practices of the class that they originally inspired. They fueled the critique of capitalist inequities and injustices. The terrible tale of capitalist development in the West is now being replayed in even more unspeakable forms in the previously colonized territories of Africa, Asia, and Latin America. Retreating into traditionalism will not help matters any more than relying on old notions of planning inherited from communist authoritarianism. Enlightenment thinking remains the best foundation for any genuinely progressive politics not simply in the West but in those states that suffered most at its hands.

~

Solidarity with the outcast and the dissident, with those whose voices are denied, is the most radical product of the Enlightenment. Its joy in experimentation and its emphasis on expanding the range of individual choices provided liberty with content. Reason in its two prime variants was employed to this critical end: scientific rationality contested traditional prejudices and religious claims to truth while speculative rationality crystallized the purposive ends that science might serve. Insisting upon the need for "absolute" foundations in order to avoid relativism and "chaos," or embracing relativism and chaos due to the lack of an absolute, has nothing to do with the Enlightenment: it cannot escape from the religious universe. Such thinking ignores the practical element within knowledge.

Much has been written about the need for a "new science" no longer defined by instrumental rationality and incapable of reifying the world. But these new undertakings always seem to ignore the need for criteria of verification or falsification; science without such criteria is, however, no science at all. Contempt for "instrumental" scientific rationality, moreover, undermines the possibility of meaningful dialogue between the humanities and the sciences. And that is a matter of crucial importance: popular debates are now taking place on issues ranging from the eco-system to cloning, the assumptions of western medicine to the possibilities of acupuncture, using animals for experiments to state support for space travel.

This shows ethical progress, again perhaps not in the sense that people have become more "moral," but surely in the sense that more questions of everyday life have become open to moral debate. Science has not eroded ethics. The Frankfurt School misjudged the impact of science from the beginning. It is still the case that science plays a crucial role in subverting religious authority—consider only the battle between evolutionists and the Christian coalition—and fostering political equality by enabling each to judge the veracity of truth claims. There is also nothing exaggerated in the claim that "the scientific revolution of the seventeenth century was perhaps the single greatest influence on the development of the idea that political resistance is a legitimate act."[6]

Critics of the Enlightenment may have correctly emphasized the price of progress, the costs of alienation and reification, and the dangers posed by technology and scientific expertise for nature and a democratic society. Even so, this does not justify romantic attempts to roll back technology. They conflate far too easily with ideological justifications for rolling back the interventionist state and progressive legislation for cleaning up the environment. Such a stance also pits the Enlightenment against environmentalism: technology, instrumental rationality, and progress are often seen as inimical to preserving the planet. Nevertheless, this is to misconstrue the problem.

Technology is crucial for dealing with the ecological devastation brought about by modernity. A redirection of technology will undoubtedly have to take place: but seeking to confront the decay of the environment without it is like using an umbrella to defend against a hurricane. Institutional action informed by instrumental rationality and guided by scientific specialists is unavoidable. Investigations are necessary into the ways government can influence ecologically sound production, provide subsidies or tax-benefits for particular industries, fund particular forms of knowledge creation, and make "risks" a matter of public debate. It is completely correct to note that: "neither controversial social issues nor cultural concerns can be settled simply by scientific fiat, particularly in a world where experts usually disagree and where science can be compromised by institutional sponsors. No laboratory can dictate what industrial practices are tolerable or what degree of industrialization is permissible. These questions transcend the crude categories of technical criteria and slide-rule measurements."[7]

Enlightenment thinking is not intrinsically committed to treating nature as an object for technical manipulation. But, if it were, the need would exist for a philosophical corrective. This would treat nature as a subject in its own right or, better, with pressing needs that underpin our own as a species. Revising narrow definitions of "evidence" will prove necessary to bring that about and it will prove necessary to revise existing standards of accountability for dealing with conditions in which human interaction with nature is be-

6. Diana M. Judd, "Questioning Authority: Sir Francis Bacon, Political Resistance, and the Birth of the Scientific Method" (PhD Dissertation: Rutgers University, 2003).

7. John Kurt Jacobsen, *Technical Fouls: Democratic Dilemmas and Technological Change* (Boulder, CO: Westview Press, 2000), 160.

coming ever more specialized, bureaucratic, and complex. In theoretical terms, it may even be necessary to move a step further.

Ernst Bloch, for example, sought to counter an unreflective mechanical materialism—empiricism and positivism—by making reference to what he considered the repressed tradition of the "Aristotelian left" that reaches back over Schelling, Spinoza, and Leibniz to Giordano Bruno and then to Avicenna, Averroes, and Plotinus.[8] This philosophical tendency posits the existence of a "life-force" (*natura naturans*) beyond the stratum of nature (*natura naturata*) that vulgar materialists reduce to its constituent parts. With this vital and "living" notion of nature, which suggests that the whole is more than the sum of its empirical parts, the idea of an ecosystem takes on new meaning. Such a stance, in principle, is less a rejection than a logical outgrowth of Enlightenment thought. It is the same when considering cruelty to animals and other sentient beings.

To be sure: Descartes believed that animals had no souls and that they were mere machines ruled by necessity. Though LaMettrie and others satirized this belief, it must have soothed the conscience of many a scientist willing to torture animals in the name of progress or, worse, many an entrepreneur willing to mutilate and slaughter them by the millions not simply for food, but for the perfect scent, a fur coat, or a piece of ivory. Enlightenment pedagogy, in any event, rests on educating the sentiments, while its concern with constraining the exercise of arbitrary power is predicated on compassion for the weak and the mute. No beings are weaker and with less of a voice in resisting arbitrary power than animals: protecting them and their environment therefore, again, does not contradict Enlightenment ethics, but instead becomes its logical extension. Natural law was seen by many of the most important philosophes as linking humans and animals. Thus Alexander Pope spoke about a "vast chain of being," utilitarians sought animal welfare legislation, Goethe maintained that "each animal is an end unto itself," while Voltaire wrote in his *Treatise on Toleration* (1763)":[9]

---

8. Ernst Bloch, *Das Materialismusproblem, seine Geschichte und Substanz* (Frankfurt am Main: Suhrkamp, 1972), 479.ff

9. Correctly, the editor of a fine anthology can note that "the ideas and values of the Enlightenment era altered the educated mind significantly, if not yet all of the public face. The general tenor of views . . . contributed to those early, if far from complete, practical advances—which is neither to ignore nor downplay the fact that many continued to treat other species as mere instruments of human purposes" in *Awe for the Tiger, Love for the Lamb: A Chronicle of Sensibility to Animals*, ed. Rod Preece (New York: Routledge, 2002), 125 and 123–76.

It seems to me that those who have the audacity to believe animals no more than machines have renounced the light afforded by nature. There is a manifest contradiction in conceiving God to have given animals all the organs of sentience while maintaining that he did not give them sentience. It seems to me equally that they must never have observed animals if they cannot recognize their needs expressed in differing tones, their suffering, joy, fear, love, anger, and all their differing sentiments; it would be very strange if they could express so well what they cannot feel.

Animal rights is still seen by many as romantic and bizarre rather than as a genuinely progressive ethical issue with political appeal. Even *The Economist* (February 15, 2003), a magazine not noted for identifying with the helpless, noted a new trend: in various parts of the United States, dogs and cats are being legally defined as "companions" rather than property; Germany now has a constitution that speaks of the right of animals to decent treatment and even more radically, in New Zealand, the Animal Welfare Act of 1999, treats great apes as "non-human hominids" and prevents experimentation on them unless the research will benefit the apes or, ultimately, seek to alleviate their suffering.

Reclaiming the Enlightenment calls for clarifying the aims of an educated sensibility in a disenchanted world. But this requires science. The assault upon its "instrumental" character or its "method" by self-styled radicals trained only in the humanities or social sciences is a self-defeating enterprise. Criticizing "bourgeois" science" is meaningful only with criteria for verification or falsification that are rigorous, demonstrable, and open to public scrutiny. Without such criteria, the critical enterprise turns into a caricature of itself: creationism becomes as "scientific" as evolution, astrology as instructive as astronomy, prayer as legitimate a way of dealing with disease as medicine, and the promise of Krishna to help the righteous a way of justifying the explosion of a nuclear device by India.[10] Striking is how the emphasis on "local knowledge"—a stance in which all science is seen as ethno-science with standards rooted in a particular culture[11] —withdraws objectivity, turns the abdication of judgment into a principle of judgment, and recalls what was once a right-wing preoccupation with "Jewish physics," "Italian mathematics," and the like.

10. Meera Nanda, "Breaking the Spell of Dharma: A Case for Indian Enlightenment," in *Breaking the Spell of Dharma and Other Essays* (New Delhi: Three Essays Press, 2002), 118.
11. Note the critique of this position with an eye on its unfortunate consequences for the economically underdeveloped world by Meera Nanda, *Prophets Facing Backward: Postmodern Critiques of Science and Hindu Nationalism in India* (New Brunswick: Rutgers University Press, 2003).

Forgotten is that those who do physics or biology or mathematics all do it the same way or, better, allow for open scrutiny of their own way of doing it. The validity of science does not rest on its ability to secure an "absolute" philosophical grounding, but rather on its universality and its salience in dealing with practical problems. There is a difference between the immanent method of science and the external context in which it was forged. The sociology of science is a completely legitimate endeavor. It only makes sense to consider, for example, how an emerging capitalist production process with imperialistic aspirations provided the external context in which modern science arose. But it is illegitimate to reduce science to that context or judge its immanent workings from the standpoint of what externally inspired its development.[12]

Too much time has already been wasted on "deconstructing" the scientific method for what Foucault termed its "dogmatic approach" and its supposedly hermetic character. That is the case not simply because the "scientific revolution" was directed against a scholastic view of nature that constrained the possibilities of inquiry or because the Enlightenment spirit influenced many nontraditional notions of science like homeopathy. It is primarily because, in political terms, the issue is not the "method" of science but the type of scientific research that demands funding and, ultimately, the ends to which science is put. Again defined by what they oppose, ironically, those principally concerned with the scientific method reflect the establishmentarian tendency to isolate science from politics. Whatever the connection between this method and metaphysics, or the status of its original commitment to benefit humanity, there is no reason to believe that science in the age of globalization has lost its ability to question previous claims or established authority: neither from the standpoint of science nor ethics is it legitimate to maintain that "the enlightenment has lost any trace of its own self-consciousness."[13]

Critical theory in the future must, once again, become more modest: it needs to specify the practices to which its categories apply. The difference between history and nature, wrote Vico in *The New Science*, is that humanity has created one and not the other. His famous statement, which looked back to Kant and forward to Lukács and the beginnings of critical theory, has serious implications. Science cannot be expected to meet either metaphysical or politically correct expectations: such concerns bring to mind the

12. Cf. Sandra Harding, *Is Science Multicultural?* (Bloomington: Indiana University Press, 1998), 39ff.

13. Max Horkheimer and Theodor W. Adorno, *Dialectic of Enlightenment*, trans. John Cumming (New York: Herder & Herder, 1972), 4.

communist believers who in the 1920s attacked Einstein for promoting relativism. The point is not to get entangled in the immanent workings of science, which most critical theorists do not even remotely understand, but instead illuminate the institutional complexes with their particular balance of forces wherein "science" receives its direction and its aims.

The Enlightenment notion of science, in the main, mirrored the more general philosophical rejection of closure and absolute knowledge. Bacon and Boyle, with their concern for methodological flexibility and provisional truth, already projected less the obsession with positive certainty than the emphasis upon "falsifiability" advocated by Sir Karl Popper. But it was surely Lessing who best expressed this general trend within Enlightenment thinking when he wrote the famous words: "if God held the truth in his right hand and in his clenched left fist the quest for it, along with all my future errors, and then told me to choose, I should point to the left and humbly say: 'Father give! The pure truth belongs to You alone!' "[14]

~

"If God is dead," wrote Dostoyevsky, "then everything is permitted." Perhaps: but enough was certainly permitted throughout the millennia in which He was alive. Looking back at the history of religion, embedded in an organic tradition and sanctified by tradition, does not make for a pretty sight. As a joke, Voltaire once tried to count the deaths inflicted by the Church: he went above a million, but he probably could not count high enough. Holy Scripture is littered with murder and from the Anabaptists to the pogroms directed against the Jews to the thousands upon thousands of witches and heretics destroyed by the Inquisition to the devastating wars of religion and terrorist acts that continue into the present: the life of God is marked by the slaughter of his supposed enemies by his supposed friends.

Everything was permitted in defense of the organic community that allowed for no division between church and state. Its proponents ultimately embraced either an integral nationalism with racialist overtones or a supranationalism predicated on the return to what Novalis called "authentically catholic and authentically Christian times" (*echt-katholischen und echt-christlichen Zeiten*). The combination of the two provides the foundation or, better, the analogue for religious fundamentalism. To be sure: brave dissidents inspired by faith have always existed, religious groups have made common

14. Gotthold Ephraim Lessing, "Eine Duplik," in *Theologische und Philosophische Schriften* (Hildesheim, 1970), 59.

cause with left movements on certain issues in the past, and it is surely the case that alliances will need to be made with such individuals and groups in the future. But the fact remains: the larger mainstream religious organizations have —historically—opposed virtually every scientific advance, every new philosophical movement, and every progressive political development. True believers still view tolerance as undermining the certainty associated with religious faith and, thus, strengthening faith calls upon the faithful to challenge liberal claims. Useful, still, to recall the words of Holbach in *Common Sense*:

> In all parts of our globe, intoxicated fanatics have been seen cutting each other's throats, lighting funeral piles, committing, without scruple and even as a duty, the greatest crimes and shedding torrents of blood. For what? To strengthen, support, or propagate the impertinent conjectures of some enthusiasts, or to give validity to the cheats of some imposters, in the name and on behalf of a being, who exists only in their imagination, and who has made himself known only by the ravages, disputes, and follies, he has caused upon the earth.

Amazing is less the assault directed against *l'infame* by the philosophes than the restraint that they showed. The young Marx and his followers may have taken the position that the Enlightenment was somehow not "radical" enough on the matter of religion. But the implications of his critique are rarely thought through: it remains both metaphysical and politically irresponsible. His argument revolved around understanding religion not merely as the "opium of the masses," but also as a "sigh of the oppressed creature." Abolishing religion is important, according to this view, because it presupposes providing solutions for the earthly problems that generated the need for faith in the first place. Considering religion from a transformative standpoint differentiated the new materialism from empiricism and positivism, imbued it with a utopian purpose, projected the end of "prehistory," and seemingly turned Marxism into the radical heir of the Enlightenment. Humanity would now be freed from its alienated subservience to a nonexistent God and in the future, with respect to religion, it will not simply "wear the chain that is without fantasy or consolation, but . . . will throw it off and pluck the living flower."[15]

---

15. Karl Marx, "Toward the Critique of Hegel's Philosophy of Law: Introduction," in *Writings of the Young Marx on Philosophy and Society*, eds. Loyd D. Easton and Kurt H. Guddat (New York: Doubleday, 1969), 250.

Everyone cites these beautiful phrases of the young Marx. But few ask about their validity. There is a good reason why Marx never returned to this theme later in his major works and, too often, his followers obediently render the proper citations without any attempt to make them relevant. In fact, no causes for religion are specified by Marx and no proposals—of even the most rudimentary sort—are made for dealing with them. There is, again, a good reason why not: Marx misconstrued the problem. For, in these famous passages, he was actually not dealing with "religion" at all but, rather, with "religiosity" or what Camus called "the longing for God" and Horkheimer termed "the longing for the totally other." The distinction between "religion" and "religiosity" is crucial: it is one thing to constrain the political power of religious institutions and quite another to eliminate religious feeling.

No political movement or policy can eradicate such an elusive phenomenon and more importantly, beyond juvenile metaphysical arguments concerning the existence of a deity, there is no concrete reason why it should. Religiosity—if not religion—is a pseudo-problem for progressive politics. Uncertainty, loneliness, meaninglessness, and death are among the reasons why this longing has remained with humanity for its entire history and why it promises to remain with us far into the foreseeable future. Recourse to the fulfillment of humanity's unrealized potential, its repressed unity, or its "species being," doesn't help matters The anthropological terms in which Marx framed the question of religious alienation—and also the division of labor—prevents anything other than a vague and indeterminate response to it in theory or practice.

Enlightenment thinkers had little use for such discussions. Usually deists rather than atheists, concerned with fostering tolerance rather than embracing any type of dogma, most philosophes considered religious faith nothing more than superstition, but they were content to leave matters of belief to the individual. Hardly any of them were concerned with abolishing religious forms of identification and most implicitly understood the difference between "religiosity" and "religion." Some of the *philosophes* saw religion as a necessary element within society: others as positively beneficial: still others as a felt existential need. The great majority of them, however, feared the bloodshed that would surely have resulted from attempting to abolish religion. Hobbes introduced what soon became the dominant political approach by counseling the sovereign against dictating "opinion" and by treating each religion as a particular interest with its own ambitions. Kant allowed for religion "within the bounds of reason," Rousseau vacillated on the role of religion and the character of his faith, Mendelssohn understood religion as a form of inner "conviction," and Voltaire believed his tailor needed a church.

Enlightenment thinkers wished to temper the power of religious institutions by privileging the secular state and, for this reason, traditionalists and dogmatic defenders of the faith—all faiths—have criticized them unmercifully ever since. The philosophes understood that conviction and tolerance are not mutually exclusive so long as a secular state is sovereign over the diverse religions, or interpretations of a single religion, in civil society. Such a stance involves recognizing faith as a private conviction. Dealing with religion then is, from the standpoint of liberal politics, actually no different than dealing with any other private interest or ideological standpoint. It becomes a matter of securing the institutional conditions for the pursuit of the one and the right to believe in the other. Faith should not be construed as a political issue. For those committed to the Enlightenment legacy, indeed, religion turns into a problem only when it strays beyond the private sphere and identifies its concerns with those of the public weal. Bringing the principles of a liberal public sphere to bear on issues concerning faith should indeed result less in a repression of "difference" than its liberation.

The Enlightenment was a movement in which the striving for truth was more important than its acquisition: its major representatives understood reality as an experiment and sought to foster conditions in which the new might glimmer. They never embraced a self-serving ambiguity: they knew what they supported and knew what they were against. Their assumptions were simple enough: they viewed tyranny, ignorance, and misery as the product of natural rather than divine forces; they believed that curing people of their vices begins by curing them of their prejudices; that progress is the enemy of cruelty; and that a fuller life lies more in exploring the rich diversity of the planet than in obsessing over the internal rumblings of the self. That general perspective retains its salience. Enlightenment thinkers assumed that society could be changed and that political engagement was necessary to bring that change about. They spoke for the lowly and the insulted, the exploited and the oppressed, and the constellation of values and attitudes that defined their undertaking are neither irrelevant nor passé. They remain with us, they underpin the struggle of every progressive movement, and —perhaps most important of all—they project the type of world that every decent person wishes to see.

INDEX

Index compiled by Fred Leise